RECONNECTED

RECONNECTED

A community builder's handbook

ANDREW LEIGH
& NICK TERRELL

IN CONJUNCTION WITH BLACK INC.

Published by La Trobe University Press in conjunction with Black Inc.
Level 1, 221 Drummond Street
Carlton VIC 3053, Australia
enquiries@blackincbooks.com
www.blackincbooks.com
www.latrobeuniversitypress.com.au

La Trobe University plays an integral role in Australia's public intellectual life, and is recognised globally for its research excellence and commitment to ideas and debate. La Trobe University Press publishes books of high intellectual quality, aimed at general readers. Titles range across the humanities and sciences, and are written by distinguished and innovative scholars. La Trobe University Press books are produced in conjunction with Black Inc., an independent Australian publishing house. The members of the LTUP Editorial Board are Vice-Chancellor's Fellows Emeritus Professor Robert Manne and Dr Elizabeth Finkel, and Morry Schwartz and Chris Feik of Black Inc.

Copyright © Andrew Leigh and Nick Terrell 2020
Andrew Leigh and Nick Terrell assert their rights to be known as the authors of this work.

ALL RIGHTS RESERVED.
No part of this publication may be reproduced, stored in a retrieval system, or transmitted in any form by any means electronic, mechanical, photocopying, recording or otherwise without the prior consent of the publishers.

9781760642617 (paperback)
9781743821510 (ebook)

 A catalogue record for this book is available from the National Library of Australia

Cover design by Design by Committee
Cover images by Josh Durham/Bigstockphoto
Text design and typesetting by Marilyn de Castro
Author photos by Hilary Wardhaugh

CONTENTS

1. Social Capital — 1
2. Dissecting the Disconnection Disaster — 13
3. Volunteering — 53
4. CyberConnecting — 91
5. Getting Active — 111
6. Fostering Philanthropy — 137
7. Social Connections and Social Purpose — 155
8. Spiritual Connections — 177
9. Politics Please — 189
10. Leadership Lessons — 213
11. Reconnecting Australia — 227

Acknowledgements — 243
Endnotes — 245
Index — 269

1

SOCIAL CAPITAL

Imagine your ideal community. One in which you've got plenty of friends, and plenty of time to spend with them. A society where your street is lively and safe, and neighbours are happy to mind your dog when you're on holiday. Local cafés where people know your name. Creative communities telling Australian stories. More local sporting teams than you can shake a cricket stump at. The kind of politics where people work together to solve local problems, rather than bickering about leaders, slurs and slip-ups.

Suppose that this sense of common purpose extended to the workplace, so that people felt fulfilled in their jobs, respected by their co-workers and valued by their managers. Imagine employment that's flexible by default, so the boss doesn't scoff when you say you'd like to work a four-day week so you can care for a relative – or just practise your favourite hobby.

Picture, too, an Australia in which friendships comfortably bridge traditional divides, in which everyone shares a pride in the nation's 60,000-year Indigenous heritage, volunteers to help those who are down on their luck and takes the time to check in on neighbours who've newly arrived from overseas. Envisage the strength that such a connected society has when adversity strikes: volunteer fire brigades at the ready, foodbanks well stocked, community centres prepared.

It's a world we'd all like to live in – but too often the reality of modern life is rushing past your neighbours (who you really must introduce yourself to one day), getting stuck in traffic, rolling your eyes at the latest social media outrage and wondering how anyone ever finds time to catch up with friends. In *Reconnected*, we look at how Australia has become more disconnected – and how together we can turn it around.

Living in a more connected way isn't just pleasurable, it enables us to tackle larger challenges. Problems such as climate change, inequality, inactivity and loneliness threaten our future. Solving them will require collective action. In all of human history, there's few instances in which a crisis was resolved by one person acting alone.

The missing pieces of Australia's community-building puzzle are hiding in plain sight. Australia is fortunate to have thousands of inspirational social entrepreneurs in our midst. From sporty types organising weekend fun runs to altruists providing laundry services to homeless people, 'social capitalists' are helping to grow a more connected community. Better yet, many are deploying tactics that can be replicated elsewhere. Identifying these common threads is the purpose of our book.

But first, there's a core concept we need to understand: social capital.

Four hundred and fifty kilometres south of New Zealand's South Island lies Auckland Island, a cold and hilly landmass. For most of human history, the island has been uninhabited. Then in 1864 something unusual happened.[1] In the space of four months, two Australian ships were wrecked at opposite ends of the island: the *Invercauld* on the north-west, and the *Grafton* on the south-east.

The *Invercauld* was under the command of Captain George Dalgarno, who when disaster struck seems to have been focused only on his own survival. Dalgarno's attitude of 'every man for himself' saw six of the twenty-four sailors under him perish in the shipwreck, including a sick young crewman. In the coming weeks, the survivors roamed the island, repeatedly abandoning those who were ill to die on their own. When they caught wild pigs, each man ate as much as he could. One night, William Hervey threw another of the shipwrecked sailors, Fred Hawser, out of their stick shelter on the basis that he was being a 'nuisance'. Hawser died. A few days later it was discovered that 'Hervey had been eating some of Hawser'. A year after the shipwreck, a rescue ship arrived. Only three of the *Invercauld*'s original twenty-five crew survived.

On the other side of the island, things unfolded differently. Commanding the *Grafton* was Captain Thomas Musgrave. When his ship hit a rocky beach and foundered, Musgrave ordered his men to stay aboard and wait until daylight. They then took ashore food, a gun and a dinghy, and even managed to transfer a critically ill crewmate. Over the coming months, the five *Grafton* sailors worked together to build a cabin with a stone chimney, dining table and desk. They made a chess set to keep themselves entertained and brewed beer by fermenting a sweet root they dug up ('It is not very good, but still it is preferable to cold water,' Musgrave wrote in his diary).[2] Under Musgrave's leadership, they built blacksmith's bellows and used them to enlarge the dinghy. Eighteen months after being wrecked, they made the 450-kilometre sea journey to New Zealand's South Island. Because the boat could only carry three safely, two men stayed behind. The voyage was a success, and a rescue vessel returned to pick up the other two sailors. Everyone survived.

The story of the *Invercauld* and the *Grafton* tells us something vital about how groups survive and thrive. While one group resorted to cannibalism, the other set about community building. It is telling that Musgrave and his men built a chess set – playing games maintained their morale and their mutual efforts forged a sense of common purpose. The crew of the *Grafton* built what is known as 'social capital', and all survived to tell their stories.

To economists, capital is an asset that can produce a valuable return. One form of capital is physical capital, such as cars and computers. Another is human capital, such as education and know-how. If you're running a company, you need both the right machines and appropriately skilled workers – a mix of physical and human capital.

But your company probably won't get far if your workers are constantly bickering, and that's where social capital comes in. Social capital is the idea that the ties that bind us together have an inherent value. In a society where people don't trust each other, you have to be on the lookout for cheats and crooks. Commerce becomes tediously complicated. But in a 'high-trust' society, things flow smoothly.

The two extremes can be found in the diamond market. In the diamond mines of South Africa, workers are heavily monitored to ensure they do not steal the stones. Pat-downs, x-ray machines and cameras are used at the end of a shift to check that employees have not swiped diamonds. Workers' uniforms do not have pockets or cuffs. Crafty employees have been known to swallow diamonds or hide them in their shoes. Employers don't trust their workers, and subject them to extreme scrutiny. But when diamonds arrive in New York, it's a different story.[3] Almost half the world's diamonds are handled by merchants on 47th Street. A diamond might pass through the hands of seven or eight people, as it is inspected and matched to the right buyer. Each person's profit margin can be as thin as 1 to 2 per cent, so the payoff from cheating is huge. But the New York Diamond Dealers Club works on trust, with diamonds exchanged based on a handshake or a signature on a receipt. Joining the club is notoriously difficult, because it involves establishing one's character. Most of the dealers are Orthodox Jews with strong religious and cultural ties to one another. Without such high levels of trust, the 47th Street diamond dealers could never have created such a successful conglomerate.

Social capital is vital for business, but it also makes for a more pleasurable life. A wide network of friends gives you more social options on a Saturday night, and more people with whom to share your joys. Friends, Marcel Proust said, are 'the charming gardeners who make our souls blossom'.[4] Being a member of a club or having a sense of belonging to your neighbourhood increases the likelihood that you feel happy and satisfied with your life.[5] Drawing support from family and friends is especially good for wellbeing.[6] Social connections can also provide a safety net when hard times hit. Those close to us provide a buffer against loss – in the words of Helen Keller, 'walking with a friend in the dark is better than walking alone in the light'. Distant connections can help too – if you're fired, a broad network of loose acquaintances can be useful in helping you find work. Sociologist Mark Granovetter argued that when it comes to job-hunting, what really helps is to have a strong network of 'weak ties'.[7]

Friends may be good for your health. There is a strong association between longevity and the strength of a person's social relationships.[8] Indeed, some have argued that social isolation is as dangerous as smoking fifteen or more cigarettes each day, and more dangerous than binge drinking or obesity. Randomised trials that have improved participants' social capital and then measured their health relative to a control group find weaker evidence of the link between social capital and health. But even among these more rigorous studies, there is some evidence that improved social capital leads to better self-reported health and wellbeing.[9]

Volunteering is also linked to a range of positive outcomes. Researcher Stephen Post found that volunteering is associated with happiness, health and longevity.[10] Volunteers feel healthier, sleep better, are less stressed and better able to adjust to change, and have a higher sense of self-worth and value to their community. Post argues that volunteering is so beneficial that doctors should prescribe it to their patients, just as many currently prescribe exercise.[11] Community-sector leader Joanne Fritz suggests that volunteering builds community, reduces loneliness, increases socialising, creates new bonds and friendships, helps people develop emotional stability, improves self-esteem, helps people cope with mental illness, increases longevity, reduces the risk of Alzheimer's, leads to graceful ageing, burns fat, saves lives, improves educational experiences, enhances job prospects, develops corporate communities and is just plain fun.[12]

Post's and Fritz's claims read like the riff of an old-time medicine show, and should be viewed with the same scepticism. After all, correlation doesn't mean causation. For example, it's possible that happier and healthier people are more inclined to volunteer in the first place. But a modicum of randomised evidence suggests there may be a modicum of truth in the causal claims. In one experiment, a group of secondary school students were randomly assigned either to do volunteer work assisting younger children or to a control group.[13] Four months later, the volunteers had significantly lower cholesterol levels and body mass indices than students in the control group. Another experiment asked primary school students to perform three acts of kindness each week.[14] Compared with a randomly selected control group, students who performed the acts of kindness were rated as more popular by their peers, gaining an average of 1.5 more friends over the four-week period. As developmental psychologist Marilyn Price-Mitchell puts it, the finding supports the idea that 'nice guys finish first'.[15]

Strong social capital may also help political institutions work more effectively. In 1993, political scientist Robert Putnam wrote a pioneering book that aimed to answer the question of why government had always functioned so much more effectively in northern Italy than in southern Italy. *Making Democracy Work* found that the difference went back to medieval times, with the north having more social institutions, such as football tournaments, choral societies and neighbourhood associations. Drawing on the work of sociologist James Coleman, Putnam concluded that local governments work best where civil society is strongest – a finding that has since been reinforced in dozens of different studies around the globe.

Social capital is also intertwined with egalitarianism. In their 2020 book *The Upswing*, Putnam and Shaylyn Garrett describe the Gilded Age era of the late 1800s in the United States as 'highly individualistic, starkly unequal, fiercely polarized, and deeply fragmented'. By the 1960s, the country had become more equal, more generous and more socially engaged. But then the trend reversed, and America today is increasingly split apart. The United States has gone from being an individualistic 'I' society to a connected 'we' society, then back to an individualistic 'I' society again. Globally, it turns out that countries which are more equal are also more socially cohesive.[16] As the French might put it, *égalité* and *fraternité* go together. If you care about reducing the gap between rich and poor, you should worry about how Australian social life is coming apart.

Recognising the importance of social capital, researchers set about tracing the trends in community life. While no single measure sums up the level of social capital in a community, a variety of indicators point in a similar direction. In his 2000 book *Bowling Alone*, Putnam documented the decline in civic community from the 1960s to the 1990s by drawing on surveys showing that Americans were less likely to know their neighbours and less inclined to trust one another. Fewer families ate dinner together or had friends over to their homes. And since *Bowling Alone* was published, the decline has continued. Americans have fewer close friends and are less trusting of each other.[17] Confidence in business, media and religious organisations and politicians has decreased.

Across many other advanced nations, research teams uncovered similar trends. Voter turnout at elections, membership of political parties, union membership and church attendance have fallen.[18] In many European nations, including Britain, Germany, France and Spain, civic institutions are fraying.

In Australia, my (Andrew's) book *Disconnected* was published in 2010, a decade after *Bowling Alone*. It found that Australians are less likely to be active members of *any* organisation than we were in the 1960s. Specific mass-membership organisations – such as Scouts, Guides, Rotary and Lions – attracted a smaller share of the population. Volunteering was also down and charitable giving had flatlined. The share of the population who were members of a union or who regularly attended a religious service had more than halved. Despite compulsory voting laws, a smaller share of Australians cast valid votes than in the 1960s. Australians are less likely to play an organised sport, less likely to use museums, galleries and gardens, and less likely to go out to watch a movie. *Disconnected* also reported a decline in the number of close friends and neighbourhood connections, and a rise in the share of people who said they had no-one to turn to in tough times.

In 1790, French philosopher and mathematician Nicolas de Condorcet observed that every generation tends to accuse itself of being less civic-minded than the previous one.[19] So it's important to ground our discussion in the numbers. In Chapter 2, we delve into this evidence, and update the findings using the latest statistics. We draw on data from the Australian Bureau of Statistics, from community groups, and from fresh surveys that we have commissioned. Alas, we are unable to report any improvement on most of these metrics. Troublingly, most have actually worsened since *Disconnected* was published a decade ago.

But the goal of this book is not to write the eulogy for Australian civic life. It is to get the patient back to good health. Over the past few years, the two of us have organised more than a dozen forums with Australian community leaders, asking them the same question: what are you doing that other community groups could learn from? These forums have met in Brisbane, Sydney, Perth, the Gold Coast, Canberra, Melbourne, Adelaide, Newcastle, the New South Wales Central Coast, Launceston, Hobart and Darwin. Over one thousand charity leaders have joined the conversations. Through conferences, meetings and site visits, we have connected with thousands more.

In the course of writing this book, a new challenge to social solidarity materialised. In 2020, the coronavirus shutdown caused the cancellation of sporting competitions, religious ceremonies and community gatherings. Social distancing prevented friends, neighbours and workmates from enjoying the friendly interactions that are fundamental to a strong society. Like the 1918 influenza pandemic, COVID-19 was not just a threat to public health, but to the ties that bind community.

Yet in the midst of coronavirus, creative examples of civic engagement arose. At the same time that people were stockpiling staples, they were moving to secure social connections. And not just for themselves. Rudimentary networks sprung up almost simultaneously with the shutdown. Isolation culture began to form, with new norms and new commonalities. And shaping these was a need to share, support and feel connected. Street by street, neighbours created groups to help with shopping, walk dogs and phone people in self-isolation. Using apps like Zoom, Skype and FaceTime, choral groups and exercise classes shifted online. Virtual happy hours, virtual birthday parties and virtual religious services emerged. A national 'Play for Lives' movement mobilised thousands of sportspeople whose competitions had been cancelled. Clubs got involved to help address an urgent shortage of volunteers, but it was also a way to sustain community networks and team identity in the absence of their usual shared purpose. If these kinds of initiatives can endure after the crisis, there is just a chance that Australia's civic fabric will emerge stronger from coronavirus.

After discussing recent trends in social capital in Chapter 2, we turn in Chapter 3 to the first set of fresh ideas, involving new kinds of volunteering – from virtual volunteering to disaster recovery volunteers. In Chapter 4, we discuss the social dimensions of new technology, from the problem of smartphone addiction to the potential of using online platforms to build trust. Chapter 5 moves outdoors, where innovative organisations such as parkrun and Greening Australia are mobilising thousands of people to stay fit and improve their local neighbourhoods. In Chapter 6, we look at new ways of giving, such as Atlassian's six-second sign-up process for workplace giving, and explore how the effective altruism movement is reshaping philanthropy. In Chapter 7, we delve into new social purpose charities, such as Orange Sky Australia, whose mobile clothes-washing vans aim to provide a tangible service to people who are homeless, as well as providing social connections. Chapter 8 is devoted to the strategies being pursued by successful faith-based organisations, as well as 'faith-like' bodies such as the atheist 'Sunday Assembly' movement. Chapter 9 explores innovative strategies for re-engaging citizens with politics. Chapter 10 profiles four social entrepreneurs whose work can provide useful lessons for the rest of us. In the final chapter we imagine what life in a Reconnected Australia could look like.

Social capital isn't just the work of worthy do-gooders. At its best, social capital can be a thing of beauty – transcending the everyday to remind us of our common humanity. One such moment occurred on 20 December 2014, when 23-year-old bride Manal Kassem was married.

A Muslim woman from Punchbowl, Kassem was wearing a white hijab, and she was nervous. Only four days earlier, a gunman brandishing an Islamic flag had taken eighteen hostages in the Lindt Café, two of whom died in the final gunfight. Kassem had chosen inner-city Sydney for her photoshoot and was worried she would be judged. After considering cancelling the photoshoot, Kassem instead chose to offer a gesture of respect to the country in which she hoped to raise her children. As soon as the wedding ceremony finished, she and her groom ventured to the Martin Place memorial, where she laid her wedding bouquet alongside hundreds of other floral tributes. As one bystander wrote: 'The crowd, who at first were staring and turning their heads as the wedding party approached, applauded as she laid her flowers down. Overwhelming and very touching.' In that moment, a multicultural Australia was united to collectively mourn the loss of lives. Martin Place – days earlier the scene of an awful tragedy – seemed to transform into a symbol of Australia's connectedness.

2

DISSECTING THE DISCONNECTION DISASTER

New words reveal a lot about an era. In the 1950s and '60s, words such as 'playscape' (a children's play area that fits the landscape), 'ridgy-didge' (genuine) and 'sickie' (taking a day off work to spend with friends) were added to Australian dictionaries. Society added new words for cheap ways of travelling together ('Kombi'), eating together ('Esky') and playing music together ('Lagerphone', an instrument made of bottle caps nailed to a piece of wood).

In the 2000s and 2010s, words added to Australian dictionaries paint a different picture. They include: 'technomite' (a child with a facility for using technology), 'showrooming' (shopping in a store then buying online), 'breadcrumbing' (sending flirtatious text messages, with no intention of forming a romantic relationship), 'face swap' (superimposing a face onto an internet image), 'doxxing' (releasing an adversary's personal information online) and 'digital detox'. These terms reflect the reality of an online world that can sometimes be colder and more aggressive than the face-to-face interactions it supplanted.

Unlike human longevity, economic growth or fossil fuel emissions, social capital is hard to quantify. But we can track surveys of civic engagement, membership statistics of large community organisations, and voter turnout rates. We also compile evidence about philanthropic donations, solo living, close friendships and more. Understanding the trends in community life is a matter of bringing together an array of evidence about trust and reciprocity in Australia.

Published in 2010, *Disconnected* reported that from the 1960s to the 2000s, Australians were less likely to be active members of community organisations, less likely to be members of political parties, and less likely to cast a valid vote. The decline was particularly large for the share attending a religious service (which halved since the 1950s) and union membership (which halved since the 1980s). The share of people donating money was stable from the 1980s to the 2000s, but people reported that they had fewer close friends and were less likely to know their neighbours. From the 1990s to the 2000s, rates of sporting participation and attendance at museums, art galleries and botanic gardens declined.

A decade on, it's time to look again at the data, and ask: are we still disconnected? What do we know about Australia's community groups and volunteering rates? How are we engaging with religion and politics? Are we playing sport and connecting with our mates? Is loneliness and isolation on the rise?

Community groups

Since the late 1970s, the Directory of Australian Associations has catalogued Australia's non-profit organisations. This means it is not only a useful resource for people seeking to find out where the Australian Lychee Growers Association has its headquarters (Mooloolah in Queensland, since you ask), but also provides a benchmark of the total number of organisations nationwide. Figure 1 shows the number of Australian organisations as a share of the total population. In the late

1970s and early 1980s, Australia had around eighty to 100 associations for every 100,000 people (the uptick in the late 1970s may simply be the directory getting off the ground). But over the ensuing decades, the number of associations has steadily declined. In 2019, there were just nineteen organisations for every 100,000 Australians: one-quarter of its level when the directory began in 1978.

Figure 1: Associations per 100,000 adults

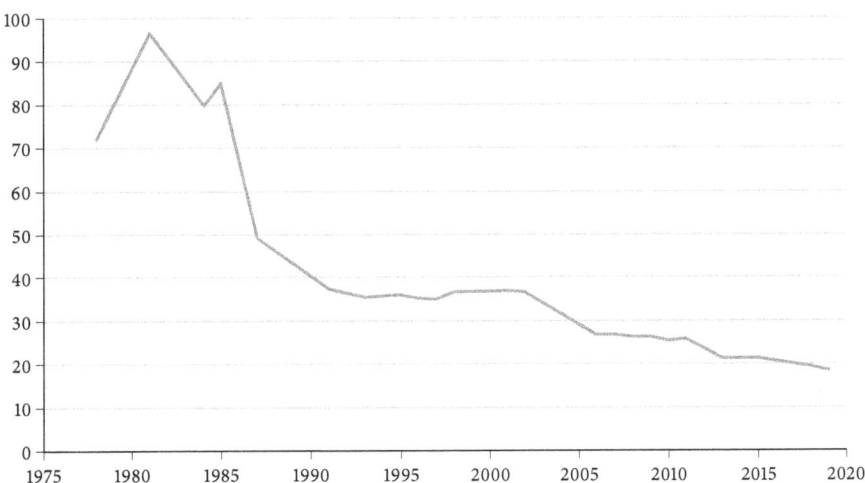

Australians are also less likely to join groups.[1] From 2006 to 2014, the share of people involved in social groups such as heritage organisations, ethnic clubs or hobby groups fell from 63 per cent to 51 per cent.[2] Over the same period, the proportion of people involved in community support groups such as service clubs and welfare organisations held steady at 33 per cent.[3]

Membership records of Australia's largest community groups allow us to track the long-term trends in organisational membership. We were able to obtain figures for twelve bodies: the Returned Services League (RSL), Apex, Lions, Rotary, the Australian Conservation

Foundation, Greenpeace, Athletics Australia, Little Athletics, Mothers' Union, Catholic Women's League, Scouts and Guides. For the Scouts and Guides, we have figures on both members and leaders. In each case, we calculate membership as a share of the relevant population. For example, Rotary membership is calculated as a share of the adult population (eighteen and over), while Guides membership is as a share of girls aged five to nineteen. Although Scouts has admitted girls since 1971, we use boys aged five to nineteen as the benchmark, since boys make up the bulk of members.

Figure 2: Membership of six Australian community groups

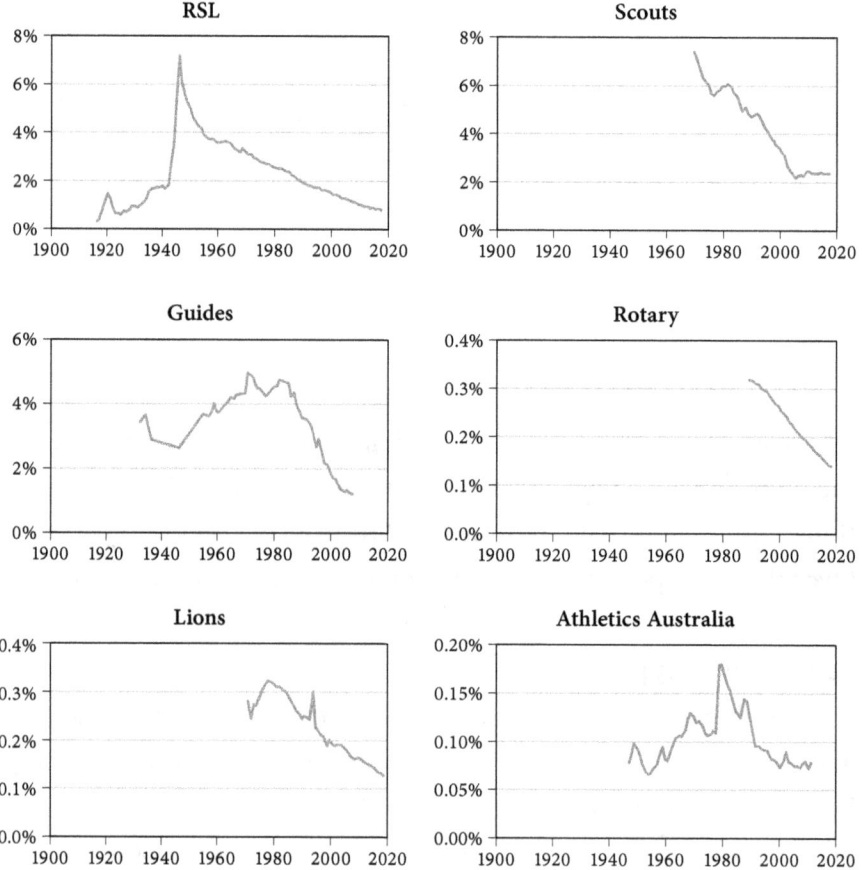

The trendlines shown in Figure 2 give a good indication of the pattern across all twelve organisations. RSL membership peaked in 1946 at 7 per cent of the adult population and is now below 1 per cent. Scouts and Guides had over 4 per cent membership rates in the 1980s, but Scouts are now around 2 per cent, while Guides are around 1 per cent.[4] Service clubs Rotary and Lions have seen their membership share fall from over 0.3 per cent of adults to around 0.1 per cent of adults. Athletics Australia's membership has, similarly, fallen.

Combining the twelve bodies that provided us with membership data, Figure 3 depicts a long-run index of membership, set to equal 1 in 1990. This shows that in the mid-1960s, organisational membership was almost twice as high as in 1990. By 2019, the index of organisational membership was down to 0.5, indicating that membership in these twelve large organisations was at half the level it had been in 1990. From peak to trough, membership of these community bodies has fallen by almost three-quarters since the mid-1960s.

Figure 3: Average membership rate across twelve major Australian community groups

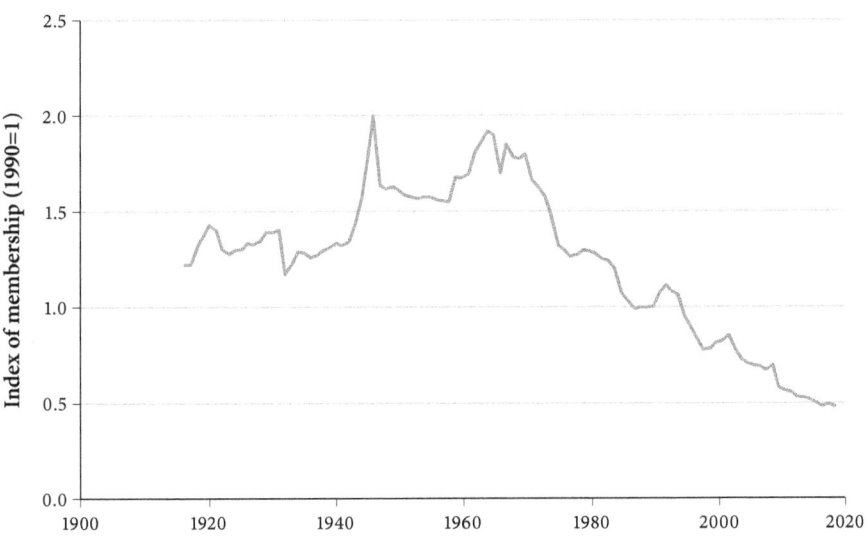

It's not as though Australians haven't noticed this trend. Asked about the decline, 74 per cent of respondents agree that 'people just aren't interested in joining things anymore', and 60 per cent agree that 'there are fewer people available to be part of local groups'.[5] Most people plead time pressures, with 54 per cent saying they 'find it impossible to give time to things outside of work and home'. Many don't enjoy membership, with half the population saying 'I just don't like joining groups'. Yet Australians bemoan the result. Eighty-four per cent say that 'the decline in membership of organisations is not a positive development'. Intuitively, the vast majority of people recognise that our society is better off when people are actively engaged in civic groups. But in our daily lives, thousands of people are steadily withdrawing from them. Across Australia, organisations are collapsing at a faster rate than new groups are being created.

Volunteering

Since the turn of the century, there has also been a decline in volunteering. The Australian Bureau of Statistics conducts two surveys on volunteering: the General Social Survey and the Australian Census. Since 2006, both measures show a decline in volunteering. We focus here on the General Social Survey, which the statistical agency believes to be the more accurate metric.[6] On that measure, the share of people who volunteered in the previous twelve months fell from 34 per cent in 2006 to 31 per cent in 2014.

The decline can be seen in figures for volunteer firefighters.[7] Figure 4 charts the share of adults who voluntarily serve as firefighters or support staff. From 2010 to 2019, this number fell by almost one-fifth, from 1.3 per cent to 1.1 per cent. This has real consequences. When massive bushfires hit in the summer of 2019–20, there were 14,000 fewer volunteer firefighters and volunteer support staff than there had been a decade earlier. Volunteers worked for weeks without a break, and many found themselves as burned out as the Australian bush.

Figure 4: Volunteering rates

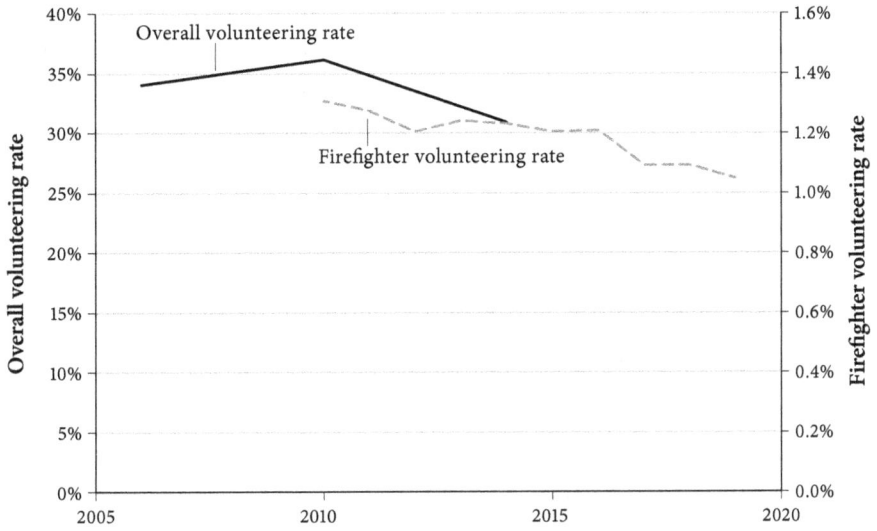

Religion

Attending religious services, participating in religious festivals and joining religious study groups are all forms of social capital that can build bonds of trust and reciprocity. Religious social capital has both direct and indirect effects. Those who are active in religious communities contribute not only to those organisations but also to secular community life. As political scientists David Campbell and Robert Putnam point out, those who are part of a religious community tend to be 'more generous neighbours and more conscientious citizens'.[8] Religiously active people give more money – even excluding their religious giving. They donate more time – even setting aside their religious volunteering. Those who are engaged in religious communities are more likely to vote and to donate blood.

Crucially, religious adherents who are most active in secular activities aren't those with the most ardent beliefs, but with the greatest level of engagement. What matters is attending church, temple or synagogue, being part of a Bible study group, a Hindu social group or a Buddhist prayer group. Someone who sits at home memorising the Bible isn't any more likely to assist on Clean Up Australia Day. But as Campbell and Putnam note, an atheist who stumbles into a prayer group meeting and decides to stay on is likely to become more civically active as a result. When it comes to neighbourliness, 'it is belonging that matters, not believing'.[9] People with many religiously based social connections are two to three times more civically engaged and generous, even to secular causes.[10] Religion creates a common point of connection. One randomised experiment found that people are more likely to trust one another when informed of a person's faith. The effect is strongest when both people are religiously active.[11] As Alain de Botton says in his book *Religion for Atheists*, 'religions understand that to belong to a community is both very desirable and not very easy'.[12]

It has been widely documented that Australians are much less likely today to believe in a higher power. In the first national census, carried out in 1911, 97 per cent of Australians reported having religious beliefs. In the 2016 census, just 60 per cent said they were religious. The most common religion in Australia today is 'no religion'. However, from the *Reconnected* perspective, what matters is the social side of religion: what people do, rather than what they believe.

At the time of Federation, approximately four in ten adults attended a weekly religious service.[13] Figure 5 shows the trends in the post-war era, when reliable surveys have been conducted. In the 1950s, one-third of Australians were weekly attendees. But today, just one in ten Australians attends a religious service every week. In 1950, almost half of all Australians attended a religious service at least monthly. In 2019, just one in seven adults (14 per cent) attended monthly or more frequently.[14]

Figure 5: Share of adults attending a religious service

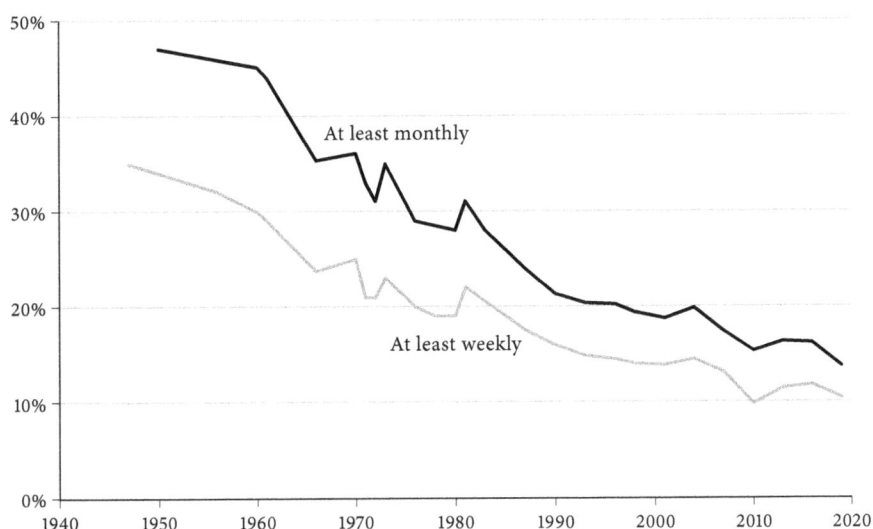

Religious leaders are alarmed. Australia's largest religious body – the Catholic Church – estimates that in 1954, 74 per cent of Catholics regularly attended Mass. That figure had fallen to 30 per cent by 1978, to 15 per cent by 2001 and to 12 per cent by 2016 (the most recent survey).[15] In raw numbers, there are more than twice as many Catholics in Australia as there were in the 1950s, but less than half as many worshippers at Mass on a typical Sunday.[16] It isn't just the lower numbers that worry the church leadership, but the age profile of Mass attendees. Mass-goers are significantly older than the overall Catholic population. Among Catholics aged in their seventies, around one in three attends Mass. Among Catholics aged in their twenties, only about one in twenty attends. When your typical congregant isn't much younger than the Pope, you know you've got a problem. One-third of parishes lack their own full-time priest, a result of both dwindling attendance and fewer priests.[17] Researchers from the Australian Catholic University observed: 'While there are numerous examples of strong, vital parish communities, in other places the viability of parishes is threatened by declining attendances. Urgent action is required if we are to save the treasure that is the Australian Catholic parish.'[18]

The Catholic Church is not alone in suffering declining numbers. Church closures are perhaps the most visible manifestation of the decline in religious civic engagement, with real estate agents selling off church buildings under signs like 'divine potential' or 'heavenly opportunity'.[19] In Victoria, Christopher Akehurst reports that since the turn of the century, Anglican churches have closed in Alphington, Brighton, Darebin, Deepdene, Elwood, Middle Park, Mont Albert, Northcote, Port Melbourne, Syndal and Thornbury. The Uniting Church in that state reports that nearly a third of its churches are redundant. One parishioner told Akehurst: 'We are cash-rich and people-poor.'[20] Soon, suburban churches may go the way of drive-in cinemas and local butcher stores.

But not all religions are experiencing declining attendance. The share of Jewish Australians attending synagogue monthly or more often rose from 15 per cent in 1967 to 32 per cent in 2008, before dropping back to 25 per cent by 2017.[21] It is harder to find mosque attendance surveys, but a 2013 poll of NSW mosque leaders reported that four-fifths had seen attendance rates grow over the previous five years. Half of all mosques said that they had insufficient space to accommodate their Friday worshippers – a problem most churches could only pray for.[22]

Politics

As Aristotle pointed out over two thousand years ago, politics is simply the art of living together.[23] Politics is how we decide as a community what rules should govern us, how much to spend on communal goods, and how to raise the money to pay for it. Democracy doesn't demand that everyone understands the nuances of every issue. But democracies work best when citizens are engaged, and the level of political activity is one marker of the level of social capital in a community.

In 1924, Australia made it compulsory for citizens to vote in elections. As Figure 6 shows, for the remainder of the twentieth century around nineteen out of twenty people on the voting roll turned up at the ballot box. By the 2019 election, that figure had fallen to eighteen out of twenty: effectively a doubling in the share of enrolled voters who failed to vote. Indeed, in 2016, the voter turnout rate fell to a ninety-year low, and it recovered only slightly in 2019.

Figure 6: Voting rates in federal elections

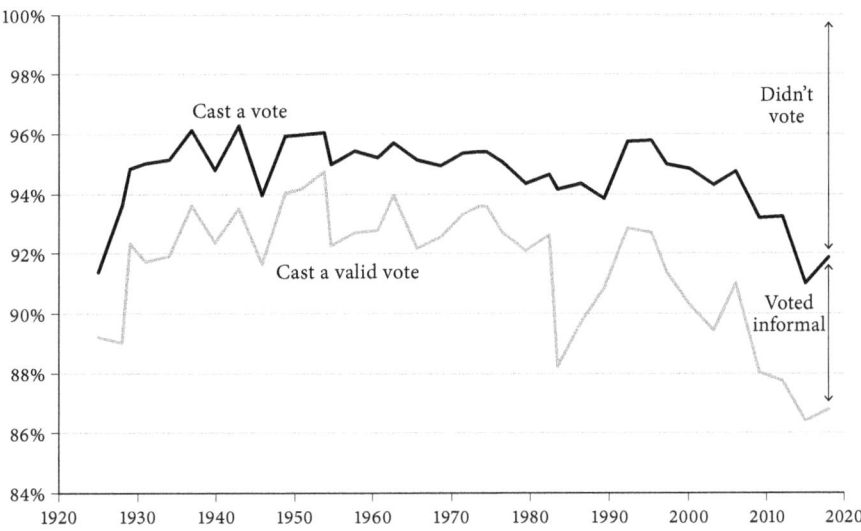

On top of this are the electors who cast invalid votes, either by making an accidental mistake or deliberately defacing the ballot paper. Accidents invariably happen, particularly after a change in the voting rules, as occurred in 1984. But the share of Australian voters who cast an informal ballot was nearly twice as high in twenty-first-century elections as in twentieth-century ones. Even though voters were more educated and informed, they were considerably more inclined to hand in ballot papers that could not be counted. In the four elections held during the 1990s, the informal voting rate on House of Representatives ballots averaged 3.3 per cent. In the four elections held in the 2010s, it averaged 5.5 per cent. Combining turnout and informal voting trends, just 87 per cent of enrolled voters cast a valid vote in the 2019 election. That is the second-lowest figure since compulsory voting began.

The Australian Election Study, a survey conducted after each federal election, paints a similar picture. Figure 7 reports some of the key findings. Since 1996, the share of people who are satisfied with democracy has dropped from 78 per cent to 59 per cent. Since 1993, the proportion agreeing that people in government can be trusted fell from 34 per cent to 25 per cent. The significance of elections to many people has waned, with the proportion who say they were interested in the election falling from 50 per cent to 32 per cent since 1993, and the proportion who watched an election debate dropping from 56 per cent to 30 per cent since 1990.

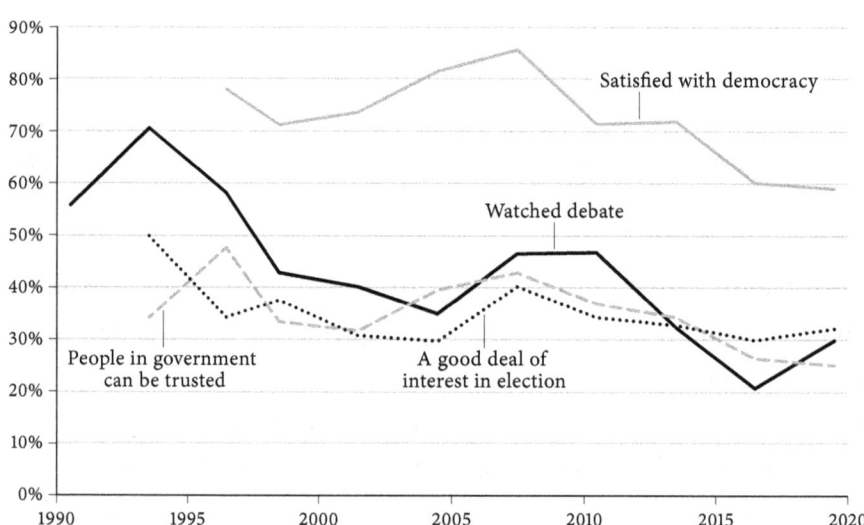

Figure 7: Engagement with politics

Is disenchantment with politics related to how much people know about politics? In the 2019 Australian Election Study, respondents were given a quick quiz about politics, comprising true or false questions about the year Australia became a federation, how the Constitution gets changed, how the Senate is elected, whether candidates have to pay a deposit to stand for parliament, and the maximum number of years between elections.[24] Analysing these results, we found that the average person got two out of five questions correct. Only 4 per cent got all five questions right.

For both trust in government and satisfaction with democracy, there is a strong relationship between political knowledge and political engagement, as depicted in Figure 8. Compared with those who got a perfect score on the political knowledge test, people who scored zero were half as likely to believe that people in government can be trusted, and two-thirds as likely to be satisfied with democracy. The trust gap is also a knowledge gap. This suggests that measures to build trust in politics may also have to increase the bedrock of political knowledge among voters who distrust government and are dissatisfied with democracy.

Figure 8: Political knowledge and engagement

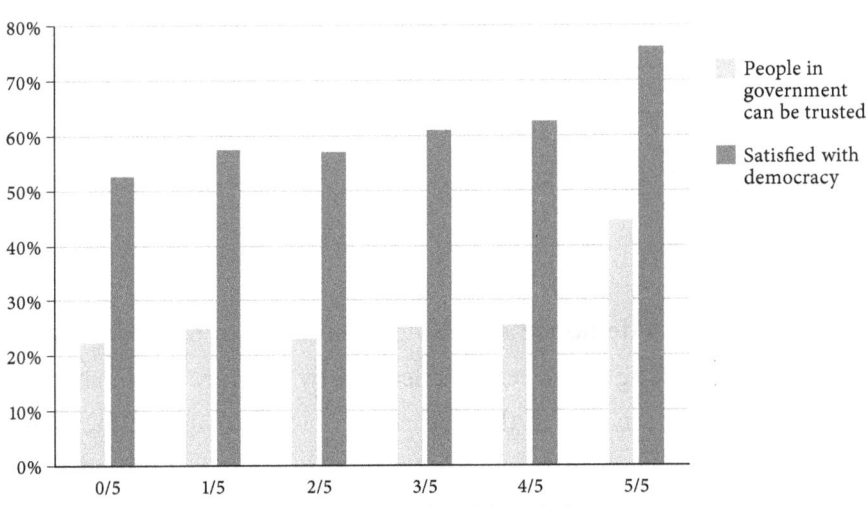

Is Australia on the right track? For over a decade, the Australian National University's ANUpoll has been asking a sample of people 'All things considered, are you satisfied or dissatisfied with the way the country is heading?' Figure 9 shows the trends. In 2008, four in five people were satisfied with the nation's direction. By 2018, that had fallen to three in five, where it remained in January 2020.[25] Amid the coronavirus lockdown, the survey showed a sudden change, with the share of people satisfied with the nation's direction suddenly leaping upwards to four-fifths in April 2020. It remains to be seen whether the April 2020 result will be sustained or temporary.

Figure 9: Attitude towards national politics

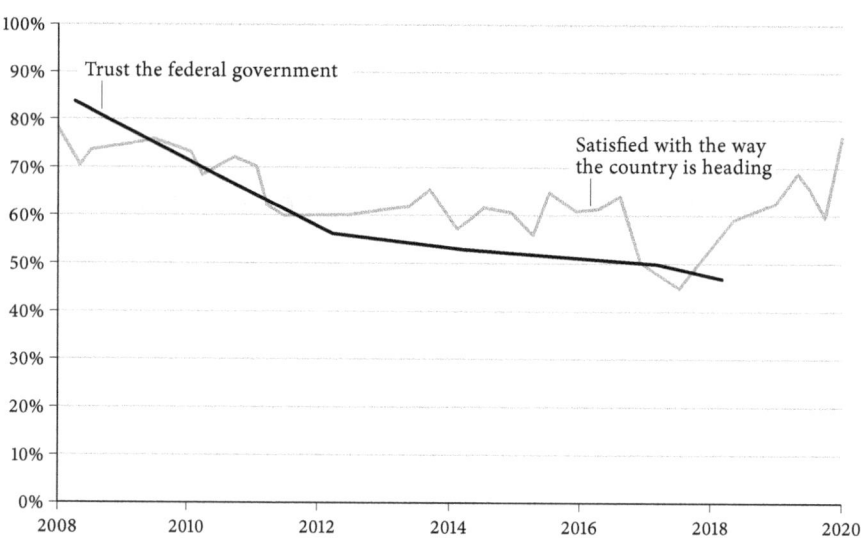

Similarly, surveys demonstrate falling trust levels in the federal government. According to surveys carried out by Griffith University and Transparency International, the share of people who say that they have trust and confidence in the federal government has slumped from 84 per cent in 2008 to 47 per cent in 2018.[26] Trust in state and local governments has also declined over this period, though not to the same extent. The share of people who think the federal parliament is free of corruption fell to 6 per cent in 2018, down from 18 per cent just two years earlier.[27] These trends match the patterns in the United States, where the share of people who say they have confidence in Congress and the presidency has halved since the early 1970s.[28]

As with distrust in government, those who are optimistic about the future tend to be the most informed. Asked whether they and their families will be better off in five years' time, 34 per cent of the mass public say yes. But among those who are university-educated, affluent and engaged with policy debates, the figure rises to 54 per cent.[29]

Another metric of political social capital is party membership. In the 1950s, more than one in 100 adults were members of each major political party. In recent years, this figure has fallen below one in 300.[30] As one commentator wryly noted, there are more people on the waiting list for the Melbourne Cricket Club than are members of all Australian political parties combined.[31] The decline in membership also shows up when we include all kinds of political groups. According to the General Social Survey, the share of adults involved in civic and political groups – a broad category that includes political parties, unions, consumer bodies, environmental groups and animal rights campaigns – fell from 19 per cent in 2006 to 14 per cent in 2014.[32]

Work

In the workforce, a key marker of the strength of community is trade union membership. Unions have traditionally played a strong role in introducing new employees to their colleagues, organising social activities at lunchtime and maintaining a sense of community. Some unions sponsor local sporting clubs and hold barbecues at community events. In other cases, unions encourage political engagement through petitions, telephone campaigns and street stalls. This political activity is not always in relation to industrial issues; sometimes it can be around environmental or social justice issues too.

For the four decades after the end of World War II, half of all workers were union members, as shown in Figure 10. But the share of unionists began to fall in the 1980s, and the decline accelerated in the 1990s. By 2000, union membership was down to one in four. By 2018, it had declined to one in seven (14 per cent). There are still 1.5 million union members in Australia, but that amounts to one million fewer unionists than in the mid-1970s, when the workforce was considerably smaller. The decline in union membership in Australia is one of the most rapid in the advanced world. Australia's union membership rate is now only slightly above that of the United States, where around one in nine workers is in a union.

Figure 10: Union membership

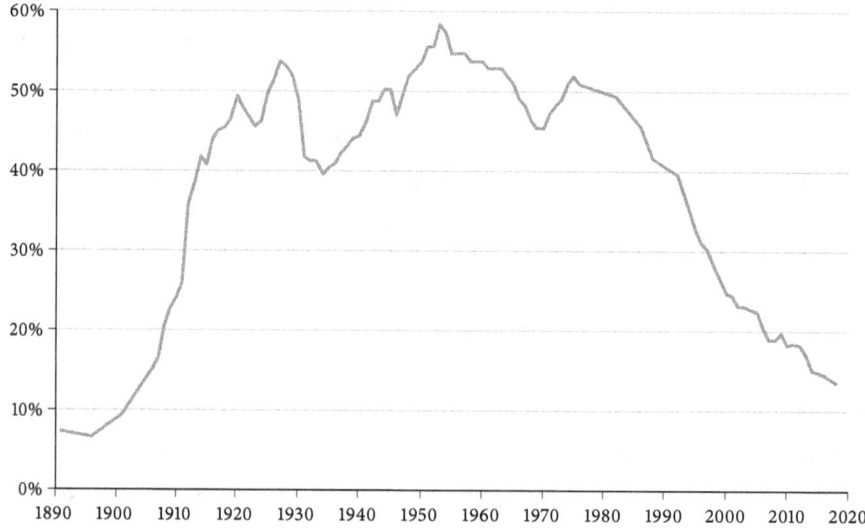

As it happens, the drop in union membership parallels the drop in religious attendance. Since 1950, the share of adults attending a religious service at least once a month has dropped from one in two to one in seven. Since 1980, the share of workers who are union members has dropped from one in two to one in seven. Regular religious attendance and membership of a union have gone from being usual to uncommon.

Sport and recreation

Growing up in Eaglehawk, a suburb of Bendigo, in the 1950s, Liz Low recalls a childhood of exploration: playing on the old mine poppet heads, climbing rooftops, and surfing a stormwater drain. It was not without risk – a stranger once attempted to attack her in a playground. But it was a very different balance between freedom and safety than many children (our own included) now enjoy. The 'free range' childhood that she describes in her memoir *Eaglehawk Girl* is a rarity today.[33]

A few years ago, British researchers approached a family who had been living in Sheffield for several generations. They asked each member of the family – a great-grandparent, a grandparent, a parent and a child – how far they had been allowed to roam unaccompanied from the family home at the age of eight. The distance was 10 kilometres in 1926, 1.6 kilometres in 1950, 800 metres in 1979, and 300 metres in 2007.[34] Subsequent studies reached similar conclusions. In past generations, primary schoolers often did not have to tell their parents where they were going.[35] By contrast, some children today could not go more than 100 metres from home on their own. They spend so much time being driven around that some have dubbed them 'the back seat generation'.

Next time you're at a family gathering, ask everyone how old they were when they were first allowed to leave the home unaccompanied. In our experience, those born up to the 1960s will say around age six.

Those born in the 1970s and 1980s will say around age eight. Those born in the 1990s and 2000s will say around age ten. Australian parents are increasingly reluctant to allow their children to roam the neighbourhood. Children are spending less time in outdoors free play and more time on indoors screen time. Some children's only sporting activities are organised sports, with little time spent physically 'mucking around'. Consequently, we might expect that Australian children would be less fit and less socially engaged.

Indeed, the numbers confirm it. One marker of the decline in sporting activity is the physical health of young Australians. Since the 1990s, the share of Australian children who are overweight or obese has risen from 21 to 25 per cent.[36] In one study, researchers looked at how far Grade 6 children could leap from a standing start.[37] In 1985, the average Australian child could leap 147 centimetres. By 2015, this was down to 130 centimetres. Even when researchers took account of the increase in body fat, they still saw a marked decline in physical ability, suggesting that there had been a decrease in muscular strength among primary schoolers. The kids weren't just carrying more body fat, they were less fit. The study was titled 'The Great Leap Backwards'.

Among adults, a similar pattern emerges. *Disconnected* documented the decline in membership for a few mass participation sports, including athletics and surf life-saving. However, we have since gained access to a treasure trove of data on sporting participation, from an annual survey conducted by polling firm Roy Morgan since 2001.[38] These figures allow us to track Australians' involvement in a whopping sixty-one different sports over a two-decade period. For some small sports, the figures can bounce around from year to year. Because Roy Morgan's survey may not capture many rowers or ballroom dancers in a given year, it's important not to put too much emphasis on a single figure. So to be sure that we are properly capturing the trends, we fit a regression trend line to the statistics for each sport using all years' data.

If the line shows a definite upward or downward slope, then we categorise that sport as rising or falling in popularity.³⁹ If the slope of the line isn't statistically distinguishable either way, we classify the sport's popularity as staying constant. We then report the average membership rate in the first two years (2001 and 2002) and the last two years (2018 and 2019), as well as the percentage change between these points.

Figure 11 shows the ten sports whose popularity has been growing, ranked in descending order of their popularity in recent years. Note that these tend to be activities that can be done alone. Walking for exercise has increased by 23 per cent, gym-going by 86 per cent, and jogging or running by around 75 per cent.

Figure 11: Sports increasing in popularity

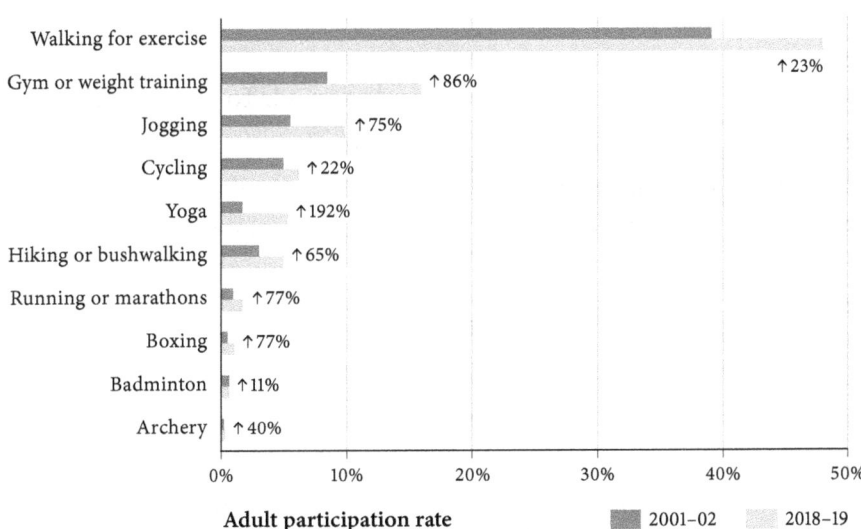

Figure 12 charts the thirteen sports for which there isn't a clear trend either way. They include a major team sport – soccer – plus several individual sports, including swimming, snowboarding and triathlons. For these sports, the data do not suggest a clear trend in

Figure 12: Sports with fairly constant popularity

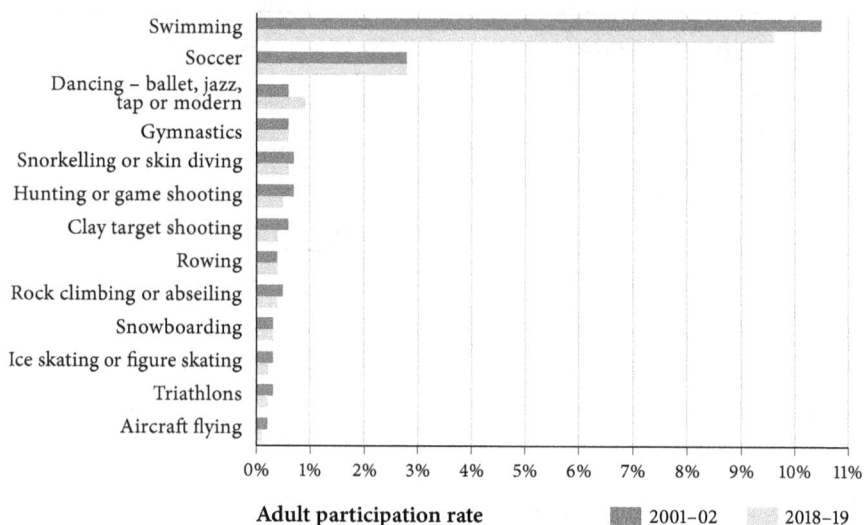

participation rates across the two-decade period. To be clear, we aren't saying that the rates are precisely the same in 2001–02 and 2018–19. Instead, what we mean is that when we look at the data for all years we cannot discern a clear upwards or downwards trend out of the usual survey volatility.

Figure 13 depicts the thirty-eight sports that have shrunk, including aerobics, Aussie rules, basketball, baseball and cricket. Among the largest decreases are for squash (down 70 per cent), rugby league (down 61 per cent) and tennis (down 49 per cent). Since Robert Putnam published *Bowling Alone* in 2000, the share of Australians who go tenpin bowling has fallen by 64 per cent, while the proportion who engage in lawn bowling is down 47 per cent.

Golf, the most popular club sport among adults, is no longer so popular. Figures provided to us by Golf Australia show that from 1970 to 2000, the share of Australians who were members of golf clubs was around 3.5 per cent. That figure is now down to 2 per cent.[40]

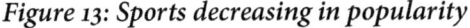

Figure 13: Sports decreasing in popularity

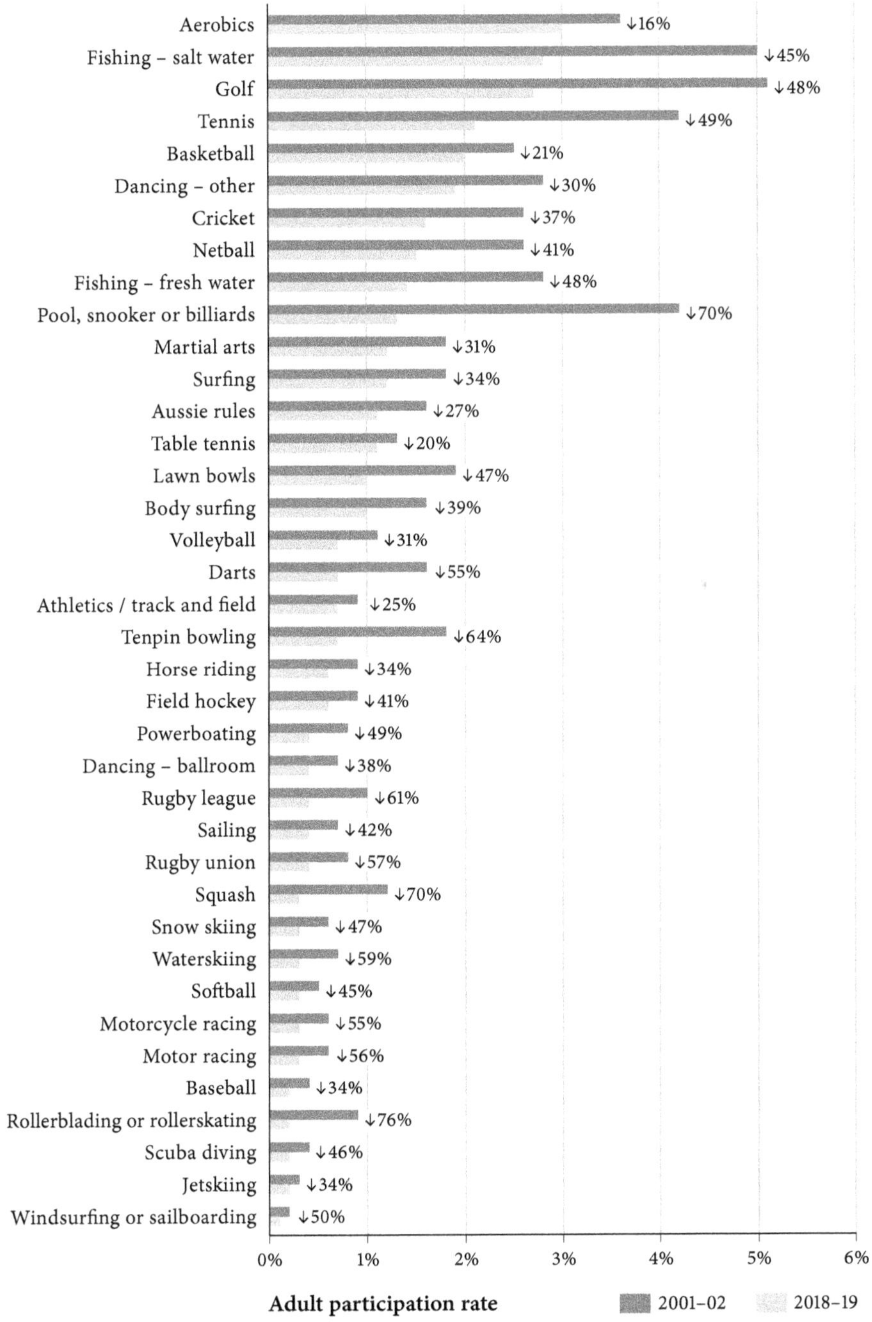

(Note that these are club membership figures, so are smaller than Roy Morgan's participation figures, since some people play golf as guests or green fee players.) Golf's problems are particularly acute in rural areas, as well as on the Queensland Gold Coast and the NSW Central Coast.[41]

What does this mean for overall sporting participation? Summing up overall engagement, Roy Morgan calculates the share of people involved in individual sports (such as surfing or horse riding) and team sports (such as hockey or volleyball). The survey firm also sums up total involvement in all sports and leisure activities, including activities such as hiking or walking for exercise. As Figure 14 shows, both individual and team sports have seen a drop-off in participation. However, because of a significant rise in leisure activities – particularly walking – overall activity levels have ticked up slightly.

Figure 14: Overall trends in sport and leisure

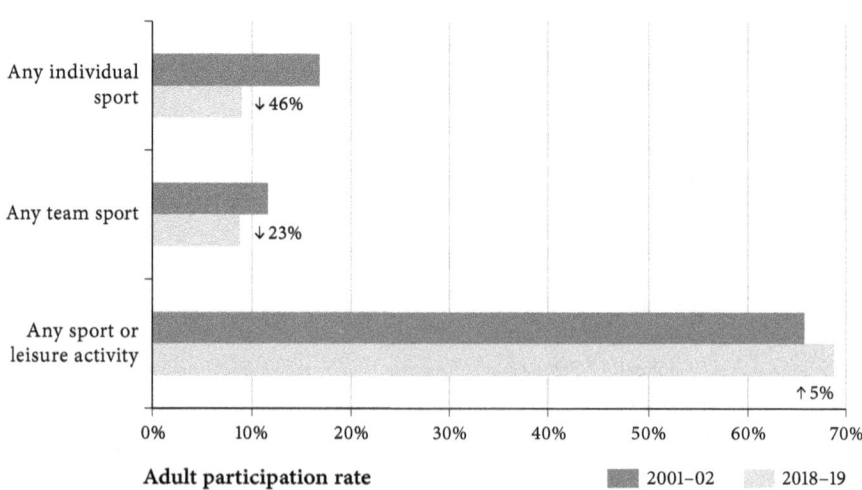

As Australians turn away from organised sports to unorganised activities such as walking, gym-going and jogging, society is losing the camaraderie that comes from sporting clubs. And the new activities may not be as good for our health, with body weights on the rise. In 1995, 56 per cent of adults were overweight or obese. By 2017, the figure had risen to 67 per cent.[42]

Friends and neighbours

When life gets busy, it's easy to fall into the trap of underinvesting in friendships. Discussing this challenge, social commentator David Brooks distinguishes between two kinds of virtues: résumé virtues and eulogy virtues.[43] Résumé virtues include titles and awards, promotions and qualifications. But at funerals, people don't typically talk about what a great CV the deceased person had. Instead, we focus on how they treated those around them, whether they were kind, how many friends they had and how they cared for their mates. Our friendships aren't résumé virtues, they're eulogy virtues.

No single metric encapsulates the value of our friendship networks. Ideally, we need close ties with a few trusted souls, solid relationships with others and the ability to get along with many. Imperfect as any measure will be, it's still worth trying to get a handle on the size of our friendship networks, and how this has changed over time.

In 1984, a national survey asked a sample of Australians a series of questions about their close friendships. In 2005, Ipsos Mackay Research fielded the same set of questions, for results reported in *Disconnected*. In 2018, we asked Omnipoll to administer the survey a third time. The result is a 34-year time series of the strength of Australians' friendships, depicted in Figure 15.

As a measure of trusted friendships, the surveys asked: 'Among your family and friends how many people are there easily available, whom you could talk with frankly, without having to watch what you say?' In 1984, Australian adults averaged nine trusted friends. In 2005, it was down to seven. By 2018, this had fallen to five.

Figure 15: Friends and neighbours

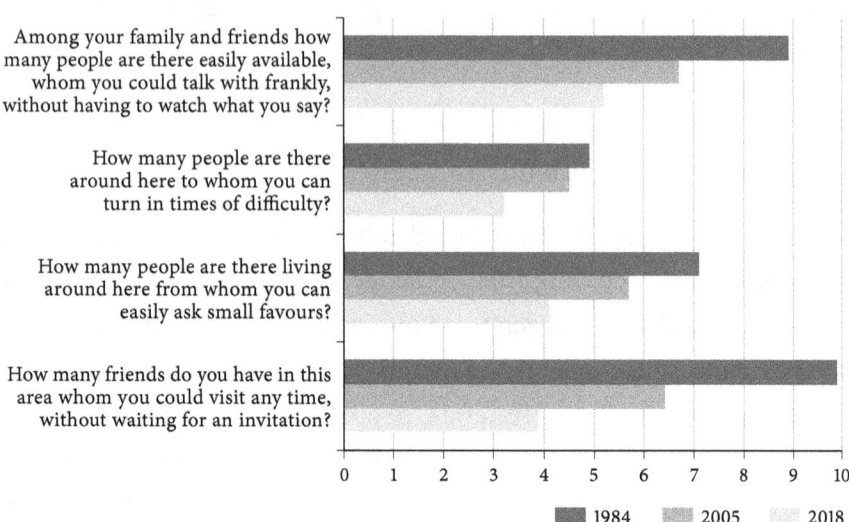

This decline matches the trends reported in the United States, where surveys asked people to list their closest confidants – the people with whom they could discuss important matters.[44] From 1985 to 2004, the average number of trusted friends fell from three to two, and the share of Americans who had zero close confidants rose from one-tenth to one-quarter.[45]

Another way of measuring friendships is to look at reciprocal friendships. Here, the Australian surveys asked: 'How many people are there around here to whom you can turn in times of difficulty? I mean, someone you could trust, and whom you could expect real help from in times of trouble (apart from those at home)?' In 1984, the average adult had five of these reciprocal friendships. By 2018, it was down to three. Since 1984, Australians have shed four of the friends they can talk with frankly and lost two of the friends who would help them in times of trouble. On these measures, Australians today have only about half as many close friends as in the 1980s.

In societies with high levels of social capital, people don't just have strong friendships, they also have plenty of acquaintances. Recall sociologist Mark Granovetter's research on 'the strength of weak ties' – referring to the value of having a plethora of people you know well enough to ask a favour of, even if they're not so close that you'd share a secret with them. One place people often find these acquaintances are in the house or apartment next door. Neighbours can be a source of tension, but they can also provide support in difficult times, and bolster our sense of civic community. A neighbour might take in your mail while you're away for a few days or offer a cup of tea when you've had a rough day. To measure the strength of neighbourly connections, our survey asked people: 'How many people are there living around here from whom you can easily ask small favours? I mean people you know well enough to borrow tools or things for cooking?' In 1984, Australians averaged seven neighbours of whom we could ask favours. By 2005, this was down to six. In 2018, it had fallen to four.

Another metric of neighbourliness is the number of people you can casually drop in on. To measure this, we asked: 'Thinking now about this area, more widely. How many friends do you have in this area whom you could visit any time, without waiting for an invitation? You could arrive without being expected and still be sure you would be welcome?' In 1984, the average adult knew ten neighbours that they could drop in on. By 2018, people averaged just four. On the 'small favours' metric and the 'drop in' metric, Australians know only about half as many neighbours as in the past.

Naturally, none of these metrics is perfect. Rising incomes and home-delivered meals might have decreased our need to borrow a potato peeler from the neighbours. Ubiquitous mobile phones may have changed the 'drop in' culture to one of 'text first'. Yet it is striking that whichever way you ask the question, it seems to point in the same direction: towards a society in which we are less connected to our neighbours than in the past. Australian Bureau of Statistics figures over the eight-year period from 2006 to 2014 show a similar decline.[46]

Ironically, these trends coincide neatly with the period that Australia's longest-running drama series has been on air. Since its first broadcast on 18 March 1985, *Neighbours* has screened over 8000 episodes; dealing with everything from alcoholism to adultery, intergenerational clashes to imprisonment. Millions have tuned in to follow the Ramsays, Clarkes, Scullys, Robinsons, Alessis, Timmins and more. Australians have loved *Neighbours*, but they know half as many of their real neighbours now as when it first screened.

Contemporary data point to some interesting features in how we think about our neighbours. Nine out of ten say we've met them, but more than half say we don't know their names.[47] This doesn't say great things about our ability to remember names, though it also points to the superficial nature of neighbourly relationships. Three out of five Australians say that we'd like to get to know our neighbours better, but we don't seem sure where to start.[48] The coming chapters will offer some ideas.

Loneliness

Before leaving the topic of friends and neighbours, it's worth saying a few words about social isolation. Our surveys found that over the period from 1984 to 2018, the share of people with zero trusted friends rose from 4 per cent to 6 per cent, while the share of people with zero reciprocal friends rose from 14 per cent to 18 per cent. Depending on how you define it, 6 to 18 per cent of Australians are friendless.

There has also been a rise in the share of people who report that there are zero neighbours of whom they could ask favours or who they could drop in on unannounced. Over the past generation, the share of people who said that they didn't have a single neighbour who would do them a favour rose from 11 per cent to 13 per cent, while the proportion who said that they didn't have a single neighbour that they could drop in on rose from 7 per cent to 17 per cent. This fits with recent research on loneliness, which finds that almost 30 per cent of Australians hardly ever or never catch up with friends.[49] Half the population report feeling lonely for at least one day a week, while one-quarter of Australians feel lonely for three or more days each week.[50] In 2017, the federal minister for aged care said that two-fifths of aged care residents get no visitors at all.[51] Former US surgeon general Vivek Murthy believes the world is suffering from an epidemic of loneliness.

A significant change over recent generations has been the falling share of Australians who live with others. As Figure 16 shows, in the early 1930s, 99 per cent of adults lived with at least one other person. This fell to 95 per cent in the mid-1970s, 90 per cent in the mid-1990s, and 89 per cent in the mid-2010s.

Figure 16: Share of adults living with others

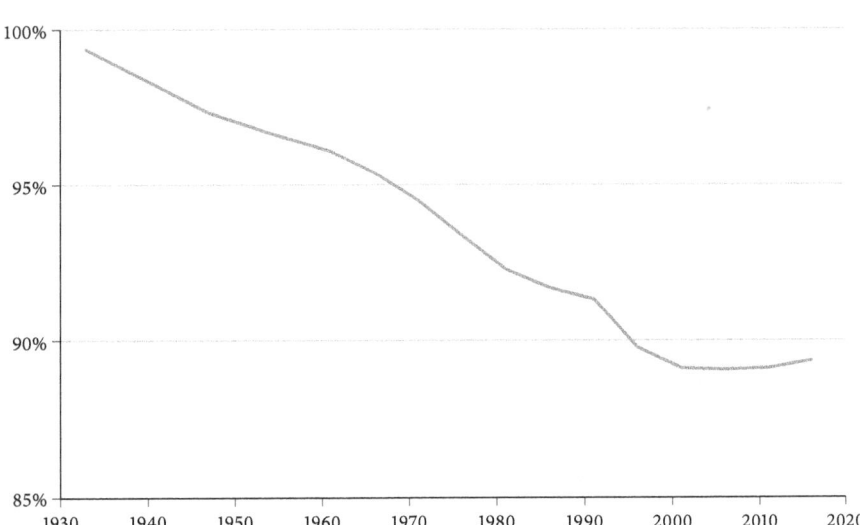

Solo living has upsides and downsides. In 1995, a heat wave in Chicago killed 739 people, shocking city leaders and public health researchers alike. Why were so many people unable to find a cool place to shelter? As a seminal study by sociologist Eric Klinenberg revealed, the answer had to do with social connections.[52] His 'social autopsy' of the disaster revealed that many of the victims died alone. US surveys suggest that those who live on their own have relatively high rates of loneliness.[53] Yet while they are more likely to experience loneliness, people who live alone are sometimes deeply engaged in civic life. They enjoy more freedom and choice and are better able to focus on their own needs. Solo living can often be the best available option. 'As lonely as I sometimes feel when I'm on my own,' an interviewee said, 'there's nothing lonelier than living with the wrong person. There's no feeling more lonely than having a domestic partner with whom one was once intimate, with whom once had a feeling of trust and connection, and coming home and feeling disconnected from that person.'[54] Many people appreciate the autonomy of a household of one, but as a society it's important to ensure that people who are living alone aren't lonely.

At its extreme, isolation can lead to suicide. Figure 17 charts the suicide rate in Australia since 1910, both as a raw rate, and adjusting for changes in the age composition of the population.[55] On an age-adjusted basis, the chart shows that the Australian suicide rate was highest in the early 1910s, 1930 and the 1960s. While other measures of social capital have worsened since the 1960s, the suicide rate has thankfully improved, falling to a low of ten deaths per 100,000 people in 2005. Since then, the rate has risen to around thirteen deaths per 100,000, a worrying trend that appears to match the pattern in the United States and New Zealand. These 'deaths of despair' are driven by many factors, including joblessness, mental illness and substance abuse, but social connections are also an important part of the puzzle. A stronger community is less likely to allow people to fall through the cracks.

Figure 17: Suicide rates

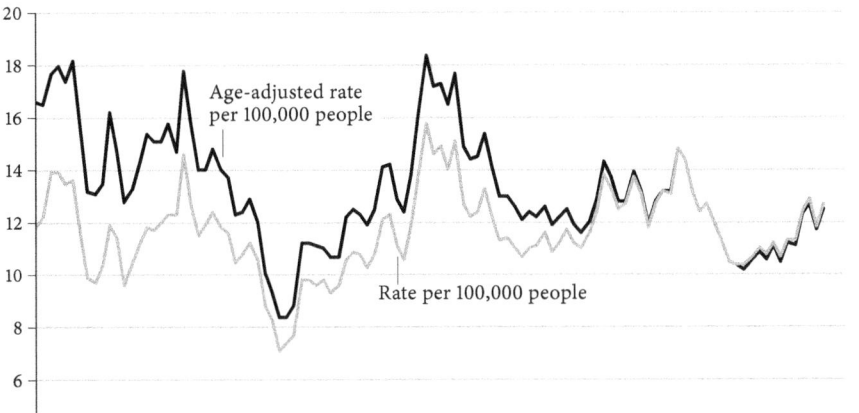

One particular cohort appears to be hard-hit. In Chapter 4, we outline the evidence on the mental wellbeing of young Australians. Across multiple surveys, the mental health of teenagers appears to have worsened considerably. Unlike much of the other evidence we review, the shift is quite recent – taking place largely in the 2010s. Although we cannot be sure about the causal link, the timing of this change coincides with a sharp rise in the prevalence of smartphones and tablets among young Australians.

Giving

In recent surveys, around three-fifths of Australians say that they have donated money to charity in the past twelve months. Among Australian donors, the most popular causes are supporting children, helping the poor and funding medical research, followed by donations to homeless people and people with disabilities.[56] Asked why they gave money, the most common answers were 'I care about the cause', 'I want to help people less fortunate than me', 'I realise I can make a difference' and 'It makes me feel good'.[57]

How has this changed over time? Because small changes in question wording can affect the outcome, we have to find a survey that asks precisely the same question on multiple occasions. From 2011 to 2018, Roy Morgan's survey shows a decline in the donation rate from 70 per cent to 61 per cent. This is only a relatively short time span, but the trend is down.

Another approach is to look at the share of Australians who claimed a tax deduction for charitable donations. This will only be a subset of donors, but it provides a way of tracking philanthropy over a longer time span. Our analysis of tax data is shown in Figure 18. In 1986, 48 per cent of Australians claimed a tax deduction for their charitable donations. A decade later, this was down to 32 per cent, and has hovered around that level ever since. In 2017, the most recent year for which these tax estimates are available, 33 per cent of taxpayers claimed a tax deduction for charitable donations. In dollar terms, total tax-deductible donations have steadily risen, but this appears to reflect the generosity of a small number of affluent philanthropists (which in turn may be a product of rising inequality).[58]

While the decline in the giving rate has been modest, international experience suggests that the standing of the entire charitable sector is at risk if organisations push too hard for money. In 2015, Olive Cooke, an elderly British woman, took her own life. Her family blamed charities, which they said had bombarded her with telephone calls and letters requesting donations. When it emerged that Ms Cooke was on the target list for around 3000 charities, the case sparked a national debate in British philanthropy about whether charities had become too aggressive in their hunt for cash.

Figure 18: Share of people who donate to charity

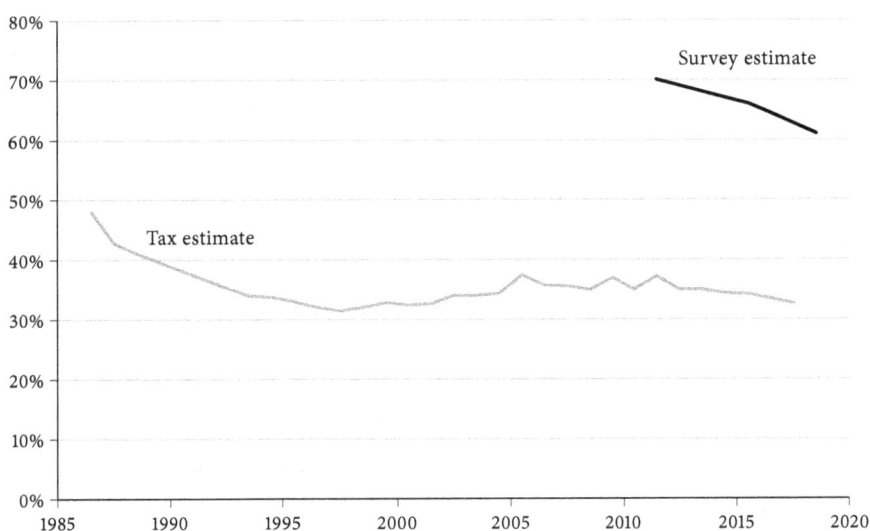

Similar issues surround street solicitation of donations – the charity workers dubbed 'chuggers' – short for 'charity muggers'. Actor Samuel Johnson describes them as 'snakes', while journalist Mary Ward related her experience of chuggers disproportionately targeting women, sometimes using sexual language.[59] Two-thirds of Australians dislike being asked for money on the street, but many hand over cash just the same.[60] About one-third of the donations go to the chuggers and the fundraising companies that employ them.[61] Even so, there have been reports of chuggers being underpaid and exploited.[62] At its best, philanthropy is 'the gift that gives twice'. At its worst, it's the gift that doesn't give at all.

A generation ago, charities raised a significant portion of their revenue through postal campaigns and doorknocking. Today, online fundraising accounts for an increasingly large share. This means that it's necessary to update fundraising laws that were written in an era when the web was something a spider wove, and online was what you did with wet laundry. But it also poses a significant challenge to charities to ensure that their fundraising campaigns are ethical and informative.

Charitable donations depend not only on having a big heart, but also on having some spare cash. That's why donations typically fall during recessions, because squeezed household budgets reduce the ability of people to translate their generosity into philanthropy. But there's one area of donation where being big-hearted is enough: blood donations. Humans have around five litres of blood, and except for the small number of people whose medical conditions prevent them from donating, we're all equally able to turn up to the local Red Cross and offer them our veins. So what share of Australians donate blood? Over the period 1998 to 2018, the annual blood donation rate fell from 3.2 per cent to 2.5 per cent, as shown in Figure 19. To some extent, this has been made up for by the rise of 'superdonors'. Some are truly exceptional, such as Sydneysider James Harrison, who gave blood 1173 times between the ages of eighteen and eighty-one, earning him the moniker 'the man with the golden arm'. Donors also give more frequently

Figure 19: Blood donors

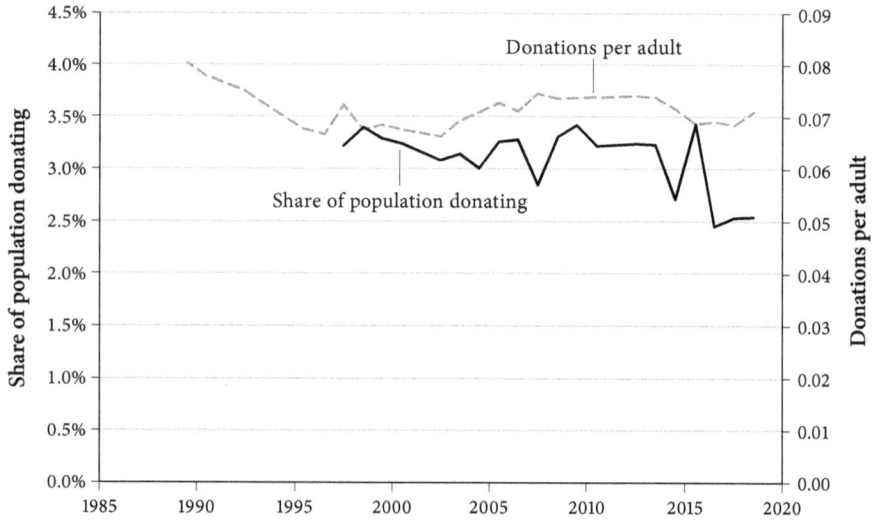

following the introduction of plasma donation, which allows donors to give every two weeks (rather than every twelve weeks for blood donation). But even despite this technological advance, the number of donations per person (including blood and plasma) dropped from eight per 100 adults in 1990 to seven per 100 adults in 2018. Consequently, Australia now imports two-fifths of its plasma.[63]

Government surveys

We were also intrigued to uncover a new trend, one that has gone largely unnoticed. Australians are substantially less likely to answer government surveys than in the past. This matters because surveys are a kind of public good. Throughout the year, the Australian Bureau of Statistics asks a sample of the population to participate in surveys about everything from housing to healthcare. Like picking up litter in your local park, filling out surveys takes an individual some time, but provides a larger benefit to the community. While participation is theoretically compulsory, the statistical boffins at the Australian Bureau of Statistics are reluctant to punish people for failing to do their civic duty.

The cost of failing to fill out surveys is both national and local. If hardly anyone agreed to do government surveys, we'd have a much fuzzier picture about everything from business startup rates to crime victimisation. But at a local level, failing to complete surveys can have a negative impact on the local neighbourhood. Government funds are often allocated based on population counts from surveys. In the United States, one study estimated that every household which failed to fill in the Census cost the community US$900 in federal grants.[64] When deciding how to allocate bus routes, state governments use demographic information from surveys, so refusing to answer surveys can reduce the quality of public services in your community. A jobless

Figure 20: Government survey response rates

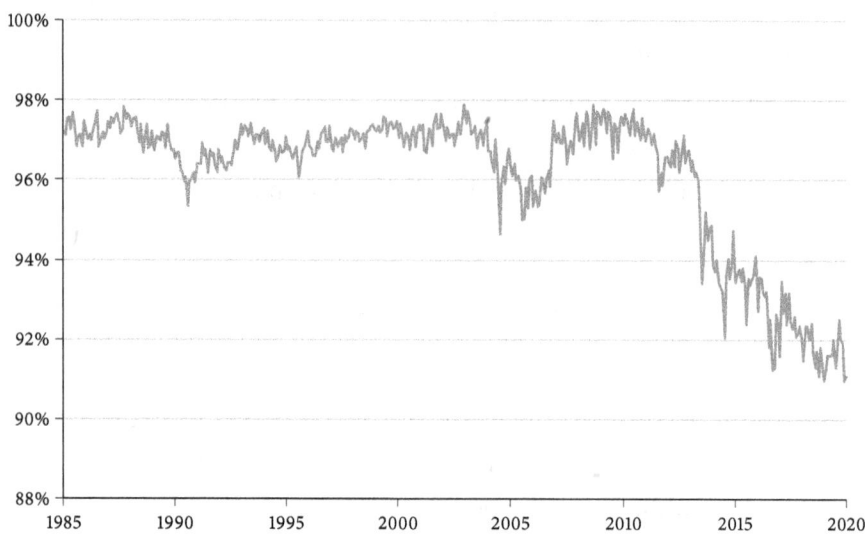

person who refuses to answer the employment survey reduces the resources that are targeted towards their community.

Figure 20 shows the response rate to the Labour Force Survey, one of the largest surveys carried out by the Australian Bureau of Statistics. The survey takes around fifteen minutes to complete, and provides a range of indicators, including the unemployment rate. From 1985 to 2010, around 97 per cent of Australians agreed to answer the labour force survey. Then in the 2010s, the response rate fell dramatically. By 2020, only 91 per cent were answering the survey. Our series ceases in February 2020, when coronavirus caused the bureau to change the way it conducted its interviews. A similar drop has been observed in response rates to the household expenditure survey, though in that case the slump appears to have begun earlier.[65] The decline in the survey response rate represents another way in which Australians are less willing to take an action that comes at a small personal cost but carries a large community benefit.

'We' versus 'me' in Australian books

If Australia has become more disconnected, we should see it in the language – not just in the new words that enter the dictionaries, but also in whether society speaks in connected language or individualistic language. A powerful source for this is the Google Books database, based on millions of scanned volumes. This is used by Putnam and Garrett in *The Upswing*, but where their analysis focuses on American books, we look at Australian books (or, more specifically, books that mention the word 'Australia'). To compare connected language with individualistic language, we estimate the relative frequency with which Australian books use the connected pronoun 'we', compared to the frequency with which they contain the individualistic pronoun 'me'.[66] Our findings are shown in Figure 21. Throughout the twentieth century, Australian books were twice as likely to use 'we' as 'me'. The ratio peaked in the 1940s – perhaps reflecting the shared sacrifice of World War II – and remained high until the 1990s. In the twenty-first century,

Figure 21: Ratio of connected words to individualistic words in Australian books

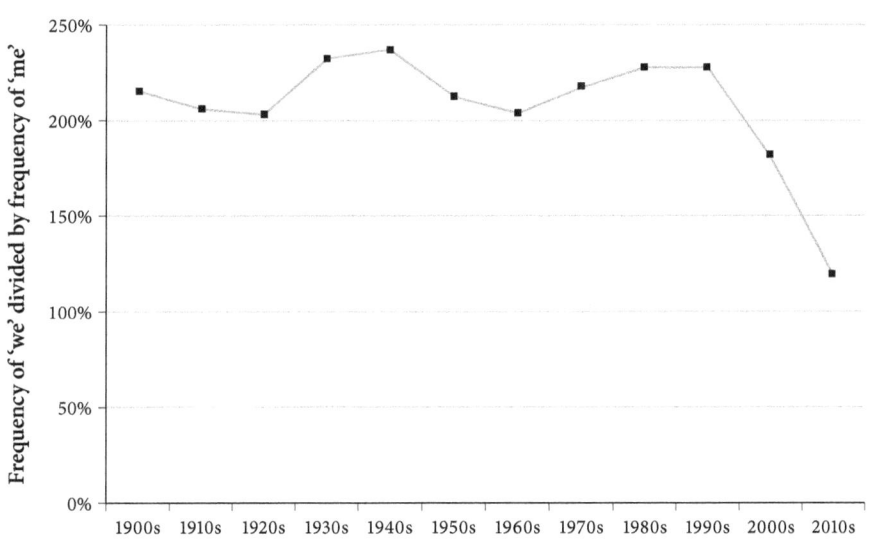

the use of connected language declined dramatically, so that in the 2010s, the word 'me' appeared in Australian books almost as often as the word 'we'. On this metric, Australian books are now more individualistic than ever before.

Indigenous social capital

Lastly, it's worth looking at the data on social capital in Indigenous communities. In these communities, the concept is often regarded differently. If you've ever spent time in an Indigenous community, you'll quickly lose track of people's aunties, uncles and cousins. Family is a broader concept, and helping out those in the community is often seen as 'just what you do', rather than a form of volunteering.[67]

Comparing social capital metrics across Indigenous and non-Indigenous Australians, a mixed picture emerges. Some studies have found higher levels of volunteering among Indigenous Australians, while other research suggests that Indigenous Australians are less likely to believe that most people can be trusted.[68] Just half of Indigenous Australians vote in national elections, compared with nine-tenths of non-Indigenous Australians.[69]

What about the trends over time? The National Aboriginal and Torres Strait Islander Social Survey asked a sample of Indigenous Australians whether they had been involved in selected cultural events, ceremonies or organisations in the previous twelve months. These included Indigenous festivals, carnivals, sporting events, NAIDOC week activities and funerals (known as sorry business). In 2002, 68 per cent of Indigenous people had been involved in such ceremonies. By 2015, this had fallen to 63 per cent.[70]

Another clue about the trends over time comes from looking at differences across generations. A study conducted among the Yawuru people of Broome found that civic connections were much weaker among younger generations.[71] Compared with those aged eighteen to twenty-eight, community members aged forty-five or older were more likely to attend community meetings or rallies, or share Yawuru culture. Older community members were more than twice as likely to vote at Yawuru community meetings. Three-quarters of older Yawuru people said they voted in state and national elections, compared with just one-fifth of younger people. While it is possible that this reflects a lifecycle pattern rather than a secular trend, the figures are consistent with a decline in civic engagement in this Kimberley community.

To recap, over recent decades, the number of Australian associations per person has fallen by four-fifths, and the share of people involved in social, civic and political groups has declined. Across a dozen large organisations, the membership rate is down by three-quarters since the mid-1960s. Volunteering rates are down. In the 1940s, almost half the population attended a religious service at least once a month – now it's just one in seven. In the thirty elections held between 1925 and 1998, the share of the population casting a valid vote averaged 92 per cent. In 2019, it was 87 per cent. Australians are less satisfied with democracy, and less interested in elections. In the decade to 2018, there was a 37 per cent fall in the proportion who have trust and confidence in the federal government.

The mainstay of workplace social capital has traditionally been the trade union. But union membership has declined from 50 per cent in 1982 to 14 per cent in the most recent survey. Among private-sector workers, twenty-somethings and migrants, fewer than one in ten are members of a union. On the playing field, Australians are less likely to let our children engage in free-range play, with the result that they are less physically fit than kids in the mid-1980s. Among adults, three-fifths of sports, including tennis, golf, cricket and rugby, are on the wane. Australians are giving up organised sports in favour of unorganised activities such as walking and gym-going.

What about social ties? Our survey research found that the typical Australian today has half as many close friends as in the mid-1980s and knows only about half as many neighbours. Indeed, half the population now admits to not knowing their neighbours' names. Loneliness is a serious social problem for many Australians, and a rise in the suicide rate since 2005 suggests that many don't get the help they need. From 2005 to 2017, the share of school students who say they are 'very stressed' rose from one-third to one-half.

When it comes to philanthropic giving, the data hint at a slight downturn. As charities switch from postal campaigns and doorknocking to online campaigns and chuggers, there is a real risk that donors' trust will be breached. Even the Red Cross, which continues to take its donations the only way possible (alas, technology cannnot displace the good old needle), has seen a drop in donation rates in recent decades.

We also found evidence that the decline in social capital is affecting communities in unexpected ways. Australians are 6 percentage points less likely to answer government surveys – a decision that can have adverse impacts on their local communities. The language in Australian books is less connected and more individualistic. Indigenous communities appear to have suffered a drop in social capital, with participation in cultural activities falling since the turn of the millennium. Gathered together, this array of evidence confirms that many of Australia's bonds of reciprocity are fraying.

Encouragingly, most Australians are unhappy about these trends. Three-fifths of the population would like to know our neighbours better. Over four-fifths of Australians believe that declining membership rates in community organisations is an undesirable trend.

A better-connected society will be a more satisfying place to live.

Such a community will also be better prepared to meet major challenges. Whether those problems are predictable, like climate change, or unexpected, like a global pandemic, they can only be solved collectively. The resilience that comes with reconnecting will be critical in keeping our communities happy, healthy and productive. These same indicators of declining social capital that we've surveyed above will also serve as yardsticks against which to measure the success of rebuilding efforts.

Creating a more connected community is about helping others. So we begin with volunteers – society's helpers – to see who's innovating, what they're doing and how the rest of us can learn from them.

3

VOLUNTEERING

Times of crisis can serve to remind us of what matters, stripping life back to the essentials of health, love and human connection. When COVID-19 upended normal life in Australia in early 2020, two-thirds of Australia's volunteers cut back on their voluntary activities.[1] Millions of willing helpers were unable to participate in their usual way, but there was a counterbalance. Isolation measures sparked a flourishing of loosely organised kindness cooperatives and spontaneous support for strangers. While the crisis exposed some frailties in our volunteering structures, its deeper message was that Australians are ready to help their neighbours. This is a hopeful sign.

To solve collective problems, we don't just need smart ideas, we need strong networks through which such ideas can spread. Volunteering bridges groups of people that might never have connected otherwise. The ideas that follow will help community builders create, extend and strengthen those networks.

Connecting in a crisis

On 21 December 2019, as residents in the Adelaide Hills prepared for the arrival of a fire front that would kill two people, injure twenty-three firefighters and destroy seventy-two homes, 76-year-old Denis Noble and his wife were monitoring the advance of the front, watching flames rolling steadily over a nearby hill and down towards their home. They had moved into the area just the previous week. When the flames began to take hold in an open paddock that led up to their residential street, an energetic posse of neighbours quickly came together to form a bucket brigade that ultimately halted the fire's advance at the road line. Noble described how 'it came slowly, inexorably towards us ... we're oldies. They're full of energy and tearing around with buckets. Everybody pitched in to stop the fire and it stopped at the roadway. It was a good way to get to know the new neighbours.'[2] This was a dramatic introduction to a new home base, but also a deeply affecting experience of gratitude and fellowship with a new community.

Large-scale emergencies boost social capital. When the fire season of 2019–20 started to consume townships and displace communities around coastal New South Wales, East Gippsland and the Adelaide Hills, the outpouring of community assistance initially outpaced the official offerings. Social media campaigns to garner money and accommodation took off. Community organisations and spontaneous informal collectives organised donation points for essential items (water, food, clothing) and partnered with small-scale voluntary logistics operations to get assistance to people who'd been forced to flee their homes. Facebook and Twitter hummed with updates from the fire fronts and with earnest outpourings of helpfulness from concerned people looking on from afar.

Organic and anarchic, every good turn prompted more. At times, the well-intentioned assistance created organisational and logistical headaches for relief operations. A community in East Gippsland received 10,000 apples. They really needed money. In other communities, donations of clothes, furniture and toys clogged up community halls, leading Jeremy Hillman from the NSW Office of Emergency Management to warn, 'We see all over New South Wales that these halls get filled up to the roof, and at the same time the community has nowhere to come together while it's full.'[3] Huge numbers of people were expressing, and maybe discovering for the first time, a desire to do something good for people they would never meet. But without the right systems in place, the chance to translate that spontaneous altruism into a lasting volunteering ethos would be missed.

When it comes to measuring the benefits social capital can generate for individuals and their communities, disaster response and recovery is one of the better researched fields. Disaster-prone areas tend to have firmly established routines of communal response. Economist Aitor Calo-Blanco and his collaborators looked at a range of regional areas in Chile with varying exposure to earthquake activity and found that 'social cohesion increases after a big earthquake and slowly erodes in periods where environmental conditions are less adverse'. Drawing on research around other disaster scenarios, they noted that when disaster struck, people had a tendency 'to create networks associated with higher social cohesion'.[4]

Disasters hit a community indiscriminately and all at once, short-circuiting the usual evaluation humans make about who deserves our help and whether a favour will be returned. There's a Darwinian rationalisation for this process, with communities in adverse locations needing to cooperate to survive. The Chilean study concluded that 'exposure to earthquakes seems to be consistently associated with higher levels of positive and lower levels of negative social cohesion indicators'. People gave more to charity, volunteered more and were more likely to vote. They were less likely to engage in crime and reported higher life satisfaction. The effects eroded gradually as the earthquake receded into memory, suggesting the crisis point was a factor in these changes.[5]

A similar pattern occurred in the United States after the terrorist attacks on 11 September 2001, which killed almost 3000 people. Social capital surveys before and after the attacks found that Americans were 6 per cent more likely to work on community projects.[6] They were also more trusting of government, co-workers and neighbours. But these effects faded over the subsequent years. Unlike the way that World War II moulded the lifetime volunteering habits of the birth cohort sometimes dubbed 'the greatest generation', the September 11 terrorist attacks did not leave a lasting impact on social capital in America.[7]

To optimise resilience and recovery, Japanese local government areas have learnt that where evacuees need temporary resettlement, they should be kept in groupings that maintain local bonds. Organised activities and volunteering can strengthen social networks among disaster-affected residents and help them maintain morale. The activity could be a tea ceremony or having an elderly resident tell a story to a group of children. One study found that regular attendees gained around one extra friend. Their sense of agency and belonging increased.[8] Participants were more likely to share their opinion in public meetings, vote and interact with elected officials.

Such studies suggest that low-cost social infrastructure investments can have better returns than physical infrastructure. The challenge is to build smart structures that turn disaster-inspired altruism into volunteering efforts that are useful in the short-term and benefit the community in the long term.

COVID-19 generated a range of spontaneous social infrastructure. In coastal northern New South Wales, Bellingen Shire Council's preparation for the oncoming challenges of the pandemic provides a good example of how local organisations can help small community units form a regional web. The Bellingen Shire Pandemic Response Group was created in early March as a precautionary collaboration to prepare the community for upheavals across social support, clinical services, council activity and local business. The group was administered and resourced through the council, and guided by community members. 'It's all about helping the community help itself,' explained the facilitator, Dean Besley. 'We don't know what we're facing, we just know we're better if we do it together.'[9] The Response Group gave a role to each of the major sectors in the town – health, council, business – and created a new Neighbourhood Care Network specifically to sustain connection and social support. A radio ad told shire residents, 'The more of us who register, the easier it will be to get help for people who really need it. And this will be important if things do really get tough.' Local 'Champions' were encouraged to take initiative in their area and set up neighbourhood networks of about fifty people: large enough to spread the load, but small enough to make communication simple – through emails, text messages or Facebook. The council hopes that the preparation has strengthened the district's resilience, making the community safer and more connected.

We'll return to some other examples of COVID-driven volunteering in the final chapter, but for now it's worth noting that Bellingen Shire Council's response both addressed an immediate need *and* helped build resilience. This kind of positive synergy needs its own name. In his dystopian novel *Nineteen Eighty-Four*, George Orwell imagined a world in which a totalitarian regime had replaced all superlatives with the word 'double-plus-good'. We think it's time to repurpose Orwell's Newspeak term for a more positive purpose. When community groups deliver a dual benefit, we call it 'doing double-plus-good'. Because setting up and maintaining local resilience networks strengthens local ties, it's double-plus-good.

How dealing with disasters changed volunteering

While her own house was flooded and uninhabitable, Sarah Borg travelled three hours to an area where the floodwaters had already receded and the clean-up process was underway. She camped out with other volunteers at a local high school so she could be on hand for the long days the teams were putting in clearing local farmland. 'It was a time when we couldn't do anything else, so while I couldn't do anything on our house, I thought if I went and helped someone else it would be a way of saying thank you for the other people helping us.'[10] Borg would wake up at first light, and by 7.30 am would have been allocated to a team deploying to flood-affected properties, where she would spend the day untangling debris from farm fences and picking up sticks to clear paddocks. 'What really stood out to me was how close everyone was. Just from looking at them and how they interacted, you would have thought they had known each other for years, but in fact they had known each other for only a few days.'[11]

Between 2008 and 2011, Queensland was hit by a series of extraordinary weather disasters. In each case, the community response was also extraordinary, with unprecedented surges of community volunteers offering to assist. While trained emergency services volunteers were integral to the response plans, there was no established mechanism to manage spontaneous volunteers. Well-intentioned people were travelling from other parts of the country to be a part of the disaster response, but there was no system to ensure that the right number of people with the right skills were arriving at the right place at the right time. Volunteering Queensland was brought in, partnering with the Red Cross and the Salvos to coordinate volunteers. With the assistance of a corporate-supplied customer relations management tool, they created the Emergency Volunteering Community Response to Extreme Weather system: EV CREW for short. When it launched in the summer of 2010–11, EV CREW handled over 120,000 offers of assistance.

EV CREW relied on the live-matching work done by Volunteering Queensland. The matching platform is adapted from the organisational structure and technology of sales and recruitment agencies. Volunteers and organisations registered online or over the phone and the software allocated people to tasks that disaster recovery organisations listed. That way, an organisation which requests ten volunteers for each of five different jobs doesn't suddenly find fifty people at one spot and zero at the others. For volunteers, EV CREW ensures people don't waste their time showing up to a task that already has too many helpers.

In emergencies, EV CREW allocates volunteers to tasks as close to their local area as possible – places where they have the best chance of fostering meaningful connections and cohesion beyond the crisis. While effective management can minimise damage and speed up recovery, it also means more people will meet and support each other during a time of high anxiety. It's an experience that many emergency management workers associate with better emotional recovery from the trauma of natural disasters. Nature can be cruelly indifferent, but the generosity of volunteers is deeply inspiring.[12]

Beyond the response and recovery phase of any specific emergency, EV CREW check in routinely with volunteers to make sure they feel appreciated and to keep databases up to date. Volunteers can also keep contributing as local community advocates for emergency preparation, sharing information and building social resilience in their area. By channelling people into this continuous program of preparation, the program creates safer communities by encouraging better connections.

Technologically, EV CREW's cloud-based system quickly matches incoming offers of assistance to incoming requests for help. Managers can segment the vast database by location, availability and skills to pinpoint the closest suitable volunteer. Julie Molloy, who played a key role in developing EV CREW, recalls a call coming in after dinner one evening, about a street in a Brisbane suburb that needed sandbagging repairs ahead of rising water that would soon pass through. Entering the location into the volunteer database, the operator got a hit on the same street. The potential helpers were a single mother and her teenage sons. The family were sitting on the couch watching television when they got the call from the EV CREW operator. Would they be available to head out and fix the sandbags? The mother asked the boys, they all agreed, got on their shoes, walked up the road and did the job. Then back to the couch. Molloy points out that these are people who don't want to turn up every week and wear a badge. They don't want to be a part of a cause, but they want to help, and will when they're asked.

The lesson has spread throughout volunteer management peak bodies across the country, who have developed a range of similar platforms. Organisations that can structure their activities to appeal to both regular and occasional volunteers stand a better chance of recruiting new (and particularly younger) volunteers. The irony of disaster management is that you hope your plans will never be tested.

Identifying potential volunteers

When Curtin University's Kirsten Holmes looked at the dynamics of volunteering in rural Western Australia, she saw that volunteering was a catalyst for sustaining reciprocity, mutual aid and social networks. But she also observed a troubling trajectory for the core group doing most of the volunteering. Regional areas often have higher rates of volunteering than urban areas, with unpaid helpers staffing the firefighting units, paramedic teams and visitor information centres. This builds community but can leave gaps. A lack of professional services can see families, older people with specific medical needs and young people moving away to areas with better services and more opportunities. In turn, this can deplete the volunteer base. In regional Western Australia, it has been estimated that 9 per cent of the most active volunteers will soon leave. Many vital services are simply not viable without volunteer support networks. And if these crucial services can't be sustained, neither can the towns that rely on them. So for many regional areas, smarter ways to recruit new volunteering populations are a first-order requirement for the community's survival. Here's where one of the neatest, most pragmatic social capital hacks comes into its own.

Holmes has developed an open-source tool that can identify the best prospects for conversion to volunteering. It recognises that not everyone is itching to volunteer. We all sit somewhere on a spectrum. Those at the volunteering end might face the same barriers to participation as those at the non-volunteering end (a busy job, family commitments and travel constraints), but when they weigh the cost of getting past that barrier against the value they place on the cause they're supporting, they choose to help out. Volunteers find it just as hard to make time in their lives as non-volunteers but choose to make the necessary sacrifices.

Holmes's analysis of volunteers and non-volunteers suggested the group of potential converts – non-volunteers whose habits and behaviour most resemble those of existing volunteers – is typically about 10 per cent of the non-volunteering population. If this 'convertible' one-tenth of all non-volunteers started to participate, Australia could increase volunteer numbers by about 1.6 million people. The key is to focus attention on people who currently sit outside the existing volunteering population, *but only just*.

Like commercial marketers trying to target new customers, this kind of analysis recognises that some people are persuadable and others intractable. The Convertibility Calculator asks questions about traits that show up as clear points of difference between volunteers and non-volunteers, and generates a convertibility score. The five-question survey asks subjects about current group affiliations, existing habits around helping others, attitudes to volunteering as a young person, whether they feel competent to help others, and past motivations for volunteering. It takes less than a minute. The calculator is a tool any organisation could use to improve volunteer attraction and retention.

Connecting people with causes

Of the world's thirty-two volunteer-matching sites, seven are in Australia, suggesting an unusual enthusiasm in the Antipodes for linking volunteers with charities.[13] One of them, Do Something Near You, is a little different to most volunteering portals. There is no need to sign up and it takes no time to get started. You simply type in your suburb or postcode and it connects you with a host of things to do. Users can then refine the initial listings by clicking on a category such as 'Disadvantage', 'Environment' or 'Youth'. The strength of the platform is the wide range of 'things to do' including markets, festivals, events, fun runs, issue-based advocacy and community gatherings. Do Something Near You provides links to everything from activities you can do in your neighbourhood to nationwide campaigns.

Volunteering Australia, the peak body for volunteers, has created its own matching website and app. GoVolunteer allows volunteers to filter opportunities by location, cause and duration. Choices range from one-off assistance for a few hours through to regular volunteering for six months or more. GoVolunteer also lets you select roles specifically suited to people from groups that may face steeper barriers to getting involved in volunteering. These include 'people learning English', 'families and children', 'people with disabilities' and 'online and remote volunteers'. GoVolunteer draws on the strategies used by leading international volunteer-matching platforms, such as Volunteer Makers in the UK and VolunteerMatch in the US (which claims over 15 million volunteers connected, and 4 million available opportunities, including in Australia).

Another hub, Communiteer, started out as a web platform specialising in skills-based volunteering. Founders Vincent Feng and Victor Lee set up a platform that gave charities access to skilled volunteers who could team up online to complete multifaceted projects. Lee likens it to an Airtasker for social good. The original Communiteer platform was designed to broker skills-based volunteer transactions, but Feng and Lee were disappointed to discover that once the transactions were completed, people often left and didn't come back. So they changed tack, turning Communiteer into a place where charities, corporate volunteers and social entrepreneurs could share their interests, work together to support causes that matter to them and stay connected long-term.

Communiteer's internal social network aims to be a space where members can 'hang out', interacting with the community and sharing its purpose without any heavier commitments. Communiteer's charity and corporate partners are encouraged to plug their staff into the network. As Lee envisages it, the site is about building a 'habit' of giving back: 'That means allowing people to do good in their own way. So whether they want a thirty-second action or high commitment, like quitting your job to go away and do volunteering in foreign aid – we want to be the space that provides all the choices.'

Communiteer's approach is a reminder of the value of organisations switching tack when things aren't working. It also illustrates the importance of volunteers feeling that they are part of a larger movement. Whether an organisation is trying to keep its volunteers engaged or attract new recruits, building a sense of esprit de corps among volunteers can be valuable.

Matthew Boyd set up Vollie after a common entrepreneurial experience: he went looking for something he thought must exist, and when he couldn't find it he built it himself. Vollie is focused exclusively on online volunteering opportunities. As Boyd puts it, 'On Vollie, you land and you get to the point: what are you good at? What do you care about? And then opportunities appear from right around Australia and you can complete the project anywhere.' Because online volunteering can start immediately, he knew it was essential that the sign-up process be quick and simple (a principle we've seen in other successful social capital activities). Vollie aims to engage skilled professionals, 'people hitting their strides, red-hot at what they do, with fresh knowledge and cutting-edge understanding in tech, marketing, comms'. When COVID-19 struck, Boyd reported that requests for online volunteers from charities doubled, but offers of assistance from volunteers increased five-fold. The pandemic, he says, 'fast-forwarded Vollie's relevance'.

Matching platforms are making episodic and so-called 'micro-volunteering' roles more available, which means more people will be able to try them out. But some in the community sector are anxious about the cultural shift that could result from increased reliance on episodic volunteers. There are also concerns that volunteer-matching sites have been slow to address the kinds of concerns over privacy and security that have embroiled social media giants such as Facebook and LinkedIn. Perhaps we shouldn't be disappointed that no website has a monopoly over Australian volunteer matching, and that charities and volunteers have multiple matching engines through which to connect.

Matching sites are especially well suited to online helping, since volunteers can log in, find an opportunity, and get to work – all without leaving their home. Even before COVID-19, virtual volunteering opportunities were proliferating. An Australian organisation has been leading the world in this space, and the lessons they've learnt along the way can help other groups get the most from keyboard altruists.

Virtual volunteering

Teresa Van Der Heul is one of the Australian Museum's most prolific volunteers, but she's only set foot inside the Sydney premises a handful of times. Teresa is an amateur fungi expert and keen natural scientist, and from her home on the South Coast she has performed more than 500,000 separate tasks in the museum's digitisation project.[14] Her secret: 'My awake hours must be spent learning something and certainly never wasting time!'[15]

The Australian Museum has approximately 19 million specimens in its collections, and many are not registered in their digital archive. Museum staff wanted to capture and preserve the data and make it available online to researchers around the world, but with little funding available they had to think creatively about mobilising volunteers. Paul Flemons, who manages digital collections and citizen science at the museum, came up with a plan to harness many small contributions of time from remote volunteers. And in collaboration with the Atlas of Living Australia, the Museum developed the DigiVol crowdsourcing platform. Rhiannon Stephens, who coordinates the DigiVol program, gives an example of how it works: 'Volunteers come into our museum labs and photograph specimens with their labels. Our virtual volunteers then work online to transcribe all the label data into text. That goes to our database and then gets harvested out to biodiversity sites like the Atlas of Living Australia.' Without the remote transcribers who power DigiVol, this work wouldn't get done.

When it started in 2011, DigiVol had 100 volunteers. It now has 6000 and is helping institutions all around the world digitise collections. During the pandemic lockdown, the number of new DigiVol helpers nearly doubled. The structure and size of the tasks mean there's always work for volunteers to do, so no volunteer goes away frustrated. The DigiVol team have developed online equivalents to the kind of rewards and incentives they can provide to on-site volunteers.

Virtual volunteers receive recognition when they reach certain milestones. These awards are distributed at the same time as the NSW Premier's Recognition awards, to reinforce remote volunteers' sense of being part of the Australian Museum community. DigiVol maintains a daily leaderboard and an all-time honour roll of the most prolific volunteers. Volunteers receive newsletters and information about the projects they're working on. Team leaders respond to questions from volunteers and make sure they feel welcomed as an important part of a project team. When a project is completed, team leaders share a final report that shows the volunteer team the outcomes of their work.[16] Behind all those micro tasks is a rich array of people who share the bond of their commitment to natural history.

Being a part of the museum's virtual community can also deliver some unique perks. The DigiVol team introduced Van Der Heul to the researchers who had produced her favourite material to transcribe, the Antarctic Diaries. 'I had the pleasure of meeting some of the geologists who actually lived on the ice and wrote the diaries,' Van Der Heul recalled. 'They are old men now (older than me, but I'm old too) and they were delightful to talk to one on one about their experiences – their time with the dogs, how they cooked their meals, the instruments used for recording, fishing, penguins, seals, etc. We could have talked for weeks.'[17]

The Australian Museum has made the DigiVol platform available to other institutions for similar digitisation projects. This allows DigiVol volunteers to help the CSIRO, Geoscience Australia, the New York Botanical Gardens and London's Natural History Museum. The open-source code developed for the DigiVol platform has been copied by replica sites in Belgium and South Africa, and adapted by the Smithsonian.

DigiVol has much in common with another Australian online volunteering platform, the National Library's Trove project. Also started in 2011, Trove has attracted thousands of virtual volunteers in the years since. Collectively, Trove editors have corrected more than 120 million lines of text in scanned newspaper articles. Trove's most prolific corrector, John Warren, has made more than 2.5 million corrections.

Volunteers have written the world's most popular reference work (Wikipedia) and the world's most commonly used operating system (Linux). Yet most organisations that rely on volunteers still expect them to be able to work to the institution's rhythms. Virtual volunteering attracts different kinds of people and different personalities. For introverts, it provides a way to be part of a meaningful community. For those who live in remote Australia, have accessibility challenges or hold down a nine-to-five job, it allows the flexibility they need to contribute. For the Australian Museum, it's been a vital way to tap into a new pool of human resources.

Combining multiple projects, virtual science volunteering hubs such as Zooniverse and the Australian Citizen Science Association invite potential volunteers into a virtual volunteering fair, purpose-built for curious minds and willing helpers. Each project is an online anthill, with hundreds of discrete research tasks being undertaken by thousands of remote volunteers. The site allows someone sitting at a kitchen table in Bronte to classify wildlife in Botswana, using footage from 'camera traps' that have managed to catch a glimpse of elusive species. Other volunteers help transcribe notes from the digitised sketchbooks of Henry Moore and Francis Bacon. This work is the kind of thing you could do on the train, five minutes at a time. This is the key process in making micro-volunteering work. To get the anthill to complete your project, you need to make sure it's in ant-sized pieces.

Citizen science is finding new ways to create enduring relationships with their crowdsourced supporters. App developers are gamifying data collection through smartphones, creating challenges and incentives so that volunteering to log wild orchids becomes a quest as compelling as Pokémon Go.[18] Even without the leaderboards and virtual gold stars, the projects can generate emotional satisfaction. Seamus Doherty, a student at the University of South Australia, expresses the pleasure of assisting researchers: 'It had always been a passion of mine to help researchers in different fields (environmental science, biology and cosmology, to name just a few of my favourite fields) to sort through and interpret mass amounts of data via online organisations, such as Zooniverse, just for the sheer joy it gave me to be helping real researchers make new and exciting discoveries. And here I am today, developing a citizen science mosquito surveillance programme of my own in an effort to help control arboviruses in South Australia as part of my honours thesis.'[19] *The sheer joy it gave me to be helping*. Flow, the helper's high, vocation, community – for Doherty these are all wrapped up together in one online network. This suggests that for Doherty, online volunteering delivers some of the same benefits as face-to-face volunteering.

For organisations wanting to tap into the micro-sphere, Zooniverse's advice to project builders is a good place to start. Break down projects into discrete tasks. Maybe one person will still take it on as a job lot, or perhaps a few people will share the work. Micro and virtual volunteering will become more important and bring new people in, but there's no reason traditional and micro volunteers can't coexist happily.

Talking it up

Digital tools and marketing approaches have been reshaping volunteer management in the image of social networks for some time. A common concern we've heard from non-profits all around Australia is that volunteering lacks prestige and profile. But social tools are already starting to change that, and new digital volunteering platforms are more assertive and self-confident in the services they're offering to volunteers and the organisations who rely on them. Image, narrative, emotion – these are the currency of influence and influencers, and they are the fundamentals of experience sharing. An easy sign-up path is critical for recruiting new volunteers, but an organisation first needs a compelling story about its purpose, followed by an engaging call to action.

A couple of years ago, the St Vincent de Paul Society realised it was struggling to connect with younger volunteers and supporters. The management knew they needed a way to get into a conversation with a generation that didn't know what the organisation stood for. So they got some advice from an image consultant, and started asking existing volunteers to tell their stories and share photos. A bearded hipster in a Batman t-shirt says, 'Everything's impossible until someone does it.' A Vinnies store worker is quoted as saying 'I love being able to give back to my local community'. Two volunteers in the sorting room laugh together in their blue Vinnies aprons. The key to collecting good stories was enlisting all staff and volunteers as researchers by providing them with a template for turning everyday encounters into usable Vinnies content. Vinnies staff would capture a good visual, take notes on the context and record contact details of anyone involved. That material was then fed back to the central content curator for polishing and publishing. Vinnies watched to see what kind of content, stories, pictures and events got the strongest audience response across different demographics and channels.

Vinnies' digital strategy doubled their web traffic and increased their traction with younger audiences. Richenda Vermeulen is the director of digital strategy firm Ntegrity, which partnered with Vinnies to reposition the charity's brand. Vermeulen believes that 'not-for-profits have a goldmine of content available to them. Stories that span their unique work, the everyday impact they have, issues they fight on the frontline for, and their volunteer heroes.'[20] It's not unusual to use volunteer stories to humanise a brand or to share the emotionally engaging narratives of its people. But the way Vinnies gave widespread organisational backing to the storytelling showed their volunteers, supporters and would-be volunteers how central their role was in the Vinnies mission.

Smarter digital outreach doesn't have to involve hiring consultants. There are lessons for organisations of any size in the Vinnies experience. As Vermeulen explains: 'Finding great content doesn't require big budgets or big teams. Neither should it rest on the shoulders of one content curator to source, create and produce all online content. What it does require is a whole community of people who have open eyes and open ears to what is going on around them. Does your team know it's their responsibility to be on the lookout for great stories?'

Mining user-generated content and cultivating a compelling social media presence can help organisations augment their volunteer recruiting and engagement strategies, build communities with a strong shared identity and create emotional bonds to meaningful causes. And Holmes's Convertibility Calculator might then tell them who they should tell that story to.

Finding a tribe

Deploying user-generated content to attract like-minded supporters encourages recognition; it prompts a personal response that can lead to identification or aspiration – 'I belong' or 'I'd like to belong'. The data science of 'convertibility' rests on the idea that the people who are most like existing volunteers are the people most likely to become volunteers. Recruitment by association can be efficient and effective, and whether the association is to a shared cause or to the kind of people that support that cause, it's a strong basis for bonds that will last.

Puddle Jumpers is an Adelaide children's charity that provides camps, holidays and get-togethers for children who don't live with their birth parents. Founder Melanie Tate and her team help the children develop the resilience, confidence and social skills they will need to 'jump over puddles' later in life, by supporting them to mess around and 'jump in puddles' as children. Tate says their strategy for expanding their volunteer pool is unorthodox, but it essentially follows the same principles as the Convertibility Calculator or a volunteer-matching search engine – they recruit by association. Puddle Jumpers asks new volunteers to bring along a friend or family member. It's a simple principle: where one person is drawn to support the work and principles of the Puddle Jumpers program, there's a good chance their close friends or family will share similar values. Puddle Jumpers asks volunteers to take on challenging work and difficult problems, and the culture and approach to volunteers reflects that. As Tate explains, 'We're more comfortable with friends and family members, so we give more of ourselves because we feel more confident and outgoing.' There are advantages for reliability too. 'It's like encouragement, like a gym membership. If you join with a friend, sometimes they don't feel like going, sometimes you don't, and so you attend more if you encourage each other'. 'Normally someone would find the organisation and think it's great, then go back and tell family and friends, then bring people along, the boyfriend or grandma, to share the positive experience. We encourage them to take the mission to their acquaintances and we organise social events for the volunteers that would encourage them to bring family and friends that they'd like to share the experience with. So we actively encourage them to expand our network through theirs.' In 2019, Puddle Jumpers doubled in size, and Tate is now planning an expansion from South Australia into Victoria.

For Tate, the aim is to challenge conventional thinking about who can contribute. Puddle Jumpers' approach has allowed them to get past some of the barriers that can stop socially isolated or disabled people experiencing the fulfilment and social benefits that come with purposeful volunteering. 'We're all vulnerable,' says Tate, 'anyone's circumstance could change, and we consistently give the message that people can contribute and we can find ways to support that.' Tate explains: 'One of our most dedicated volunteers is housebound because she has a fear of leaving her home and is anxious about driving. Our volunteers drop food to her house and she cooks and prepares the food for our Free Food night. We pick up the finished product and bring it back for the kids. She's been volunteering for three or four years and has never been physically on our site. She found us through social media, identified with the cause and has become an important resource.' Tate tells another story about a young man who is non-verbal and has several disabilities, but who was determined to help. The team tried a few things, without success. Eventually, working with the young man's support team, they hit upon a plan where he would use his time with paid carers to do delivery drives for the organisation's food service. He was satisfied and his carers were delighted – he now has a tribe and a new purpose. Puddle Jumpers' approach proves that the best volunteers can sometimes be found by thinking creatively.

Overcoming obstacles

Remoteness, cultural and language barriers, and disability can make it challenging for some people to get involved. Virtual volunteering provides some pathways, but it also takes creativity, commitment and time to figure out how to bring people in from the margins. 'In the service centre at Volunteering Queensland we had two women come in separately,' recalls Julie Molloy. 'One lady was partially sighted and one lady was partially deaf. So we were able to match them up and they worked together so that one would read the script for the other lady to type out. They became really good friends and went on to do things outside of that. You could see all sorts of people connecting in a social way with a sense of purpose. The platforms enabled them to participate in these community mobilisations in a way that was structured and needed, and that they hadn't been able to do before.'

The Deaf Society found a way for deaf volunteers to contribute to emergency management and preparation, devising a world-first program of Deaf Liaison Officers. Deaf volunteers and emergency services personnel worked together to build knowledge, awareness and networks to support deaf people in emergency situations. Roberts explains that 'this in and of itself was ground-breaking – that type of ongoing role-based volunteerism was virtually unknown in the deaf community'. Along with the resilience structures they were building, the Deaf Liaison Officers strengthened the identity of the deaf community and created new connections to the wider community. Through collaborations with the NSW State Emergency Service, NSW Rural Fire Service, Fire & Rescue NSW and the Red Cross, Deaf Liaison Officers now help train emergency services personnel. As one officer puts it: 'I'm passionate about providing information to others where they do not have the ability to rely on radio messaging, or newsletters where English isn't their first language.'

In Brisbane, Maia Tua-Davidson found herself facing another kind of participation challenge. As the manager of Welcoming Sport, Tua-Davidson builds community connections and inclusion through structured sporting activities. She recalls: 'I was approached by a group of young Somalis who wanted access to facilities and support for their community football in a park. They invited me along and I expected to find ten people kicking a ball. But there were over 150 people, all playing different roles. They had uniforms – a box of t-shirts the kids put on to play in and then left behind at the end of the day. They had the mums sitting in the shade with their friends and young children. And around the park on the benches, the older men, all the community elders, were doing their social thing. And the community was doing that every day of the school holidays.' Tua-Davidson was struck by this structured organisation sitting outside the grassroots system. It was flourishing and internally strong, but isolated. It mirrored formal structures but received none of the benefits of connecting into wider community networks or the traditional sporting systems that can be a meeting place for diverse communities.

In many migrant communities, the top sport is soccer. Yet established clubs have traditionally expected people to integrate into their structures and culture. Tua-Davidson was part of a new initiative, known as Welcome to the Game. It worked with local community groups, multicultural organisations, councils and clubs to make football more accessible for more people. Regular low-cost, community-driven tournaments were scheduled to coincide with national days of celebration. During the fasting month of Ramadan, kick-off times were shifted. Uniform fees were subsidised. For players who were ready to move beyond their informal sporting community, Welcome to the Game offered accredited coaching and referee training.

Welcome to the Game established arrangements with local clubs where membership fees could be waived for some of the young players if they volunteered to coach the junior programs. This not only removed a financial barrier, it ensured that the volunteer coaches quickly became valued members of the club's community, boosting cross-cultural understanding in clubs with minimal cultural diversity.

It's still sometimes a fraught process for young people at their first club. Tua-Davidson notes, 'For the first part of the season they might struggle to get to training with public transport – but by the end of the season they're getting lifts, getting picked up by teammates and going out with club members after the games.' And seeing the new connections those volunteers were making also encouraged other groups in their community to be more open. A group of Somali women, who had been nervous about being active in public, started their own organisation. 'The effect rippled through the whole community,' Tua-Davidson reflected. 'Now kids attend local homework clubs and women visit Neighbourhood Houses.' By giving community members skills they could trade on outside their close networks, Welcome to the Game helped a whole range of people in the community see new opportunities. But one of the clearest lessons from Welcome to the Game's bridging activities is for mainstream sporting clubs. In the face of waning participating rates, why not reach out to participants from underrepresented communities? And to increase the chance new players will make the transition to formalised club structures, make sure you know where the obstacles might arise and let your new recruits know they're welcome.

In the Kimberley region, Garnduwa was created in 1991 as a central organisation to support sport. Working with the West Australian Football Commission, they have helped develop competitions among thirty teams across the region. On a typical dry-season weekend, that means up to 800 men and women taking the field. While Aussie Rules is Garnduwa's largest program, they also support basketball, athletics and general fitness programs. Once a year, they run a festival that brings teams from across the region into Fitzroy Crossing for a tournament and celebration of culture, with participants travelling up to 1000 kilometres to join in.

Garnduwa also have a role that has nothing to do with health or fitness. With few other structures supporting formalised volunteering, Garnduwa's sporting programs boost community cohesion and provide a valuable outlet for members to take on organisational and leadership roles. As chief executive Michael Albert explains, 'If a community has a footy team and they're training twice a week and playing on the weekend that's three occasions people are getting together to achieve a common goal.'

'We help build volunteers,' Albert explains, 'that idea, the culture in sport where in a metro area like Perth, your mum and dad go down to support, be coach, cut the oranges, that's what's happened for a long time. And we're developing that. Because there haven't been these clubs in remote communities, so they're still developing that culture. We identify people to coordinate that and develop the culture and be the glue. We need people to do all those roles and we help by building up that idea of volunteering.'

While Welcome to the Game and Garnduwa generate extra benefits around their core activities by recognising and supporting the volunteers who want to help them do good things, some migrant and refugee services are making similar progress by creating formal volunteering roles specifically for their client communities. The Mount Druitt Ethnic Communities Agency is a settlement service providing individual case management for new Australian residents. They provide information, local knowledge, advice and referrals to services. They also work to give new migrants and former refugees the cultural grounding that will help them establish themselves in their area, and the confidence to connect with communities outside their own. Volunteering is widely recognised as a way to gain skills, experience, connections and confidence, and to prove some basic workplace savvy. But if you're facing language and cultural barriers, it can be difficult to land a mainstream volunteering role. The agency found that a major obstacle to its graduates getting work (a key part of the settlement journey) was migrants' inability to find the volunteering roles that might make their résumé look more attractive to potential employers. So they set up their own volunteering program, drawing directly from the local communities they were servicing.

The Mount Druitt Ethnic Communities Agency is another example of double-plus-good social capital. The organisation benefits from the assistance of their volunteers, while the helpers themselves receive a structured volunteering program, and a stronger résumé.[21] Unlike most volunteer organisations, this one wants its volunteers to leave – it's actually the goal of the program. The lesson is a valuable one: community organisations working with clients who find it hard to access mainstream volunteering programs should look at how they could include them in their own operation.

Corporate capital

Workplace volunteering days are a standard activity in many companies' team-building toolkit. They can be the start of deeper partnerships and can bring corporate employees, non-profits and their clients together to learn from each other. The benefits for the community are also real enough. But a team of accountants doing a food rescue session has a fraction of the value of a team of accountants giving non-profits a day of pro bono bookkeeping. And from an institutional perspective, when an organisation gives staff paid leave to voluntarily share their professional experience, they're taking on a categorically different kind of social responsibility. Corporate volunteering that lends out the expertise of employees effectively moves some of the running costs of a non-profit onto the balance sheet of the business which pays the volunteer's salary.

As more businesses get serious about corporate social responsibility, more will realise their potential to make significant and lasting impacts. Workplaces contain a stock of skills and experience, and are a reservoir of career and networking savvy. Deploying these resources in the service of a non-profit will create more good in the world than lending out professional staff to clean up litter and paint fences. Here's a few examples we think can point the way.

As a part of their corporate support for drought-stricken Lightning Ridge, the NSW NRMA, a member-owned mutual organisation, partnered with Outback Links to provide free repairs for farming equipment, tractors, utes, and motorbikes.[22] NRMA roadside patrol officers have visited farmers in the area annually since 2014, volunteering their time to make sure farmers don't fall behind in the upkeep of vital equipment while waiting for the drought to break.

Ardoch, an education charity, aims to improve school students' skills and workplace connections. The charity runs several corporate volunteering programs – including Literacy Buddies, Learning Through Lunch, and Engage – which pair schools in disadvantaged areas with corporate workplaces. In the Literacy Buddies program, students and their buddies exchange letters throughout the school year and meet up at the school and in the workplace. The program seeks to improve students' literacy and connect vulnerable children with mentors. In Learning Through Lunch, a small group of students go to a restaurant for a meal with their corporate mentors to learn how to be at ease with unfamiliar authority figures and how to handle themselves in social situations they may not have encountered. Children from comfortable homes will probably be at ease in fancy restaurants. But for someone who's grown up in a disadvantaged setting, making a good impression at a business lunch while using the correct knife to butter your bread can be a stressful experience. The Engage program has a similar approach, with corporate volunteers providing mock job interviews, leadership training, career advice and study tips.

Seventy-eight per cent of Australian companies have a volunteering program, but only 15 per cent of employees volunteer through their workplaces.[23] Put simply, most workers could volunteer through their workplaces, but choose not to. If Australia can get better at facilitating corporate volunteering and make it easier and more rewarding for workers to get involved, we'll have happier workers and stronger communities.

GoodCompany, a workplace volunteering facilitator, produces an annual ranking of corporate volunteering programs. In 2019, the top spot went to Origin Energy, which offers employees unlimited paid time off for volunteering. Food services company Sodexo and consulting firm Accenture took the silver and bronze medals. Yet even among the companies that are further back in the ranking, there has been a significant increase in the number of paid volunteering leave days. In 2018, 34 per cent of the companies participating in GoodCompany's survey offered two or more days of paid volunteering leave. In 2019, that figure swelled to 49 per cent.[24] GoodCompany hopes the annual publication of their 40 Best Places to Give Back list will spur a philanthropic arms race among top corporations, with social impact budgets expanding in a competition to provide employees with the best opportunities to volunteer. Companies are responding to the expectations of customers and staff that they should invest in the wellbeing of the communities that generate their profits. Having a good story to tell about what a company is doing to fulfil its corporate social responsibility has become an important way to build brand loyalty and compete for the best employees. GoodCompany chief executive Ash Rosshandler believes that companies are now beginning to understand that 'by not putting a budget aside for team-building volunteering opportunities they actually might fall behind companies who are willing to spend a few dollars on it'.[25]

Third-party platforms such as GoodCompany, Communiteer, BeCollective and Vollie aim to help businesses get greatest social impact from their social responsibility dollar by linking them to suitable charities, offering payroll administration tools and facilitating social impact reporting to shareholders. Charities in turn get access to high-value pro bono skills. Companies can offer some hours from their graphic design or tech team, or lend out accountants and lawyers. Charities can put out an in-kind tender for the expertise they need: 'senior professional required for board position'.

BeCollective's platform tracks volunteer engagement and verifies the outcome. The goal is to provide volunteers, non-profits and corporations with an authoritative record of their input and impact. 'All the data is live online,' says BeCollective's Mark Campbell, 'we're looking at it and so are the charities. BeCollective is about facilitating that community connectedness and goodwill and measuring everything.' The social record that BeCollective provides to its volunteers has been described by the New Zealand government as the best volunteering passport to employment they've seen. The verified outcomes also provide a solid reporting basis for corporates measuring their social impact, and for non-profits preparing grant applications.

Professional associations can also play a pivotal role in setting industry norms for pro bono contributions. After devastating bushfires hit the east coast of Australia in 2019–20, the Australian Institute of Architects established Architects Assist. The program matches professional architects who are willing to offer free services with individuals and businesses who need advice on rebuilding. So far, over 600 firms have signed up. The Australian Institute of Architects hopes that carefully designed structures will have a better chance of surviving future disasters. While the bushfires crystallised the initiative, Architects Assist is intended as an ongoing facility that will match pro bono assistance with disaster-affected communities. It will build a lasting knowledge base and share expertise with developing countries, where architectural skills could have similar benefits for safety and resilience.

Organisations can also mobilise their members. The NRMA has established a DriveTime Program that recruits volunteers from among its 2.6 million members as driving mentors to help refugees living in Western Sydney and the Illawarra practise driving and get their licence.[26] The program helps refugees connect to their new communities, and taps into the skills of the many experienced drivers who make up the NRMA membership.

Among animal and plant breeders, there's a principle known as 'hybrid vigour'. That's when different parents are bred together, producing a cross-bred offspring with qualities that are superior to both parents. At its best, corporate volunteering partnerships provide a chance for hybrid vigour in the social context. When talented volunteers join forces with mission-driven charities, the resulting partnership can produce something that neither organisation could deliver on their own.

Achieving this result requires work on both sides. Charities can press corporates to share not just volunteer hours, but also valuable skills and connections. Firms can do a better job of measuring impact and engaging their workforce. Companies that want to get serious about workplace volunteering should set an engagement target that at least matches the average level of volunteering across the community (one in three) and provide the right incentives to get employees involved. Professional associations have a role too. They should seek to match the pro bono ethos of the legal profession, which has a proud record of providing skilled assistance to charities and non-profits. Effective corporate volunteering is about doing good better.

Creating culture

In the junior Aussie Rules leagues in Western Australia's south-west region, there's been a long-standing tradition that younger players from the home club volunteer as boundary umpires for the senior games. But researcher Kirsten Holmes found this culture had been put under strain in the area when some clubs started offering payment to fill traditionally voluntary roles.[27] The south-west region, taking in Bunbury, Manjimup and Boyup Brook, is a spread-out network of communities supported by mines, wines and tourism. Some high-school students in the area travel two hours each way to school, leaving little time in their lives for sport or volunteering. Finding regular volunteers is a real challenge for many grassroots competitions. But when some clubs were seen to be paying their volunteers, long-time Aussie Rules volunteers worried that it signalled a cultural shift, with young players no longer expected to give back to the bouncing game.[28] They also feared the shift would have adverse implications for the future of community volunteering more broadly. Whether or not to pay volunteers is a challenging question not just for West Australian Aussie Rules teams, but for other community organisations too. Volunteers don't expect to get paid, but they also don't expect their commitment to bring significant personal cost.

As we saw in Chapter 2, volunteering rates are declining. Some traditional volunteering models seem less and less suited to twenty-first-century lifestyles. Many young people complete their education without the experience of giving back to the community through school-based volunteering. Episodic volunteering platforms, experience-based volunteer challenges and clever engagement strategies can hook young people, but will these experiences be sufficient to create a culture of lifelong volunteering? To sustain the services and the social connections volunteering supports, Australia's culture of volunteering needs careful cultivation.

Volunteering Australia has been arguing for volunteering to be included more prominently in formal, organised school activities – because if we want future generations to help out in the community, we should start the habit young. Meanwhile, volunteering and philanthropy programs for children are catering – sometimes literally – to the needs of young volunteers. In the Sydney suburb of Bondi, Our Big Kitchen offers holiday volunteering programs and school group experiences. Parents can book their children in for a day of food preparation and cooking, as a contribution to the charity's main purpose as a food provider for people in need.

In order to create 'the next generation of generosity', Carole Schlessinger and Ruth Tofler-Riesel created Kids Giving Back, a charity which facilitates family volunteering opportunities. Schlessinger and Tofler-Riesel believe that when young people volunteer, they develop respect, resilience and leadership skills, and become better at engaging in the wider community. The organisation's Connect4Good programs run on weekend afternoons, partnering with organisations such as the Horn of Africa Relief and Development Agency. Kids Giving Back even extends its mission to a workplace volunteering pitch – offering companies the opportunity to combine corporate social responsibility activities with family.

Volunteering with a parent also helps organisations deal with duty of care legalities which can make engaging under-eighteen volunteers too tricky for some. Facilitating family-based volunteering could mobilise a new volunteer pool. Introducing young people to the benefits of volunteering is a smart investment for community builders.

Conserving culture

How do you fire a volunteer? It's not the first question you'd think of when planning an enterprise that will rely on people power, but it turns out to be crucial. Elaine Bensted, chief executive of Zoos SA, which operates Adelaide Zoo and Monarto Safari Park, puts the value of their volunteer workforce at $4 million. Zoos SA invests significant effort ensuring their volunteers understand the values of the organisation. Applicants go through a detailed recruitment, training and induction process. They then need to pass through an assessment process before they can get the green light to be a part of the team. Finally, volunteers receive the same mandatory training in the values of the zoo as the paid staff.

The charter of values ensures the culture of the organisation remains consistent as the volunteer pool changes. It allows volunteers to pledge a kind of allegiance to the overarching purpose of the zoo. But it also makes it clear that where any individual is detracting from that overarching purpose, they will be moved on. An organisation should never be so grateful for the generosity of any one volunteer that they would compromise their values rather than reject that gift of time. Zoos SA have maintained the established values of the organisation by being willing to let volunteers go, just as they would with staff. So every now and then, volunteers must be 'exited'. Or, to put it another way, fired.

What's going on here? The approach reflects an institutional seriousness about the role of the volunteer workforce. There's a pragmatic courtesy to the majority over the outlier. For every volunteer that is failing the values test, there's a whole pool of people around them who are soaking up bad vibes. That initial formal agreement between the organisation and the new recruit underpins a social compact of mutual respect between Zoos SA and its volunteers, which Bensted fulfils as chief executive by meeting with the volunteers on a monthly basis to fill them in on her plans for the zoos.

Every group doesn't have to sustain every individual to be building community. Establishing simple guidelines that keep the volunteer pool in sync with the values of the organisation creates a better experience for effective volunteers and avoids the productivity drain of handling personnel issues without a clear framework. With their charter of values in place, Zoos SA have found it easier to attract new volunteers to their team and their volunteer numbers have increased significantly.

Getting the lions out of the giraffe enclosure is one way to build a healthy culture in a volunteer team. Another way is to manage that valuable resource properly. Volunteer management is a human skill as well as a software challenge. A look at the ups and downs of volunteer engagement in the Landcare movement gives a sense of why attentive management is a clever path to productive and fulfilled volunteers.

Since the 1980s, Landcare has been bringing people together to tackle conservation projects and address local community challenges. 'Landcare is often viewed through the lens of conservation and sustainable agriculture,' explains Landcare NSW's Leigh McLaughlin, 'however it's all about people.'[29] Landcare groups work to sustain local habitats, but they also nurture the social health of their communities, addressing mental health in drought areas as readily as infestations of weeds and pests. 'In rural communities Landcare is often the main community group, and sometimes the only one. It's a place to meet up with neighbours and talk over problems, as well as getting people outside and into nature.' But that social element is typically built on a project, and without proper support many Landcare groups were struggling. 'About five years ago', explains McLaughlin, 'we got a letter from a Landcare group saying they just couldn't do it anymore. "We've got a grant from the government but we're sending it back, we can't do it without support." That coordinating support had diminished, so people were wondering why they were bothering.' That's when the organisation knew they needed their Local Coordinators back. 'As a volunteer movement, we can't do what we do without these coordinators. You have to have someone coordinating the local teams.'

Local Coordinators had been active in facilitating Landcare's early growth, but their impact had diminished since the early 2000s as the organisation's funding shrank. When Landcare NSW went to members to ask what they needed to get their network active, the members put Local Coordinators at the top of their wish list. In 2015, a state government grant allowed Landcare to make that wish a reality. Coordinators boosted morale among the groups and allowed them to work on local programs that mattered to them. One NSW Landcare group set a goal of zero suicides in their community. Others engaged more volunteers in their local area. Each coordinator has a multiplier effect.

Professional volunteer managers are out of reach for many non-profits, but there are some basic self-assessments any organisation can do at no cost, to check whether they're 'hot or not' in the eyes of volunteers. Kirsten Holmes's Convertability Calculator has a partner – the Recruitability Tool. The tool presents a simple matrix charting whether volunteers find it easy or hard to join, against whether the organisation finds it easy or hard to recruit. Based on data collected from eight exemplary volunteering programs, the tool then provides a handful of suggestions about simple, practical steps to make that move happen. For example: 'Talk to existing volunteers and ask them why they think recruitment numbers have changed.' There's also a set of questions to prompt self-diagnosis, such as: 'How many recruitment steps are there for new volunteers?' 'Is there a waiting list to volunteer at your organisation?' 'Can anyone apply?' 'Do your volunteers need special skills?' With its modest prompts to self-assessment, the Recruitability Tool can help organisations take some simple steps towards that basic principle of wisdom: know thyself.

Organisations that provide volunteers with great experiences can create a chain reaction, in which volunteers go on to become social entrepreneurs. As a 21-year-old, Anna Donaldson volunteered as a life story writer for older community members. Donaldson was connected with a lady called Patricia who wanted her life story recorded. She recalls, 'I started visiting her on weekends and it started as that project but became a friendship and an offer of companionship. I ended up visiting her for a couple of years before she passed away. I was twenty-one years old and I got a huge amount out of it in terms of what I learnt but it was also a really confronting experience. She was so isolated and alone, and towards the end I was the only significant person in her life. Seeing what that's like for someone to be so alone at the end of her life was eye-opening for me.' Donaldson went on to found Lively, a charity that combines employment opportunities for young people and social support for isolated older Australians. Lively is an example of a double-plus-good organisation, and it owes its existence to Donaldson's life-changing volunteering experience.

Like non-profits that make use of the professional expertise of corporate volunteers, some organisations are seeking out volunteers with special skills. Noticing that people looking after dementia patients often feel burnt out and underappreciated, the Australian Centre for Social Innovation created the notion of 'weavers'. Weavers are volunteers who've cared for someone in similar circumstances and have experience navigating services and dealing with the emotional burdens of being a carer. Weavers draw on their own experiences to reduce the stress of carers, improve their wellbeing and social connections, and increase their capacity to care.[30]

Another Centre for Social Innovation program that taps into volunteers' special expertise is Family by Family. The program's goal is to support at-risk children without removing them from their home or parents. The program matches 'seeking families' who need help with 'sharing families' who have been in similar situations and made it through. The sharing families support the seeking families on a voluntary basis. If the sharing families need advice, they can call on one of the professional Family by Family coaches, each of whom supports around fifteen sharing families. The sense of being supported, rather than managed, and the subtly corrective influence of the sharing families would not have been possible through more conventional approaches, such as paid counsellors or support workers.

After managing thousands of emergency volunteers, Julie Molloy still believes this was a role that showed her the best of people. As she recalls: 'A local Islamic group in Brisbane contacted EV CREW during the floods saying the wives are making sandwiches in the kitchen, the men have got the chainsaws ready to go and we've all given blood. That outpouring of generosity you see in these times, it restored my faith in humankind seeing what people would be willing to do to help each other. And what that does for resilience in the community in itself, the social memory that's created.'

In the energy, resilience and resourcefulness we've profiled in this chapter, there's plenty to be optimistic about. When it comes to recruitment, Kirsten Holmes's Convertibility Calculator and Recruitability Tool show the value that can be gained from straightforward surveys of existing volunteers. Online volunteer-matching platforms provide organisations with fresh sources of volunteers. Recruitment is also about simplicity – a theme to which we'll return. Charities should streamline their sign-up process and get new volunteers active as quickly as possible. There are also ways to make volunteering easier. Local recruiting means volunteers don't have to travel far, while offering helping opportunities outside regular business hours makes it easier for full-time workers to volunteer. It's also worth considering untapped sources of volunteers – like the partially deaf and partially sighted duo who teamed up as helpers to assist a Queensland organisation, or Mount Druitt Ethnic Communities Agency's use of volunteering to help provide work experience for new migrants.

When it comes to marketing, enthusiasm counts. Organisations should celebrate the good their volunteers do and the benefits they get. Compared with the bombast and bravado that marketers routinely use to sell sugary drinks or fancy cars, it's striking how modest Australia's non-profits are about their achievements. Much as we admire their humility, we think charities can afford to boast a little more. Alleviating poverty, averting homelessness, supporting crime victims and cleaning up the planet are incredible goals – and can be turned into effective selling points when organisations are looking for helpers.

Vinnies' enthusiastic showcasing of its volunteers is just one model for this, and its partnership with a commercial public relations firm is an approach that other organisations could adopt. We hope that the next generation of advertising professionals will feel an obligation not just to sell more sweet and shiny things, but also to provide pro bono assistance for charities seeking new volunteers.

Finally, an effective volunteer culture cannot be taken for granted. Volunteer inductions should leave helpers with a clear understanding of the organisation's purpose and their role in achieving it. Only when volunteers are reminding each other about the mission of the organisation can you be confident that the purpose is broadly shared. It's also worth creating a sense of esprit de corps, through sharing success stories, facilitating networking among volunteers and listening to volunteers' ideas about how the organisation can do better. We all like to feel like we're part of something bigger than ourselves, and building a volunteer tribe can create a self-sustaining identity for non-profits that seek to make the world a better place.

4

CYBERCONNECTING

At Cherry Bar, on AC/DC Lane in Melbourne, owner James Young finally decided he'd had enough of patrons 'holding their arms up like two f---ing windmills with their phone seven feet in the air'.[1] Rather than experiencing the gig, people were recording low-quality videos of it. So he banned mobiles. In order to 'protect what's right for rock and roll', Cherry Bar now advertises 'phone-free shows'. It's not excessively strict. As Young told us: 'People are asked not to film for over twenty seconds at a time unless the band approves filming. We want people to live in the moment.'

Many people sympathise with Young's approach. Pocket-sized supercomputers are having a seismic impact on social interactions and civic ties, especially for the generations who have grown up only knowing digital connectivity. Email has transformed office jobs. One in three new relationships starts online.[2] Social media has upended teenage socialising. More Australians are addicted to smartphones than smoking.[3] In the future, smartphones and tablets will only grow more powerful and useful, so it's essential that they are used in ways that make our lives more meaningful and engaged.

In this chapter, we take a deep dive into the evidence on how devices are affecting social lives and communities and discover fresh strategies for ensuring that electronic devices serve us – not the other way around. We call our approach 'CyberConnecting', because it's not simply about logging off. Instead, it's about users becoming more intentional, designers crafting software that strengthens society, and community groups harnessing digital technology to strengthen social capital.

But first, let's take a look at the problem.

Antisocial media

Peter Zimmerman was fifty-one years old when he died. He worked sixty-hour weeks as a lawyer and often used drugs to stay focused. His funeral was so packed that many mourners had to stand. While the tearful eulogies were delivered, many of Peter's co-workers stared at their phones. As his ex-wife Eilene recalled: 'Quite a few of the lawyers attending the service were bent over their phones, reading and tapping out emails. Their friend and colleague was dead, and yet they couldn't stop working long enough to listen to what was being said about him.'[4]

Australians use phones everywhere. One in three of us checks our phone within five minutes of waking up.[5] One in five admits to checking it while on the toilet.[6] As a result, one-sixth of mobile phones are contaminated with faecal bacteria.[7] Behind the wheel, one in four checks text messages while driving.[8] In busy cities, up to a half of pedestrians are distracted by smartphones when they cross the road.[9] At home, nearly three-quarters of Australians admit to using their phone during dinner with family or friends.[10] One in ten Australians admits to checking their phones during sex.[11] Perhaps it isn't surprising that sexual activity among Australian couples fell by one-fifth in the decade to 2013.[12] Indeed, an American survey found that one-third of respondents would prefer to give up sex than be without their smartphone, while almost half would work an extra day a week in order to keep the device.[13]

Apple says its users unlock their phones an average of eighty times a day.[14] Add on the times people check unlocked phones, and it turns out that smartphone users check their phones over a hundred times a day.[15] Total daily usage time has been estimated at 2.5 hours for Australian smartphone users. US research, which includes tablets, puts the average at four hours a day.[16] Much of this is on social media. Over a lifetime, one study suggests that people would end up using Instagram for eight months, Snapchat for fourteen months, Facebook for nineteen months, and YouTube for twenty-two months. That adds up more than five years on social media, considerably more than the typical person spends eating and drinking (three years and five months) or socialising in person (one year and three months).[17]

Smartphones are phenomenal. Mobiles make it less burdensome to be stuck in a long queue and easier to locate a friend in a busy city. They let us snap a beautiful moment, videoconference with our family, keep up with the news, check the weather and track our fitness. A world without smartphones would mean relinquishing music on demand, ubiquitous podcasts, ride sharing, mobile payment, and augmented reality mobile games. Sometimes, mobile phones even save lives. When 58-year-old Mark Lee suffered a heart attack in the Perth CBD, the St John First Responder app put a signal out to trained responders nearby.[18] Danny Rummukainen, a block away, arrived within minutes and was able to get Lee's heart started again before an ambulance arrived. Phones can help with diagnosis too: the SkinVision app claims to have identified over 40,000 skin cancers among more than one million users.

But are people using devices too much? Many people think so. When Australians are asked whether they use their mobile phones more than they would like, two-fifths say yes.[19] Office workers fear that their job description has become 'email answerer'. Parents fret that rather than invent new games, children think of imagination as something you download from the app store. An experiment by photographer Eric Pickersgill depicts people in everyday settings, with their smartphones photoshopped out.[20] The surreal series – 'Removed' – shows newlyweds, families at the dinner table and friends at barbecues, all staring dully at their hands. In 2017, Pope Francis urged Catholics not to take their phones to Mass. He told an audience in St Peter's Square, 'At some point, the priest during the Mass says, "Lift up your hearts." He does not say, "Lift up your cellphones to take pictures."'[21] Many worshippers ignore him, and surreptitiously check their phones when the sermon doesn't move the soul.

In the political realm, technology has been linked to political polarisation. If you have extreme views, it's never been easier to consume your news solely from people who think like you. YouTube's rules prohibit hate speech and harassment, but there is evidence that its algorithm keeps users addicted by taking them down radical rabbit holes.[22] Misinformation, trolling and cyberbullying have a corrupting influence on social media platforms, which privilege insults over ideas. Political conversations on Twitter have been compared to a debate in which a group at the back of the room are constantly shouting 'fight, fight, fight'. Unsurprisingly, many users retreat to like-minded online communities. Marc Dunkelman, author of *The Vanishing Neighbor*, argues that technology 'makes it much easier for us to connect to people who share some single common interest'.[23] Conversely, he argues, technology makes it simpler to dodge 'face-to-face interactions with diverse ideas'.

iGen

Today's teens are the most digitally connected people the planet has ever seen. Researcher Jean Twenge refers to those currently in high school as iGen – a cohort born after the internet, who have mostly grown up in a smartphone-dominated world. In her interviews with members of iGen, social psychologist Sherry Turkle shows that the one thing they hardly ever seem to do with their phones is make phone calls. Instead, teens communicate through texts, Snapchat, WhatsApp and Instagram. Some use Facebook, though its uptake has slumped among under-25s.[24] One interviewee told Turkle: 'I never really learnt how to do a good job with talking in person ... Even when I'm with my friends, I'll go online to make a point.'[25]

In 2012, half of American teens said that their favourite way to communicate with friends was in person. Today, only one-third feel that way.[26] From 2006 to 2015, computer and phone usage among 15- to 24-year-old Americans rose by seventeen minutes a day, to sixty-one minutes.[27] Meanwhile, socialising fell by twelve minutes, to sixty-nine minutes daily. Young Americans may now be spending more time on devices than socialising.[28] Binge watching is so addictive that the chief executive of Netflix believes his company's main competitor is sleep.[29]

As the first generation to be born into a world of ubiquitous connectivity, iGen are different from previous generations in unexpected ways. For example, American teens are less likely than young people in previous generations to leave the house without their parents.[30] The share who get together with friends nearly every day has fallen by two-fifths since 2000. Adolescence seems to be lengthening. By the end of high school, almost all American baby boomers had their driving licence. Today, only three-quarters of Year 12 students can drive. Among boomers and Generation X, about 85 per cent went on dates. For the current crop of Year 12 students, the figure is just 56 per cent. In recent years, US high-schoolers are also less likely to have a paid job than previous generations.

In *The Coddling of the American Mind*, Greg Lukianoff and Jonathan Haidt argue that the changes occurred rapidly, over the six-year period from 2007 to 2012. The iPhone was released in 2007. The first commercial Android touchscreen phones launched in 2008. Key social media platforms had their genesis around this period, including Facebook (publicly launched in 2006), Twitter (founded 2006), Tumblr (2007), WhatsApp (2009), Instagram (2010), Snapchat (2010), Pinterest (2010) and TikTok (2012).

Coinciding with these changes, the American researchers document a significant increase in the share of adolescents who say they feel lonely or depressed. US adolescents today are more likely to self-harm, and more likely to commit suicide. The shift occurred largely in the 2010s, and was most pronounced among girls. Lukianoff and Haidt argue that this is because boys tend to be physically aggressive (they punch and shove) while girls are more relationally aggressive (they try to hurt rivals' social standing). If a malevolent demon put a handgun in every adolescent's pocket, they say, the harm would be worst for boys. But if the same demon put a social-media-enabled smartphone in every adolescent's pocket, the damage would be worst for girls. Although it is difficult to link digital device use and mental wellbeing, the fact that the decline has been worst among girls is consistent with a causal connection.[31]

Does the same pattern exist in Australia? Young Australians are certainly prolific device users, with virtually all teens owning a smartphone or tablet. As to the lengthening of childhood, the share of Australian twenty-somethings living in the family home rose from 23 per cent in 1981 to 30 per cent in 2016.[32] There has also been a drop in the proportion of twenty-somethings who know how to drive a car.[33] But not all the Australian trends point in the same direction as the US patterns. Prior to the COVID-19 downturn, there was not a noticeable drop in the share of school students with part-time jobs. We were unable to find Australian data on trends in dating, getting together with friends, or leaving the house without a parent.

On the mental health front, the Australian data paint a disturbing picture. A survey of school students in Years 2 to 12 found that in 2005, 33 per cent reported feeling 'very stressed'. By 2017, 49 per cent of all school students said they were very stressed.[34] According to an annual survey of nearly 30,000 school students aged fifteen to nineteen, the share of young people in psychological distress rose from 19 per cent in 2012 to 24 per cent in 2018, with the increase being sharper for girls than boys.[35] The 2010s also saw an increase in suicide among Australian teenagers, from seven deaths per 100,000 in 2010 to ten deaths per 100,000 in 2017.[36] Focusing on a wider age group, the Household, Income and Labour Dynamics in Australia survey, conducted by the Melbourne Institute, found that the rate of depression and anxiety among 15- to 34-year-olds rose from 9 per cent in 2009 to 16 per cent in 2017.[37] Depression and anxiety among other age groups also increased, but not to the same extent as among younger people.

Advances in video game technology are tempting people away from regular employment. Today's massive online games are realistic, immersive and engaging. The software adjusts to your skill level so they're accessible for novices yet engaging for experts. Players can use headsets to chat with one another for hours on end. Four-fifths of Australian men aged fifteen to twenty-four are gamers, averaging two hours of daily play.[38] For a sizeable cohort, these games have come to replace work. Employment rates for American men in their twenties without a degree dropped markedly from the mid-2000s to the mid-2010s. Three-quarters of their newfound leisure time went into gaming, and they were increasingly likely to live with their parents.[39] As one commentator warns: 'Young men content to remain outside the labour force and play video games – while their parents provide food, shelter and health insurance – may begin to desire something else as the years pass. But, having been out of employment during a crucial period of life – early adulthood, when friendships and contacts are made, experience and skills cultivated – such gamers may find themselves unable to build the lives they come to realise they want.'[40]

New technologies are also reshaping sexuality. More than nine in ten Australian boys (and more than six in ten girls) have seen online pornography.[41] Many have viewed hundreds of online videos before they have held or kissed a partner. Online pornography is nothing like the magazines that past generations hid in their bottom drawers. Videos have replaced still images, and those videos are often explicit and rough. Analysing the most popular online pornography, researchers found that 88 per cent of scenes included physical aggression, such as gagging, choking and slapping.[42] When sex education comes from internet pornography, teenagers don't just get a warped version of what a healthy body looks like – they can also get a distorted perspective on what is normal in the bedroom. As experts Maree Crabbe and David Corlett found when they interviewed young men and women, those who have binged on online pornography often find it difficult to form an honest connection with their partners.[43]

Smarter smartphone use

Smartphones provide immediate entertainment, but can harm relationships. From 2005 to 2018, there was a significant rise in the share of Australians who agree with the statement 'I find myself occupied on my mobile phone when I should be doing other things, and it causes problems'.[44] Australians are increasingly likely to say that they have tried and failed to spend less time on their phone. Our devices have changed sex, politics and religion. They have coincided with a lengthening of childhood and a frightening drop in the mental wellbeing of young Australians.

Realising the ways that technology hotwires neural circuits is essential to figuring out how to become smarter smartphone users – the process we dub CyberConnecting. One aspect of this is the way that technology is often designed to hook us rather than serve our deeper needs. Snapchat's Snapstreak feature shows how many days two users have continually snapped one another, leading many Snapchat users to simply message their friends pictures of blank walls with the word 'streak'. As one user remarked, 'streaks quickly went from a fun, novelty feature of the app to one that caused me stress and anxiety'.[45] Former internet marketer Tristan Harris likens the features that make social media addictive to the way sugar, salt and fats keep people eating junk food.[46] Smartphones are often defaulted to vibrate or ping when a message arrives. Social media notifications that pop up on an unlocked screen have been compared to the 'variable rewards' that characterise poker machines. Overuse can change our brains.

After spending hours online every day, blogger Andrew Sullivan wrote that the skill of reading books began to elude him. 'After a couple of pages, my fingers twitched for a keyboard.'[47] He began to fear 'that this new way of living was actually becoming a way of not-living'. For Sullivan, part of the solution came in recognising the trade-offs: 'Every hour I spent online was not spent in the physical world. Every minute I was engrossed in a virtual interaction I was not involved in a human encounter. Every second absorbed in some trivia was a second less for any form of reflection, or calm, or spirituality.'[48] He attended a meditation retreat and started a practice of daily silent contemplation. His daily silences slipped from an hour a day to around half an hour a day, and then every other day. But it helped restore some balance.

Another insight is to recognise that multitasking is a myth. People can switch tasks, but it comes at a price. In one experiment, subjects took sixty-eight seconds to return to their main task after checking email.[49] As the University of Missouri's Nelson Cowan puts it, 'It can be exhilarating to flit from one conversation to another on Facebook, but people don't realize what's missing in the process. It's like having a delicious soup poured on your head.'[50]

Understanding the psychology underlying technology is essential to CyberConnecting. In one experiment, 124 busy professionals were randomly split into two groups.[51] Half were asked to turn on email notifications and permitted to check email as many times a day as they wished. The other half were asked to turn off their notifications and only check email three times a day. The limited email group didn't comply perfectly, but averaged only five email checks a day, compared with fifteen for the unlimited email group. Importantly, they experienced lower levels of stress, felt more productive and slept better. They were using email as it was designed – as an asynchronous technology that lets the recipient reply at a convenient time.

As well as turning off unnecessary notifications and checking email less often, smart organisations are trying to reduce the burden of email by discouraging use of the 'reply all' feature, and encouraging people to use the CC field judiciously.[52] Other research suggests that most people would save time by avoiding the use of dozens of multiple folders, and instead relying on the search function to locate old messages.[53] Other common tips include unsubscribing from unwanted newsletters, dealing with messages immediately, and trying to send fewer emails.[54] More radically, some people advocate 'inbox zero', a system in which you deal with all your emails by the end of the day, leaving the inbox empty. Intuit chief executive Brad Smith says that he does this by forcing himself to do one of four things with every incoming message: 'read, act, file, or delete'.[55] His goal is to 'Never touch something more than once'.

Some compare email to a zombie movie: you keep killing them, and still they keep coming.[56] In academia, email has been described as 'a kind of digital water torture for the scholar struggling to think without interruption'.[57] If this is how you feel, an 'email holiday' might be in order. In one study, thirteen information workers were cut off from email for five days.[58] Researchers monitored their behaviour and found that they became more focused on the tasks in front of them. Without email, their heart rates were more constant. As one participant noted, 'I was surprised at how much all that human interaction came in to fill the vacuum.' Similar results emerged when an Italian home textiles firm asked employees to cease internal emails for a week. Employees were encouraged to raise issues in person. Company president Michele Moltrasio acknowledged that it wasn't easy at first, but people appreciated 'rediscovering the pleasure of meeting and talking rather than writing. Even if from next week we all go back to using email, these days of experimentation are very worthwhile, to understand and rethink the methods and pace of working.'[59]

More radically, Microsoft researcher danah boyd carries out an 'email sabbatical'.[60] For a fortnight, she sets up her computer to delete all incoming messages and let senders know that if it's important, they should resend their message in a fortnight. In an emergency, they can reach boyd via her mother. Not everyone loves it when boyd bounces their messages. But she reflects: 'The folks who bitch about my email sabbatical are folks who don't know me. My boss gets it; my collaborators get it; my friends get it. And they like me a lot better when I've taken a vacation recently.'

Avoiding addiction

CyberConnecting means not being enslaved to devices. Turning the screen to black and white makes the device feel less enticing – akin to watching 1950s television. If you don't think removing the colours would matter, consider the fact that Facebook's notification icon started out blue, and was hardly used. Then the designers switched it to red, and usage exploded.[61]

To get a better rest, experts advise using the iPhone's Night Shift or Android's Night Light mode to cut down on blue light before bedtime. If you don't want to be tempted by social media in bed, charge your phone in the kitchen and buy an old-fashioned alarm clock. Silicon Valley consultant Nir Eyal goes one step further. His home internet router is connected to a timing device that cuts off the internet at a specific time each night.[62] Eyal should know – his book *Hooked: How to Build Habit-Forming Products* explores the subtle psychological tricks that firms employ to engage users for as much time as possible.

In 2018 (Silicon Valley's 'year of apology'), a number of developers – responding to calls to build less addictive products – rolled out products that let users self-limit. In that year, version 12 of Apple's iOS operating system added a Screen Time feature, allowing users to restrict the hours when they use their phones, or set a maximum time on particular apps. Google followed a similar path, with the Digital Wellbeing features included in the Android 9 Pie update. 2018 also saw Facebook and Instagram release dashboards enabling people to limit notifications, track their time on the platforms and set a timer when they hit a specified amount of time on the app. But they're soft limits, since nothing stops you keeping on using the app after this.

Following the Cambridge Analytica scandal, the hashtag #DeleteFacebook briefly trended on Twitter (proof that social media has no sense of irony). Most users aren't ready to give up the platform, but some have deleted the app versions of Facebook and its social media counterparts. As one computer scientist puts it, this means removing from your phone 'any apps that make money from your attention'.[63] The rationale is that the browser versions of social media platforms tend to be less addictive. Without the app, you might be able to gaze at a beautiful sunset without thinking which Instagram filter to use when posting it.

If logging off permanently or deleting apps is too much, you could consider a 'Facebook holiday'. In a Danish randomised experiment, those who were asked to take a week off the platform reported significantly higher levels of life satisfaction.[64] A similar randomised trial in the United States paid people $100 to deactivate Facebook for a month.[65] Those paid the bonus spent more time in offline activities, including television and socialising with family and friends. They were happier, less politically polarised and more inclined to self-limit their Facebook usage in the future.

Hit 'Refresh'

In the physical world, French schools ban smartphones entirely – requiring students to keep them in lockers or bags, at risk of confiscation.[66] Some Australian schools take a tougher stance: requiring students to check their phones in at the front desk at the start of each day. Those who advocate banning phones argue that frequent use of social networks is incompatible with the role of a great school. As sociologist Monique Dagnaud puts it, learning is about delayed gratification – you gain knowledge now that will be useful in the future. By contrast, she contends, social networking is often about immediate pleasure.[67] When McKinnon Secondary College in Melbourne implemented an all-day ban on phones, people noticed that the schoolyard became noisier. Principal Pitsa Binnion observed: 'There was laughter, people were actually interacting and socialising.'[68] You can see the same chatty dynamic at a pub trivia event – one of the few moments in the modern world when pulling out a smartphone remains taboo.

A handful of restaurants – including Bistecca and Pazar in Sydney, and the Frankie and Benny's chain in the UK – ban phones entirely.[69] Woolloomooloo eatery Contact gives a free glass of wine to anyone who can go without touching their phone for the whole meal.[70] Other establishments gently nudge their customers. At Hearth, an Italian restaurant in Manhattan, small decorative boxes adorn each table, with a polite note suggesting that diners might stash their phones inside.[71] Writer Andrew Sullivan suggests a simpler rule: next time you're out with a friend, put both smartphones face down on the table. Anyone who touches their phone pays the bill.[72]

For app designers, the Center for Humane Technology lays down eight design principles, including 'Does your product enhance relationships, or keep people isolated?', 'Does your product respect people's schedules and boundaries?' and 'Does your product eliminate detours and distractions?'[73] Plenty of apps are built specifically to help you use your phone to help you break your addiction to your phone. With time management apps such as HabitLab, OFFTIME, Moment, Quality Time, Lilspace, Flipd and Freedom, you can not only set hard limits on your smartphone usage, but also turn the psychological tables on your naughty self, with features including email updates to your family members letting them know how much you used your device. Other addicts prefer low-tech solutions, such as putting a rubber band around your phone as a reminder to ask yourself: 'Do I really need to check it right now?' One of the reasons Kindles and Kobos remain popular in the tablet era is that e-reader devices are only good for one thing: reading books.

Are people overreacting about the risk that electronic devices pose to society? Over the generations, every new technology has led to some degree of handwringing from society's elders.[74] In 360 BC, Plato feared that writing down speeches would ruin people's ability to remember them. In 1494, Johannes Trithemius said that the printing press would create a culture of disposable books. In 1775, there were fears that newspapers would lead to isolated citizens reading in 'sullen silence'. In 1839, one artist responded to seeing early photographs with the cry: 'Painting is dead!' In the 1920s, radio was forecast to lead to 'the death of conversation'. In the 1950s, television was feared to rot our brains and destroy 'patterns of family living'. Yet in the end, society managed to find a reasonable balance. Why should the internet be any different?

A clue that today's technologies might pose a bigger challenge to social capital is the number of technology experts that are part of the movement to curb excessive use. Bill Gates would not let his children have a phone until they were teenagers, and his wife Melinda believes they should have waited longer.[75] Apple chief executive Steve Jobs would not let his children use iPads, and insisted on device-free family dinners.[76] His successor, Tim Cook, discourages his teenage nephew from using social networks.[77] Evan Williams, who co-founded Blogger, Twitter and Medium, doesn't let his children have iPads, preferring books instead.[78] Stanford University's Donald Knuth, author of the world's leading text on computer programming, had an email address from 1975 to 1990, and then cut it off, saying, 'Fifteen years of email is plenty for one lifetime.'[79]

Tim Berners-Lee, who invented the World Wide Web, warns of the way in which artificial intelligence has been used by sites such as YouTube and Facebook to keep people engaged for as long as possible. 'People are being distorted by very finely trained artificial intelligences that figure out how to distract them.'[80] Sean Parker, Facebook's founding president, admits that the goal of the platform was to consume as much of users' time as possible. 'And that means that we need to sort of give you a little dopamine hit every once in a while, because someone liked or commented on a photo or a post or whatever. And that's going to get you to contribute more content, and that's going to get you ... more likes and comments ... It's a social validation feedback loop ... exactly the kind of thing that a hacker like myself would come up with, because you're exploiting a vulnerability in human psychology.'[81] Parker now describes himself as a 'conscientious objector' to social media.

Justin Rosenstein, who helped invent Facebook's 'like' button, admits, 'I find myself getting addicted – yes, in some cases, by the very things I've built.'[82] He fears for a world in which people are constantly distracted from their most important goals: 'These are our precious, finite, mortal little lives. The idea that we are spending them distracted, not accomplishing the thing that we're trying to do, is just painful. It's crazy.' Roger McNamee, an early Facebook investor turned critic, argues, 'Facebook, Google and others compete for each consumer's attention, reinforcing biases and reducing the diversity of ideas to which each is exposed.'[83] These social concerns dovetail with privacy critiques, such as Shoshana Zuboff's *The Age of Surveillance Capitalism*.

Perhaps the most anxious insider is former *Wired* magazine editor Chris Anderson, who says of excessive screen use: 'On the scale between candy and crack cocaine, it's closer to crack cocaine.'[84] He argues that technologists have been slow to recognise the addictive power of their products, which directly target 'the pleasure centres of the developing brain'. After making what he describes as some 'bad decisions' as a parent, Anderson's five children are now subject to a dozen 'tech rules', including no phones until high school, no iPads, no screens in bedrooms, and screen time schedules.[85] As journalist Ross Douthat points out, policy-makers used to worry about a 'digital divide', in which the poor lacked access to the internet.[86] But when it comes to curtailing screen use, more affluent families often have the strictest rules.[87]

CyberConnecting isn't about logging off, it's about using technology more intentionally. We need to recognise that social media is created by savvy designers who often exploit human biases (one company that blended technology and neuroscience even called itself Dopamine Labs).[88] As with alcohol, gambling and painkillers, many people find it hard not to overconsume. Like Norman Lindsay's magic pudding, devices offer a ceaseless supply of content. Community builders need to know the best strategies for managing email, limiting social media and keeping device use in check.

Turning Facebook friends into true ties

Community organisations also need to take advantage of the ways that devices can be used to establish and strengthen connections. When COVID-19 hit, thousands of neighbourhood support groups sprang up online to help those who were self-isolating: providing them with help shopping, watering the garden or walking the dog. Psychologists set up websites on managing anxiety during lockdown. Educators compiled the best educational resources for home-schooling. Brisbane-based charity Aurous linked over 500 older Australians with volunteers for a weekly video chat: a kind of 'adopt a grandparent' model that proved especially helpful for those in aged care homes.[89] Melbourne charity Lively offered isolated seniors up to four hours a week of free social support and technology training, provided by their friendly young support workers – 'like a grandkid with more patience'.

The coronavirus pandemic led to other online innovations too. Community Builders held a webinar with Beechworth Bakery founder Tom O'Toole on building good businesses in small towns. Elton John and Lady Gaga threw online benefit concerts to raise money for healthcare. Using the JustGiving platform, Britain's Tom Moore set himself the goal of raising £1000 for the National Health Service by walking 100 laps of his backyard by his 100th birthday. On the day of his birthday, he had raised £30 million. Moore was honoured with a flypast by a wartime Spitfire and a Hurricane, 150,000 birthday cards and a knighthood. We might also think of him as the world's most venerable CyberConnector.

As we've discussed, Facebook can be an addictive time-sink, but it can also connect the disconnected. Chief executive Mark Zuckerberg says Facebook has helped to connect people worldwide who have the rare disorder epidermolysis bullosa, military families in San Diego who want to make friends with other spouses, and Berlin residents who volunteer to help refugees find jobs and homes.[90] Zuckerberg estimates that

100 million Facebook users are part of what he calls 'meaningful communities'. 'These communities don't just interact online,' he maintains. 'They hold get-togethers, organize dinners, and support each other in their daily lives.'[91] One such example can be found in Canberra's Kingston, where Eternity Hausen found herself struggling to make friends after moving from Brisbane.[92] So she started the Facebook group 'Say Hello Kingston', which acted as a hub for community get-togethers. The group now has over 900 members, and has held wine tastings, get-togethers for new parents, coffee catch-ups and games nights. Hausen counts among her close friends at least five people whom she met through the group.

It isn't always possible to connect in person with online friends, but the best community groups see 'clicktivism' as a starting point, not an end goal (something we return to in Chapter 9). Just as devices can worsen political polarisation, they can also improve civic engagement. Even in an age of Russian trolls and the Cambridge Analytica data breach, US activists are using technology to involve more people in politics. Brooklyn-based non-profit Democracy Works has partnered with Facebook to register new voters. Mobile apps are allowing people to text their friends about politics. As commentator Sue Halpern notes, texting apps like Hustle on the left and CallHub on the right 'enable supporters who may not want to knock on doors or make phone calls to still engage in canvassing activities directly'.[93]

Technology also provides new donation channels. One day a year, Uber partners with the Australian Red Cross in major cities. Users simply tap the app and Uber arranges to pick up their unwanted clothing free of charge, delivering it to the nearest Red Cross shop for reuse or resale. When natural disasters hit, Airbnb's Open Homes platform allows people to open up their spare room to someone who needs it.

With outsize profits and a keen eye for potential innovators, the technology giants are well-placed to support social startups.

In Australia, Google's annual 'Impact Challenge' aims to identify the next generation of social entrepreneurs, providing a handful of organisations up to $1 million in grants and support. Winners of the Australian Impact Challenge have included Hireup, a platform that helps people with disabilities hire support workers; software produced by the Australian Literacy and Numeracy Foundation to help communities preserve Indigenous languages; machine-learning technology produced by the Nature Conservancy to protect fish stocks in the Asia–Pacific; and the Xceptional app, which reduces anxiety among people with autism and encourages their move into employment.

Xceptional is also a reminder that when it comes to online engagement there's no 'one size fits all' solution. Brandon Isleib, a Seattle-based author and legislative reviewer, describes how his level one autism creates a strong need for solitude. On *Letter*, a website dedicated to hosting in-depth discussions, Isleib noted that: 'Conversation by screen, like this lovely one, is about as good as I can maintain regularly for everyone except a handful of people closest to me, for whom I promise my energy even when I don't have it. (At the same time, all of this makes my writing conversations closer to how I would speak in person than most people – I would say there's less lost in translation between digital and analogue me.) So I've had to learn how to cut things out and then what to let back in, and digital reach-out is the pale imitation I can take most often, sort of like unseasoned food to a weak stomach.'[94]

If everyone can be as thoughtful about the pros and cons of online engagement as Isleib, we can avoid the digital pitfalls. Better yet, Australia can turn the next generation of technological advances to our advantage and use them to forge a more connected country.

5

GETTING ACTIVE

Inactivity isn't just a health problem, it's a social challenge too. Most sports are declining in popularity. Adult obesity has risen. Primary schoolers don't roam far from home and can't jump as far as they once could. But there are organisations that have been able to buck these trends, and they are also strengthening our social muscles. In this chapter we'll explore strategies for increasing activity, boosting endorphins and making new acquaintances.

Sutton's Law of Social Capital

Every Thursday after school, at a public park in a new part of Canberra's north, six-year-old Zaina and her big sister are learning a new sport. Zaina is among more than a hundred children in the area who've signed up. Her parents migrated from Pakistan and they want Zaina and her sister to have the confidence to get involved in team sport. Zaina is a tiny dynamo, says local community development officer Karlya Parnell, 'the most energetic go-getter you could come across. She runs with the bigger kids and throws herself around. She's always so keen every week to know what sport we're playing – and for the first ten minutes she'll be a bit timid, figuring it out, and then she's off and into it, getting involved with all the others.'[1]

From 2016 to 2018, the population of Zaina's suburb, Moncrieff, expanded thirty-fold, from 100 to 3000. The houses are new, the streets are new, the school is new and the neighbourhoods are new. Many of the families are also new to Australia. In looking for ways to help their children build confidence and belonging, the parents have encountered one of the key dimensions of Australian community culture: sport. Along with the usual barriers that can keep kids out of sport (cost and convenience), many families lacked the experience of finding, registering and involving themselves in a local sporting team or club, but they wanted their kids to have the social involvement it brings. As Parnell puts it: 'We have families who grew up in the Pacific Islands, India, Sri Lanka, Pakistan and Australia – and we hear a lot from the parents about how much they value the diversity of the people their children get to play alongside at our After School Sport program. They see it as a way to get their kids meeting new friends in the area and interacting away from the cliques that form at school.'

The program is provided by Northside Community Service and runs close to the local school. Participation is free. The Northside team regularly invites representatives from a variety of local sporting teams and clubs. The club coaches bring their equipment and expertise to lead an afternoon's activities. And while they're introducing the kids to a new sport, they're also showing families how to take steps towards more formal participation. Children get used to playing with different age groups, boys and girls aren't separated, and the ethos is supportive rather than competitive.

In high-income families, 84 per cent of children participate in organised sport. In low-income families, it's just 58 per cent.[2] Northside's program runs in neighbourhoods that have higher diversity or newly built pockets of social and affordable housing. 'Once a child can access sport,' Parnell explains, 'it's all about his or her skill and interest and much less about household income or cultural background. For children, sport is a great equaliser.' Bringing these families and their children into the orbit of community sport isn't just about fitness. As Parnell puts it, 'Sport is the means to an end. I know it's a really good tool to make the connections. You don't tell them to come and meet new people, you tell them to come for the sport.'

Adults see lots of benefits too. Parnell continues: 'We're seeing some really great friendships build. During the sessions we set up a chill-out space for the parents to hang out. There's one group of parents who knew each other before they came down, but they're expanding their circle through these regular after-school meet-ups. They'll all come down together and have a barbecue afterwards and catch up while the kids are occupied. Most of them first and foremost are there for their kids – but they also come along hoping to catch up with new friends. They start talking about their kids and it's an immediate connection point. We've seen people coming back regularly off the back of those first connections.'

Asked why he stole from banks, convicted bank robber Willie Sutton reportedly answered, 'Because that's where the money is.'[3] In the same spirit, we propose 'Sutton's Law of Social Capital': focus on disadvantaged communities, because that's where the need is. Providing migrant children with their first sporting experience is more valuable than serving affluent families, where children may already be playing two or three sports. Moreover, the barriers to engagement in marginalised communities may be small, such as a lack of familiarity with the sign-up process. By guiding families through the registration process, and taking them to their first activity, Northside Community Services shows the value of targeting underserved communities.

Dirty love

Landcare would like to attract more twenty-somethings. Traditionally, the environmental volunteering group has had a core workforce of retired members, plus a strong program of school-aged Young Landcarers, but it has struggled to engage those in between. To fill the gap, Landcare initiated new programs aimed at raising participation rates among younger adults.

In 2005, Ella Maesepp from Katanning in Western Australia met her husband through a Young Farmers Landcare event. Maesepp notes, 'The great thing about Landcare is that it is just as much a social network as it is an environmental movement, so you end up meeting a diverse range of people joined together by a common interest. Landcare has given me many great friends, laughs and memorable moments – plus the unexpected bonus of my life partner too.'[4]

Inspired by stories like Maesepp's, Kim Boswell ran the inaugural Landcare for Singles speed planting events in Victoria in 2011. Over 100 participants attended, and most were new to Landcare. Landcare have their routine channels for promoting planting days and recruiting volunteers, but Landcare for Singles generates extra buzz. Boswell developed a standard event kit, which includes branded promotional artwork for fliers and online promotion. The novelty of the events made them an easy pitch to local media: Valentine's Day Speed Planting, anyone? While the combination of social and environmental payoffs is already an enticing proposition, the quirkiness of the event ensures more people hear about it.

The model soon spread nationally, winning hearts in Perth, Darwin, the Gold Coast and the Illawarra. ACT Regional Landcare Facilitator Rebecca Palmer-Brodie describes the pitch: 'Rather than spending all that time swiping left or right on Tinder, or trawling through internet dating profiles, come along and plant a new tree with a new person every eight minutes on a beautiful Canberra farm.' The Landcare facilitators rotate the 'dates', and each new sapling comes with a conversation starter, such as: 'Where in the world have you been that you thought was paradise?' Landcare for Singles focuses on the social aspect of Landcare's reforestation project. Perhaps, like Ella Maesepp, you'll plant the seeds of a new relationship. Failing that, you'll definitely find a whole crowd of people that share your love of nature. It's a clever mix of incentives, side effects and unexpected rewards. While Landcare for Singles has been the start of lasting relationships, it also introduces people to the rewards of volunteering and the joys of spending time in nature (and gets some trees planted). Events regularly book out in advance. Who could resist the opening line, 'So, do you plant here often?'

There's a similar alchemy at work in Hunter Intrepid Landcare's waterway weeding projects. These activities take place as canoeing expeditions to waterways that would otherwise be unreachable. Participants clear weeds from catchments and creeks and contribute to the health of the ecosystem. At the same time, they enjoy a paddle with friends and an adventure with a purpose. Naomi Edwards, co-founder of Intrepid Landcare, observes: 'We've become so disconnected in who we are, we live in this rapid social world, it's important to slow down. We give young people connection to others, authentic relationships, connection to country, feeding the appetite to understand Indigenous Australia. Connection to conservation, doing the activity. Connection to adventure, the fun and the recreation: come mountain-biking and at the same time we're going to map weeds. And then there's the connection to place which grounds us about where we are in the world. We get to take people into pristine and iconic places you wouldn't normally get to experience.'

The dual benefit delivered by Landcare for Singles and Intrepid Landcare is another example of double-plus-good social capital. These services help participants find love *and* plant trees. Get fit *and* clean up waterways. When your organisation is trying to attract busy people, it's useful to be able to promise new members that they'll meet multiple objectives by signing up.

Part of a tribe

Organisational identity matters too. Hunter Intrepid Landcare is one of the fourteen programs that have been established since the Intrepid model was founded by Naomi Edwards and Megan Rowlatt. Edwards lived on the Gold Coast, where she was a regular Coast Care facilitator. She began to notice that while young people were engaging with the program in healthy numbers, they weren't stepping up and creating their own projects. Edwards saw that most volunteers had come to Landcare through similar paths. She started thinking about ways to draw in people with different interests and skills. Rowlatt had been having success doing youth engagement in the Illawarra, so Edwards reached out to her with a proposal.

As Edwards recalls, 'I said I'd like to run a weekend camp for people between sixteen and twenty-six with the idea that we give them a weekend taste-test of what Landcare is. We'd introduce them to a range of projects – community gardens, quarry restorations, conservation of endangered plants, bird watching walks, bush tucker expeditions, tree planting. We'd have heaps of fun. And on the second day there would be a condensed try-out of community planning. They'd come up with ideas, we'd do some planning and then I would partner with them to complete those projects ... One group decided they were going to plant 800 trees – they got their school behind them, their local member of parliament, their council, they raised money and got people backing them in a short period of time to get it done. And people were like, "This was so fun." And I said to Megan, "What if we did that all around Australia?"'

So that's what they did. Edwards and Rowlatt held retreats across the country to train young leaders and start them on a path to running their own Intrepid groups. They set out, explains Edwards, to build 'the agency of individuals, and then they create a tribe, so they're leading together. It builds confidence and opens employment pathways to meaningfully contribute. And it's designed to engage those who don't traditionally come from conservationist communities.'

Ellie Gillet, a former president of Hunter Intrepid Landcare, described Intrepid tribes as 'roaming Landcare groups' for their region, linking up with other conservation groups to pitch in across a range of initiatives. Intrepid Landcare activities are designed to combine conservation volunteering with a rewarding outdoor experience. For Gillet, the model provided an engaging way 'to encourage young people to respect the environment, get outdoors and off their phones'.[5] Each tribe creates its own organisation structure to reflect its principles. Some rotate leadership roles every six months to reflect their egalitarianism and collective commitment to their tribe.

Intrepid Landcare isn't overtly environmental in its leading pitch to new participants – it promises to help young people find a like-minded band of adventurous souls by connecting them with local groups led by young people. Initially, the emphasis is on the social experience, not the cause. The key offerings are connections to other people and a path towards belonging and community. Edwards stresses how important the weekend retreats are in giving members confidence in their ability to work together and bring about change: 'We looked at what the top passions are for young people – music, art, environment, social justice and climate change – and we encourage groups to really work on including those in their activities. It's never-ending, the cool events people come up with.'

In *Tribe: On Homecoming and Belonging*, Sebastian Junger argues that humans are at our happiest when we are part of a group that provides a sense of belonging and solidarity. A lesson of the Intrepid Landcare model for other Australian community builders is the way that their tribes build a sense of loyalty and identity. People don't just want a cushy life; humans take pride in making sacrifices for causes that are bigger than ourselves.

As Edwards notes, the Intrepid program has helped tap back into the demographic Landcare was losing. 'We break down the barriers of youth engagement, provide a supportive environment and a legacy community of practice for the individuals to set up their local Intrepid tribe. It creates a buzz for them that what they're doing in Gippsland, say, is contributing to the larger picture of sustainability. Young people are concerned about what's happening globally and by getting involved locally they can see they're helping with that bigger problem. And at the same time, they're opening up their world to personal development.'

Edwards reflects on the success of the program: 'We ran a canoeing weekend experience in partnership with NSW National Parks and put the event up online. Within fifteen minutes it was sold out. We had 1500 people on the waiting list, we could only take fifteen. That was one of the weeding waterways canoeing expeditions, and afterwards, when people looked back on the experience, my favourite piece of feedback was this simple line: "I was happy".'

Making gyms green and good

Not everyone can give up a weekend, but the blend of physicality, purpose and time outdoors is also being packaged up into shorter, routine activities that can fit neatly into a busy life. In the UK, The Conservation Volunteers have created a volunteering model that combines conservation activity with social participation and exercise. It's called Green Gym and has already been adopted on a small scale by Conservation Volunteers Australia. Sessions structure the physical tasks of conservation projects as a workout. Participants start with a supervised warm-up before the vigorous conservation activities commence. The workout might involve carrying saplings to a planting site, digging a hole and planting them. It could be clearing weeds and rubbish from native vegetation, rejuvenating parks and gardens, or creating wildlife habitats. Green Gym activities have conservation value foremost, but they are selected to also provide a physical workout. The sessions are free, social and outdoors.

Like the speed planting activity and the waterway weeders, heart rates are up, new people are involved and the events take place outdoors. The mood-heightening effects of exercise are well known, with serotonin and endorphins boosting feelings of wellbeing. It's yet to be rigorously evaluated, but after a Green Gym session, participants rate their own wellbeing higher and report feeling less stressed and anxious. Green Gym claims that more calories can be burnt in some Green Gym sessions than in an aerobics class, and it seems capable of generating the same kind of wellbeing effect that's associated with more structured exercise.

Similarly, GoodGym is a thriving UK charity that aims to get people off treadmills and out into their communities to rebuild social bonds. GoodGym was born out of frustration at the failure of normal gyms to capitalise on the human potential they marshal. The idea was to channel exercise routines towards community tasks in order to support people who were falling through the cracks. They developed a model that capitalises on the modest commitments volunteers could make on a regular basis, allowing GoodGym to tap into a large pool of ongoing supporters. Here's how it works for one GoodGym member: 'Every Saturday morning for the last eighteen months, I've run to go and see Vera. So she's my running coach in a sense ... The reason I get out of bed on most Saturday mornings is because I know Vera's there, and it's actually quite a refreshing way to start your weekend ...

Running clears your mind but I can promise you so does sitting having a chat with a ninety-year-old woman who's going to show you photos of things she was doing fifty, sixty, seventy years ago that just completely change your perspective. I guess I always forget that there's a health benefit to me, because I always think of it as just me going to visit Vera, which has just become normal.'[6]

GoodGym offers runners three options, each of which involve members running to a specified location, completing an allocated task, then running home. Mission Runs help older people with specific tasks, such as changing a light bulb or pruning an overhanging branch. Coach Runs are social visits to isolated older people, whom the GoodGym refers to as 'coaches' because they provide the motivation. Group Runs muster several runners at a central meeting point, from which they run off together to assist a community organisation.

GoodGym's slogan is 'Do good, get fit'. Some GoodGym members were runners already and were attracted by the chance to combine an activity they already love doing with giving back. Other runners were attracted by the chance to make a difference to people's lives and recognise that the exercise element commits them to a healthy habit. Whichever way you look at it, the model is double-plus-good.

GoodGym's iconic package, the Coach Run, involves a weekly commitment. Participants run to the home of an isolated older person, then spend thirty to sixty minutes talking, playing cards or having a cup of tea. Then they run home. Runners set their own route, but the 'coaching' component is scheduled. The 'coaches' provide the runners with the motivation to run. Once a GoodGym member has a weekly Coach Run in place, their exercise routine becomes tied to the quality of life of a vulnerable older person. When your visit is an important fixture in the life of someone who spends most of the week alone, ditching a run is not an option. As one runner, Michael, explains: 'Regardless of how I feel on my way there (tired, unenthusiastic, stressed), my visits to

Sheila are guaranteed to pick me up and leave me smiling.' And for the coaches? Clara is a 98-year-old still living independently who has outlasted many of her friends. Her family live far away, but she delights in human contact: 'See, when I am around people, I come alive!'[7]

Coach Paul was confined to his house by health problems and felt his attitude to life becoming increasingly negative. He sought help and was put in touch with GoodGym. 'It has, along with better health and improving my outlook on life, meant that my runner, Beth, has become a permanent and very loyal mate.'[8] The routine visit also serves as a regular check on the coach's wellbeing and plays a part in helping people age in their own home.

GoodGym coordinators work with local service providers to identify worthwhile tasks they can schedule as missions or group activities, and they take on 'coaches' by referral from aged and healthcare providers. It's a model with some extra organisational complexity given the clients are frail and vulnerable. Group Runs are larger jobs with more runners, and the work is not in someone's home, so anyone can take part. But to be able to do Coach Runs and Mission Runs, runners must have completed a background check.

GoodGym is free, though most members make a monthly donation equivalent to around $20. Members are given a branded red t-shirt to wear on their outings, and as they pass milestones (100 runs, for example) their increasing status in the movement is recognised by a new t-shirt colour.

Many kinds of community activities are good for your heart. The lesson of Green Gym and GoodGym is that with a few structural tweaks, this can be turned into a selling point to attract new recruits. Think about Green Gym's warm-ups and their deliberate selection of activities to get the blood pumping. Or the way that GoodGym matches people with coaches who live just far enough away to get a good workout, but not so far as to be exhausting. Structured the right way, could more volunteering activities – from mental health support to meal delivery – promote themselves as workout options?

Running free

Paul Sinton-Hewitt was preparing for the London Marathon in 2004 when the accident happened.[9] He turned right, his dog jumped in front of him, and Sinton-Hewitt somersaulted over, badly injuring his left leg. Doctors told him he wouldn't run for a couple of months. But his friends were runners and running events were where he got his fix of belonging. To make matters worse, Sinton-Hewitt had recently been fired from his job and his love life was a mess. Losing his running tribe was unthinkable, so Sinton-Hewitt devised a plan to keep himself engaged with his running club and maintain his social ties. He decided he would invite all his running club mates to the same park every Saturday morning at 9 am. He'd organise a run for them and then they'd all go for coffee together afterwards, when volunteers and participants would share a story and a laugh. That was the spark for parkrun.

That spark was carried to Australia by Tim Oberg, a recreational runner who caught the parkrun habit in Britain just as he was packing up his life to return to the Gold Coast. At that point, in 2010, parkrun had about sixty events in Britain and a few in Denmark, run by the UK team. Oberg chanced his arm and suggested to Sinton-Hewitt that he take a parkrun franchise to Australia. Oberg had a business background (he'd been running a travel company in London) and had studied human movement at Queensland University of Technology. Sinton-Hewitt took the chance that parkrun could have an independent life outside the UK and that Oberg was the right person to lead it in Australia.

In April 2011, parkrun Australia launched at Main Beach on the Gold Coast, with 108 runners. To date, parkrun in Australia has held over 60,000 events across more than 300 locations and has over half a million registered runners. In other words, one in forty Australian adults are registered parkrunners. The Australian parkrun franchise has grown by following the same key principles that turned Paul Sinton-Hewitt's catch-up with thirteen running mates into a global network of community runs. All parkruns are weekly, free, five kilometres long and open to everyone. If there's a key lesson of parkrun, it's simplicity.

As Oberg explains, the social side of parkrun is essential: 'Looking in from the outside, you'd say first and foremost this is just a funrun like any other running event. But the run is actually of secondary importance to a lot of people who participate in parkrun. It's primarily an opportunity to connect to their community. That could be immediate friends and family or completely different people. It's all about the community connection that is fostered through the parkrun itself, along with the post-run coffee or breakfast.'

Like GoodGym, parkrun has a colour-coded hierarchy of running tops to mark the number of events a runner has participated in. These are soft incentives, a bit of extra tribal swag. The main reason people keep coming is the magic formula that maximises enjoyment, removes financial obstacles, minimises the time commitment and ensures a non-competitive, inclusive event. 'It's a run, it's not a race.' Every parkrun event is timed, which is an important value-add for regular runners, but participation is emphasised over competition. 'We do that in a number of ways,' explains Oberg. 'We don't recognise first, second, third, nor do we recognise last. There's nothing in our vocabulary or formal process that highlights performance. The way we speak to our members and the terminology we use is very specific. We never talk about who "won" on the weekend. If we want to refer to the person who crossed the line first, we refer to the "first finisher" and the "second finisher". We don't talk about winners and we don't talk about losers. We've completely cut from the vocab of parkrun the idea of losing or being last. That's why we've attracted a lot of people that would be intimidated by traditional running club structures and also by other areas of physical activity, like joining a gym, that can be intimidating for some people.' In parkruns, Oberg points out, no regular entrant comes last: 'Whenever possible, parkruns also have a tail walker ... A lot of people we speak to who haven't come to parkrun say, "I don't want to be last," and we actually say to them, "Don't worry, you won't be, because it's actually someone's job to come last."'

Structurally, parkrun operates on a distributed model, with localised organisers assisted by a central operations team. Its 'ambassadors' work between the regular event organisers and head office. Setting up a new location requires a commitment to sustain the volunteer support structure needed and an upfront fee to cover equipment costs. The fee is typically covered by a partnership with a local business or council, or from fundraising among supporters in the community. Once that startup cost is met, the events are sustained by volunteer labour. Oberg sets out the dynamic: 'The free forever model is absolutely essential to what we do, because it just completely removes this barrier to participation. Running events are getting more expensive each year, but parkrun maintains that "free forever" model. It's important because it means anyone can participate, but it also means people are much more willing to give back to the organisation. So, we have that perfect circle of people coming in. They walk or they run. They enjoy it. They make friends and become part of the community. And then they start looking at the other part of what we do, which is volunteering. Each event needs from four up to sometimes even twenty volunteers to operate each week, so there is a huge amount of volunteer time. And mostly that's our runners, because people feel they are being given something that's meaningful and important in their lives and they're happy to give back.'

The lowercase name (it's parkrun, not Parkrun) gives a clue to its modesty. That egalitarian, inclusive ethos comes from its founder.

When he was five years old, Paul Sinton-Hewitt was put in a South African boarding home after his parents separated. A small child, he was targeted by bullies: other boys hung him by his neck, cut him and threw darts at his back. Even in the face of such cruel treatment, children in the boarding home were not allowed to show any emotion. In 1995, a few years after coming to Britain, Sinton-Hewitt had a breakdown. He identifies these experiences as the reason why he determined that the parkrun ethic would be accepting: 'I treat everyone as I would treat myself; give everyone the right to do what they want.'[10] One of Sinton-Hewitt's favourite moments came when three men approached him after a race to confide that parkrun had enabled them to beat their addiction to alcohol.[11]

A neat indicator of parkrun's ongoing success is the fact that the average time for participants across all courses has been steadily going up. In 2011, participants were averaging a 27:42 finish; in 2018 it was 33:21.[12] While many regular participants are getting quicker, the slower average tells the story of an ever-expanding pool of new participants. Because it costs nothing to participate, even the most cash-strapped runners can get the benefits of joining in. That's Sutton's Law of Social Capital in action again.

Exercise and social capital go together like bacon and eggs. And unlike bacon and eggs, they're good for your heart as well as being heart-warming. For those who prefer a ramble to a run, though, you don't have to get your pulse racing to find a healthy shared activity.

Growing communities

As we've seen, the Green Gym model owes part of its appeal to the fact that spending time in green spaces is inherently satisfying, which adds to the physical, social and community benefits of the activity. For many, particularly those who aren't enthusiastic about vigorous exercise, gardening projects provide a good way to experience those same benefits. Shared community gardens, offering hubs of neighbourhood ownership and identity, have attracted increasing numbers of participants over the last decade.[13]

Garden-centred communities have multiple benefits. When Kirsten Holmes and her team from Curtin University were looking at the stresses on rural volunteers in Western Australia, they were routinely confronted by survey results showing how fragile many longstanding activities and services had become. But then they visited Greenbushes, a 300-person timber and mining town in the state's south-west. There, they came across a project that had energised the locals. 'A number of volunteers reported that the volunteering landscape had become increasingly vibrant in recent years, with community groups undertaking a wider range of activities that benefited their town. The community garden was seen to be at the centre of much of the change, with the enthusiasm that had been created since its inception transferring to other groups and positively impacting volunteer recruitment and retention.'[14] As one of the Greenbushes locals put it, 'It just sort of took off and everyone got interested in it and little branches, things came out from that.' Whatever was going on in the Greenbushes community garden, the locals liked it and, at least anecdotally, it increased trust and cooperation.

Community gardens have been around for a long time, often ignored or barely tolerated by formal planning and local government models. These days, community gardeners are supported by a movement that has mainstream credibility and clout.

Compared to other outdoor activities that bring people together in a common space, the bar to participation in a garden is low. There's no need to speak fluent English. If you can carry the weight of a watering can and heft a shovel-load of compost, you're in prime condition. Adaptations such as raised garden beds and modified tools allow people with disabilities to participate too. Gardens call for problem solving and strategic planning. A shared garden needs cooperation, communication and commitment. According to one study, community gardens foster six 'social processes': social connections, reciprocity, mutual trust, collective decision-making, civic engagement and community building.[15]

Still, there's no guarantee that the benefits will be widely or evenly spread. A study of one Melbourne garden showed that while it generated cohesion and connection, the benefits had not spread outside the garden group.[16] The garden was a privilege, but the gardeners had not been able to share that privilege more widely by bringing new people in to enjoy it. To maximise their social capital yield, community gardeners need to be as diligent in cultivating links to the broader neighbourhood as they are in cultivating their crops. It's easy to invite new people to share the space, and for many people the invitation is all they're waiting for. One of the most common reasons people give for not participating in local activities is simply 'I was never invited'. Let's look at two existing gardens that serve the wider community.

Nestled in the U-bend of Belgium Avenue, Richmond, Cultivating Community has supported the residents of the adjacent public housing complex to plan and sustain a productive garden. The garden provides residents with a healthy way to keep food costs down, as well as being somewhere they can mingle with no pressure and grow food that's part of their culture. Cultivating Community supports community gardens that are either directly linked to community housing or provide a resource for housing tenants, diverse communities and the disadvantaged. In Melbourne they support twenty-one community gardens, sustaining around 700 gardeners, linked to inner-city housing commission blocks. That's Sutton's Law of Social Capital in action again. Cultivating Community plots are for public housing tenants, but anyone can volunteer to support the gardeners and play a part in providing access to healthy, affordable, culturally appropriate food. For many of the gardeners, limited English makes it difficult to extend their social networks, but the garden provides a point of intersection with other residents and members of the nearby community to start building networks.

Also in Melbourne, just next door to Luna Park in St Kilda, Veg Out has maintained its grip on a piece of prime real estate (an auctioneer's dream, one block back from the beach) by consistently proving the public value of its community garden.[17] Veg Out's block was set aside for public use in 1881 – what is now a garden was formerly a bowling green. As urban gardens go, it's big. It hosts events and sustains itself financially with a weekly farmers' market on-site. But from the start, there were concerns that the property market would sweep the garden aside, and the early approach was to guard the plot closely. The garden's coordinator, Rob Taylor, has a simple explanation for the neighbourhood's commitment to the garden: 'In the early days it was about locking the gate, but then we realised we needed to open it up. This is essentially public parkland and it's now open every day of the year.'[18] 'If you lock these places up,' Taylor continues, they 'become elitist and exclusive. A community garden is not a fashion accessory – that's not what community is about.' The garden has over 1000 members and the non-gardening community takes an active interest in what's growing at the plot. Taylor sees successful gardens as having an instructional role that extends beyond their direct membership: 'You become like a beacon and we get people all the time. They go: "Oh, that's how you grow that. What about the soil? How do I build these raised beds?" ... We put in solar power and water tanks and all this stuff and people are always coming down and asking questions or taking photos.' It adds an extra dimension to the 'social benefits of people getting together' that Taylor attributes to the garden.[19]

Every garden serves its own local purpose. Behind most thriving community enterprises are people who, having experienced the benefits themselves, want those benefits to be available to as many people as possible. As the community garden movement has gained momentum, the Australian City Farms and Community Gardens Network has emerged to support it. There is also a handy Community Garden Social Impact Assessment Toolkit – produced by the University of Minnesota – that community gardeners can use to assess their garden's standing as a social hub.[20] Aside from useful strategies for consultation and planning, the toolkit contains a ready-made survey that will help any dirt community get a sense of how well it's doing on inclusion, building relationships within the garden and working to expand networks out from the garden. The social impact survey is a measuring tool, but it's also a prompt. It aims to help community gardens do community building better. Gardens that build stronger bonds will last longer.

Veg Out's large block helped the garden become an anchoring presence in its neighbourhood. But resourceful gardeners don't need oversized blocks of prime real estate to create a neighbourhood talking point. For 3000acres, the underutilised green patches scattered throughout Australia's suburbs are an opportunity to grow social connections. The organisation has an ambitious approach to community gardening, targeting empty parcels of public and private land. It has created a toolkit to manage the risks and opportunities of taking on public space for gardens.

Biologist Edward O. Wilson believes that humans have an innate love of nature, an urge he dubbed 'biophilia'. But urban farms can satisfy other goals too, with community gardens supporting food swaps, fostering friendships, dispensing horticultural advice and assisting public meal programs.[21] All of these interconnections involve people working together and creating ties with other groups. For example, a Melbourne community garden might take its excess to the monthly Urban Harvest food swap events run by Cultivating Community. The gardeners might also provide surpluses to Open Table or FareShare, charities that rescue food and transform it into free meals for the disadvantaged.[22]

Most community gardens aren't generating a significant share of the food consumed by their growers. Instead, they tend to be relaxed, meditative spaces where people can go to spend some time outdoors with other green thumbs. They're spaces that aren't home and aren't work, where people can share projects, conquer small planning challenges and enjoy serendipitous conversations.

While some studies suggest people in community gardeners will mostly meet people like themselves, that needn't be the case.[23] Garden plots can be melting pots too. If they provide a site for new encounters outside existing work, family and friendship groups, there's a better chance they'll foster diverse interactions. A lesson of the community garden movement is that social entrepreneurs can maximise their impact by starting new enterprises where the need for community building is greatest, such as inner-city public housing communities.

Bring the beat back

Alice Glenn and Heidi Barrett were Melbourne dancers who had become frustrated by the lack of safe, non-judgemental spaces to move. 'Our experience of clubs and bars, as women, was it wasn't always a safe space.' Dance classes, on the other hand, felt regimented and controlling. So Glenn and Barrett created an alternative. They started No Lights No Lycra with a handful of friends in a small yoga studio hall in Fitzroy – they turned the lights off, put the music on and danced. The simple formula delivered joy and soon spread across the country. 'It grew so rapidly,' says Glenn, 'within two months we knew it was bigger than us, and that what we wanted, many people in the community also craved.' As a sixty-year-old woman who participates regularly put it, 'Dancing makes me feel good and it's no fun doing it by yourself.'[24]

Participation rates suggest that as people get older, those same obstacles Glenn and Barrett encountered take the enjoyment out of dance. No Lights No Lycra removes those obstacles. After the strong initial response confirmed the wider appetite for a judgement-free dance environment, Glenn and Barrett took time to consider how No Lights No Lycra could grow without losing the integrity of the experience. Glenn explains the approach they settled on: 'We drew up a licence agreement so anyone who wanted to start a No Lights No Lycra event could get the rights to do that but had to follow our guidelines. That was about maintaining the consistency of experience wherever it was. If the playlist or demographic were different, the basics were always there. It had to be open to all ages, demographics and backgrounds. We never wanted any limits on who could be involved. It needed to be dark and drug- and alcohol-free – we always saw it as a positive safe place for a healthy experience.'

Ambassadors sign up to run an event through No Lights No Lycra's website. They pay $200 a year to licence the name and for the support resources. No Lights No Lycra connects all ambassadors through an online forum, where they can share playlists and information. Dancers pay around $10 per class, and the central office only begins taking a share of this once attendance consistently exceeds a set threshold. Most No Lights No Lycra events don't reach that mark, so aren't contributing funds back to the central office. The larger events subsidise the ones that don't reach the threshold. There are now No Lights No Lycra events in more than a dozen countries, and in Australia more than half the events are in regional or smaller towns.

To expand the influence of the model, No Lights No Lycra has worked with VicHealth to build the Dance Break app, which provides a version of the experience to people who can't make it to a weekly session or don't have a community in their town. They also partnered with the Heart Foundation and took No Lights No Lycra on tour through drought-affected Victoria and ran free events in ten small Victorian towns. 'We connected with new communities and promoted No Lights into the health sector.'

Glenn points out that some women are using No Lights No Lycra as a transition back into physical exercise after having a child. It's a time when their lives have changed dramatically, they've often lost their sense of their own body and feel disconnected from the person they were and the way they moved before the birth. Similarly, people recovering from injury or illness have found it helpful. As Glenn recounts: 'We had a No Lights No Lycra dancer in Perth, a lady who was going through cancer treatment and had previously been very fit and active. She didn't have the ability to do that anymore, or any enthusiasm for exercise, but she found No Lights was an amazing and uplifting experience, letting her be active and social but also to move at her own pace, without worrying about what others were thinking.'

Lifeline picked out No Lights No Lycra to become a community fundraising partner after recognising that this kind of dancing provides a gateway to inclusion for people feeling isolated in the community. As Glenn explains, 'Like a preventative measure, before they really struggle they can come to a No Lights experience, where it's safe and welcoming and there's no pressure to talk or socialise and yet you feel very connected, you're all in the experience together.' One survey found that of the more than 1000 people across Australia who attend No Lights No Lycra each week, more than half have a medical diagnosis of depression, anxiety or other mental health conditions. Ninety-seven per cent of these dancers felt No Lights No Lycra improved their mental health.

No Lights No Lycra has cleared away obstacles that were keeping some people isolated and inactive, but the events also increase the time people are routinely spending with others and provide a basis for new connections and new friendships. Glenn sums it up: 'At No Lights No Lycra, you dance in the dark and then the lights come up at the end and you see the same people each week, and they become daily friends. People have found support, familiarity, acceptance. Some have even found a partner.'

Throw your arms around me

In almost every human society, people sing – leading some anthropologists to argue that singing could have evolved as a mechanism of social bonding. As one team of researchers put it, 'synchronous activity increases subsequent prosocial behaviour and feelings of affiliation'.[25] On Brisbane's gig circuit, a group of social entrepreneurs are using the power of song to create a more harmonious society. Pub Choir is a mass musical event where the audience are the central players in the performance. The events are led by Astrid Jorgensen, a musician and qualified schoolteacher, who relishes her choirmaster role, teaching up to 2000 people to sing 'Solid Rock', 'Everybody Wants to Rule the World' or 'Life in a Northern Town' in three-part harmony.

Jorgensen set up Pub Choir to help 'regular people reclaim music in their lives', free of pressure or judgement. 'I think music can be seen as really elitist for lots of people and that's a real shame because it's something everybody deserves.' In Pub Choir, everyone is a performer – often to their own surprise. 'From the first show you could see people were shocked at how it came together. We never repeat the show, so at the end when it comes together and everyone has learnt their part and contributed to the final performance, the audience know they've experienced something unique.' The full choral rendition that ends the night is filmed for distribution through the Pub Choir website.

The responses to these videos, explains Jorgensen, reflect the hunger for connection that's out there. 'Things like "It must feel so amazing to work together with that many people", "I wish I could experience that togetherness", "This is what the world needs more of". People see how fun it looks and they want to experience it, they're intrigued and they want to feel that joy.'

Pub Choir has a strong following. 'People have met and gotten married through Pub Choir,' says Jorgensen, 'they've made friends and started social meet-up groups.' In 2019, Pub Choir sold 60,000 tickets to its events around Australia. In 2020, it was scheduled to tour the United States when COVID-19 hit. Instead, they created Couch Choir, asking people to upload clips of them singing a particular song from their living room. We challenge you to watch Couch Choir's video of 3500 people singing Stevie Wonder's 'Love's in Need of Love Today' without a tear coming to your eye. The combination of music and community is a perfect example of hybrid vigour.

You can't have a choir without lots of people, but like No Lights No Lycra there's also a permissive anonymity to the event. As social psychologists have noted, people behave differently in crowds – submerging our individuality and enjoying the social identity of the group. The show is funny. You can have a drink (or not), and a lot of people bring their regular Pub Choir posse. It's also a leap of faith. 'I'm the only person who knows where it's going to end up,' Jorgensen explains: 'No-one has access to the three-part plan. The audience put faith in the unknown process of the show and people express a lot of surprise – they had no idea it would come together but they felt so good when it did.'

Pub Choir has also incorporated an element of collective giving, with a charity nominated at each event to receive a share of box office profits. It's a lesson in how giving can be a social multiplier. As Jorgensen puts it, 'That really steps it up for our audience, the idea that the feeling of euphoria and the sense of community we get at the show can be translated into something real for the broader community. It adds this extra dimension where people are feeling connected not just by singing together but by giving together.'

Getting acquainted while getting active is good for both emotional and physical health. Social contact with others plays a part in wellbeing, but it also builds our reservoir of generalised trust. Meeting more people is an important step in countering prejudice and reminding ourselves that most people are generous, kind and trustworthy. Activities such as running, planting, dancing or singing help us get to know people outside our usual work and family networks, creating bridges across traditional divides of class, ethnicity or ideology.

Each of the groups we've discussed has specific strategies to meet community needs. Northside Community Service's sports programs for migrant children and Cultivating Community's public housing gardens prove Sutton's Law of Social Capital: there are huge benefits from focusing on underserviced communities. Intrepid Landcare has built tribes that provide young participants with a strong sense of ownership and identity. GoodGym's runs to check on isolated seniors and Landcare's tree planting for singles are double-plus-good. A parkrun is super-simple and always free. And if there's a community initiative that's more inclusive than No Lights No Lycra, we're yet to hear about it.

There are key lessons here for community builders looking to get people active. Don't create a bland service in the hope of mass uptake – instead, build a dedicated tribe of enthusiasts. Create activities that aren't just good, they're double-plus-good; offering an irresistible mix of endorphins and altruism. Keep your model simple – and, if possible, free. Use Sutton's Law of Social Capital to guide you towards the neediest. It's time to slip the sneakers on and start reactivating Australia.

6

FOSTERING PHILANTHROPY

The obituary was blunt. 'Dr Alfred Nobel, who became rich by finding ways to kill more people faster than ever before, died yesterday.' But there was just one problem. Alfred Nobel was very much alive. It was his brother, Ludvig, who had died. So Alfred Nobel had a rare opportunity: to see how the world summed up his life. He had no wife and no children, and now he had read an obituary that told the world, 'The merchant of death is dead.'[1]

Nobel made his fortune by inventing dynamite, which combined the destructive power of nitroglycerine with diatomaceous earth – producing an explosive that could be handled safely. It revolutionised the mining, construction and demolition industries. During his life Nobel obtained hundreds of patents, and established dozens of armaments factories. When he read the premature obituary, he was fifty-four. In his remaining years, Nobel focused on philanthropy. His will set aside nine-tenths of his estate to establish the Nobel prizes. Today, his gift has grown to over 4 billion Swedish kronor, equivalent to more than half a billion Australian dollars. The Nobel prizes in Chemistry, Literature, Peace, Physics, Medicine and Economics are considered the most prestigious awards in their fields.

Major philanthropic gifts often stem from thinking about our legacy. We've already mentioned Our Big Kitchen, a Sydney charity that engages young volunteers to cook food for those who are down on their luck. Rabbi Dovid Slavin, who founded Our Big Kitchen in Sydney with his wife Laya, told us that instead of dictating to donors, he asks the donor what is important to them. Donors typically reply that their goals are to reduce poverty, promote understanding across cultures or strengthen communities. 'Great!' Rabbi Slavin replies. 'That's what we're doing. So if you donate to us, we can help implement your wishes.' Mischievously, he adds, 'Really, they should thank me for taking their donation.'

These are tough times to be asking for support, and not just because the COVID-19 pandemic has put the financial squeeze on donors. As we've seen, philanthropy is shifting away from mail solicitation and doorknock campaigns and towards online giving – an environment where people feel less social pressure to donate. Over recent decades, the share of people giving to charity has been flat or falling, depending on which metric we use. There's more competition for donations than ever before. So what are the savviest charities doing?

We found that three strategies underpin the most effective charitable donation drives: enthusiasm, ease and evidence. Let's start with enthusiasm.

Enthusiasm

There are many reasons to be negative about the way the world is heading. The world economy is suffering the worst downturn since the Great Depression, inequality is rising and carbon emissions keep increasing. Problems like racism and homelessness can seem intractable.

The public conversation seems dominated by extremists peddling slogans, rather than reasonable people trying to find common ground. For every optimist like Stephen Pinker or Hans Rosling, who argue that the current generation are the richest, healthiest and happiest people ever to walk the planet, there are dozens of pessimists pointing to sluggish economic growth, rising terrorism or (in our case) declining social capital.[2] However, when it comes to asking for donations, guilt only takes you so far. Sure, a pedestrian might give a few dollars to a charity worker who shows them a picture of a sick child. But if you're an organisation seeking large donations and a long-term relationship, you're better to take a more optimistic tack. Like Rabbi Slavin, the best philanthropic requests come from organisations with a sense of confidence about their ability to change the world for the better. As *Wired* magazine founder Kevin Kelly puts it, 'Being enthusiastic is worth 25 IQ points.'[3] The best philanthropy is empowering, not gloomy.

Surveying over 200,000 people in 136 countries, researchers find a robust positive relationship between charitable giving and self-reported happiness, even controlling for income levels.[4] Experiments suggest that the relationship is causal. In one study, participants were given a small sum of money and asked to spend it that day. Half were randomly assigned to spend it on themselves, while the other half were instructed to purchase a gift or charitable donation. At the end of the day, those who gave the money away were happier than those who spent it on themselves.[5] The happiness benefits of giving start early. Another study gave a handful of goldfish crackers to two-year-old children, and then offered them the chance to share some of their treats with a monkey puppet. When they shared their treats with the puppet, toddlers were significantly happier than when they ate the crackers themselves.[6]

The benefits of giving even translate into health. In another randomised experiment, a group of adults was assigned to spend the equivalent of $130 either on themselves or others. Those who spent it on themselves purchased massages, sweaters and face cream. Those who spent the money on others bought cookies for neighbours or toys for grandchildren. A man who had served in Vietnam donated to a school built in honour of a fellow veteran. Three weeks on, the group who donated the money had significantly lower blood pressure. The health benefits of philanthropy were commensurate with the gains from regular exercise or taking hypertension medications.[7]

Not all giving is equal. A novel experiment randomly offered participants the chance to donate to one of two charities. The first group were asked whether they wanted to give money to UNICEF, a global body with 'some 10,000 employees working on international priorities such as child protection, survival and development'. The second group were invited to donate to Spread the Net, a charity that provides bednets to children in Africa, and told that every donation provided another bednet. There was no increase in happiness for those who gave to UNICEF, but a marked improvement among those who gave to Spread the Net. What is striking about the study is that Spread the Net is a UNICEF program. Participants didn't respond emotionally to a generic appeal but loved being told that their donation was about 'saving lives, one net at a time'.[8]

If we want to increase giving, says lead researcher Elizabeth Dunn, we need to stop thinking about altruism as a moral obligation, and start regarding philanthropy as a source of pleasure. Dunn urges charities not to reward donors with pens or calendars, but 'with the opportunity to see the specific impact that their generosity is having and to connect with the individuals and communities they're helping'.[9] She gives the example from her own life of supporting a refugee family through Canada's community sponsorship program, which allowed Dunn and her family not only to give money, but also to build personal connections with a family from Syria: picking them up from the airport, buying groceries, taking the children ice-skating. Humans evolved, says Dunn, 'to find joy in helping others'.

Transforming giving from a worthy activity to a joyous one might sound difficult, but it is worth remembering how past public campaigns have changed Australian attitudes. In the early 1980s, the 'Slip! Slop! Slap!' campaign challenged the notion of the 'bronzed Aussie', and helped reduce melanoma rates.[10] In the late 1980s, the 'Grim Reaper' campaign confronted the idea that HIV only affected marginalised communities. Since the 1990s, family violence campaigns such as 'No Respect, No Relationship', 'Safe at Home' and 'Stop It at the Start' have worked to change perceptions of family violence. These public health campaigns demonstrate that public attitudes can be shifted.[11] In Canada, Governor General David Johnston spearheaded the 'My Giving Moment' campaign in 2013, partnering with charities, businesses and media organisations to boost support for philanthropy.[12] Philanthropy Australia argues that a similar 'National Giving Campaign' could work here too.[13]

We've seen that children get joy from giving, so to reshape the culture of philanthropy around the pleasure it can provide we should build better ways for young people to participate as early as possible. Kids in Philanthropy has to date engaged 1000 Australian children as 'Agents for Change' and involved over 5000 children in volunteering activities. The model involves parents and families, which allows the experience to extend beyond any one activity and into family discussions about purposes to support and how best to give back to the community. The Agents for Change program is tailored for schools to provide to students aged five to fifteen. It develops empathy and inspires giving by showing children that philanthropy isn't just for the wealthy but for anyone who cares enough to be strategic about their giving, be it time or money. Kids in Philanthropy's 'Hangout for the Homeless' takes the CEO Sleepout and brings it down from the corporate level. Children do the sleepout with their parents, alongside homeless young people, to see the kind of social problems giving can alleviate. The 'Made With Love' food preparation and giving circle enlists family groups to provide groceries and prepare nutritious homemade meals for the homeless and disadvantaged. They work with Youth Projects in Melbourne to support the clients of that program. Kids in Philanthropy's mission is to engage, educate and empower children and their families through hands-on experiences that help communities in need.

Another aspect of enthusiasm is setting bold goals for giving. In 2010, Bill and Melinda Gates and Warren Buffett created 'the Giving Pledge', in which they asked billionaires to commit to giving away at least half their wealth. Beginning with forty signatories, the pledge now includes over 200 billionaires. Among them are Elon Musk, Sara Blakely, Mark Zuckerberg and Priscilla Chan, Mo Ibrahim, Michael Bloomberg, and Australians Leonard Ainsworth, Nicola Forrest and Andrew Forrest. After committing to give away all but 1 per cent of his US$75 billion fortune, Warren Buffett said, 'I couldn't be happier with that decision ... my family and I will give up nothing we need or want by fulfilling this 99 per cent pledge.'[14]

Giving isn't just for billionaires. Philosopher Peter Singer points out that if you are paying for something to drink when safe water comes out of the tap, then you have money to spend on things you don't really need. Singer, who gives over one-third of his income to charity, tells his readers to try a level of altruism that is 'significantly more than you have been doing so far'.[15] Then see how it feels. If it feels good, keep doing it.

An emerging model that has helped engage new philanthropists is the 'giving circle', in which participants decide collectively how to give their money away.[16] By providing both information and inspiration, giving circles such as Impact100 and the Melbourne Women's Fund are helping to raise the quality and quantity of philanthropic donations.

Many creative altruists are seeking to boost corporate giving. In 2014, a handful of technology companies formed Pledge 1%, an organisation that asks firms to commit to giving back 1 per cent of equity, profit, product or employee time. Some companies choose to aim for all four objectives, while others focus on a single goal, such as giving 1 per cent of profits back to the community. Thousands of firms in over 100 countries have taken the 1 per cent pledge, with signatories ranging from Aussie Broadband to Zylo.

Such targets reflect the optimistic view that philanthropy is an essential part of living well. The Sikh principle of *daswandh*, the Christian principle of tithing and the Jewish practice of *ma'aser kesafim* each require adherents to donate one-tenth of their income in the name of God. In Islam, the principle of *zakat* is more complicated, involving giving away 2.5 per cent of wealth, 5 to 10 per cent of income (depending on how it is earned) and 20 per cent of found treasure. In each faith, giving is an inherent aspect of a good and honourable life – indeed, the Hebrew word to signify charity, *tzedakah*, simply means 'justice'.

Ease

In its early years, Sydney technology company Atlassian had a workplace giving program. Employees could choose to support any charity they favoured, but because of a lack of promotion and a cumbersome sign-up process, only around 2 per cent of Atlassian staff were part of the program. So in 2015 Atlassian revamped the program.[17] They minimised employees' ability to choose which organisation they would donate to, and focused on supporting the work in Cambodia of Room to Read, a charity that works to improve girls' literacy. The sign-up program was massively simplified, so it took just two clicks and could be done in six seconds or less. The first 100 employees who signed up to the revised program were given an Atlassian Foundation sweatshirt.

A literacy charity wasn't the obvious partner for an Australian enterprise software company, but the firm has built ties by encouraging a group of staff each year to fund their own travel to Cambodia to assist with the charity's work. Because the sign-up process was quicker and simpler, enrolments increased twenty-fold. Over 40 per cent of Atlassian employees now participate in the program. Room to Read has expanded to over a dozen developing nations, and the option to join Atlassian's workplace giving program is now embedded in the sign-up process for all new employees.

Behavioural economics has shown how powerful default settings and habits can be in our daily lives. Many Australians are stuck in underperforming superannuation funds because they feel they don't have the time to switch. Energy companies, credit card firms and mortgage providers exploit this psychological bias by luring new customers in with special deals. When the introductory offer lapses, inertia means that existing customers end up paying a 'loyalty tax'. If switching is costly, we often stick with the status quo.

Even small costs can deter people from taking up a promising opportunity. The 'power of free' was illustrated in a famous experiment which showed that when people were asked to choose between a nice chocolate priced at 26 cents and a basic chocolate costing 1 cent, equal numbers chose each. But when the prices were dropped to 25 cents and 0 cents, nine-tenths chose the basic chocolate. Participants couldn't resist the free chocolate, even though the price gap between the two had remained the same. In the previous chapter, we saw how parkrun puts this insight to work: promising their participants that runs will be 'free forever'. The same principle also applies to making giving effortless. To boost donation rates, never underestimate the value of ease and simplicity.

Atlassian's six-second sign-up worked because it overcame the frictions that were stopping employees from signing up for workplace giving. Similar insights are being used by other organisations.

In the area of finance, Hearts and Minds Investments is an investment fund with a twist: the people choosing the stocks do not charge a fee. Instead, the fund takes a share of its assets every year and gives them away to charities and non-profit groups that are doing medical research. The result is that people can 'set and forget' their investments, knowing that part of their share market returns will be directed towards the charitable sector. At present, Hearts and Minds Investments gives away 1.5 per cent of its assets annually to ten charities, including MS Research Australia, the Black Dog Institute, the Sydney Children's Hospital and the Florey Institute.[18] Investment fund Future Generation takes a similar approach.[19]

In other areas, complexity acts as a deterrent to philanthropy. When people sign up for a superannuation account, they are asked to nominate a beneficiary for any assets left after they die. It is simple to leave the money to a spouse or child. But there's no easy way to leave the money to charity. To do so, you need to first sign a superannuation form that directs your unspent retirement savings to your estate, and then write a will that says the money is to go to a charity. Unsurprisingly, few Australians take this approach: charitable bequests out of superannuation are rare.

Simplicity is also relevant when it comes to in-kind donations. In Chapter 10, we profile Brisbane's Juliette Wright, who established GIVIT, an online platform that matches donors with charities and individuals in need. What makes GIVIT simpler than other donation channels is the concept of a 'virtual warehouse'. Instead of moving goods into a physical warehouse, they are listed online. Typically, the goods only start moving when they have a home.

This is not to say that warehouses are always a bad idea. When it comes to food distribution, organisations such as Foodbank (established by Jeanne Rockey), SecondBite (founded by Ian and Simone Carson) and FareShare (founded by Guido Pozzebon and Steven Kolt) have set up warehouses to store food that has been donated to them by supermarkets, grocers and manufacturers. On a similar model, Good360 (started by Alison Covington) distributes excess goods from retailers, such as toys, stationery and homewares.

In Chapter 4, we discussed some of the downsides of technology for social capital. But when it comes to matching up donors and recipients, nothing beats online platforms. The simpler it is for people to donate items, the easier it becomes for charities to source the items that their clients need, and the more in-kind donations will flow to where they are most needed. Technological platforms are also making it simpler for charities to engage with potential donors. GiveEasy offers pre-filled donation forms, SMS donation ('text FREEZE to 0400 064 064 to freeze motor neurone disease') and real-time updates on donation totals for live events. Similarly, Good2Give offers a fundraising armoury equipped with social media artwork, how-to guides for charity campaigns, and 'tap to give' terminals (which allow people at an event to simply tap their credit card to give $5). Using Raisely, GoFundraise or everydayhero, organisations can quickly set up donation pages for special events. A variety of retailers and apps even allow customers to 'round up for charity', donating the spare change from their transaction to their favourite charity.

For charities who see fundraising as a necessary evil, all these newfangled plug-ins and gizmos might seem like a distraction. But non-profit organisations ignore them at their peril. Lisa Grinham, chief executive officer of Good2Give, has a simple message: 'disrupt yourself before someone else does'.[20] In 2015, when the organisation changed its name from the Charities Aid Foundation, Grinham notes, 'I could see the market was changing, customers were demanding it, and donors were becoming far more tech-savvy and wanted to make donations online. We had a lot of paper, a lot of cheques [and] it was clear we needed to invest in tech if we wanted to survive and thrive.'[21] Over the next few years, the organisation renewed the board so that three out of seven members have a technology background. Good2Give now looks more like a technology company than a charity. Its growth is centred on making philanthropy straightforward.

Evidence

Imagine the fire brigade comes to you with a problem. There are two burning buildings on opposite sides of town. Inside one is a family of five. Inside another is a beautiful painting, worth $20,000. Which fire should they extinguish?

This thought experiment, devised by Scottish philosopher William MacAskill, is a provocative pushback against the notion of philanthropic pluralism: that all giving is equally valuable.[22] When it comes to the burning buildings, MacAskill notes, most people would save the family. Yet when the decision is between donating money to a local art gallery or providing deworming treatment to children in Africa, many choose art. MacAskill is part of a growing movement known as effective altruism, which aims to compare charities based on their impact.[23] The movement had its genesis in 2009, when MacAskill joined with fellow ethicist Toby Ord and Ord's wife Bernadette Young to found Giving What We Can, an organisation that aimed to persuade people to donate a tenth of their income to combat global poverty. In 2011, a dozen people inside the movement, sick of the tag 'do-gooder', voted to call their work 'effective altruism'.[24]

On the other side of the Atlantic, something similar was brewing. In 2006, Holden Karnofsky and Elie Hassenfeld, hedge-fund analysts in their mid-twenties, established GiveWell, an organisation that reviews and rates charities. Karnofsky recalls his frustration with the initial conversations: 'I called up a charity to ask them what they did, and they would say, "$20 will provide a child clean water for life."

And I would say, "what does that mean? How do you do that? Do you dig wells? Where do you dig those wells? How long do the wells last? Why did the children need clean water? What happens to them if they don't get the clean water?" And to those things they didn't have any answers. They would offer the same – the vague generality, by and large, of "$20 gives a child clean water for life. Clean water is a necessity, you should donate to us."'[25]

But some charities were willing to engage with the analysts, providing information about how their programs made a difference. Karnofsky and Hassenfeld found the work increasingly absorbing, and eventually the pair quit their six-figure jobs to pursue it. As Hassenfeld recalls, 'I found myself staying up Friday nights till 3:00 in the morning, reading academic papers about diarrhoea. If you ever find yourself doing that, you know it might be time to look for something new.'[26]

In assessing charities, GiveWell focuses on four criteria: evidence of effectiveness, cost-effectiveness, transparency and room for more funding. At the time of writing, their top charities include the Against Malaria Foundation, which provides bednets at a cost of US$2 apiece; the Helen Keller International's vitamin A supplementation program to prevent child mortality; and GiveDirectly, which distributes cash to Kenyans and Ugandans living on less than US$1 a day. These preferred charities have often conducted randomised trials to prove the causal impact of their programs. GiveWell now shifts around A$200 million a year to its recommended charities.[27]

As it found its niche, GiveWell began exploring charities that focus on policy advocacy. This began with a discovery by GiveWell researcher James Snowden that at least one-eighth of those who take their own lives each year do so by drinking pesticides.[28] It can be frighteningly easy for people in developing countries to access lethal pesticides. So GiveWell made a grant to the Center for Pesticide Suicide Prevention, which works to tighten laws around the sale and storage of highly hazardous pesticides. GiveWell is now assessing other charities that work on policy advocacy, recognising that the evidence on cost-effectiveness may not be as solid when the outcome is law reform rather than program delivery.[29]

Meanwhile, the effective altruism community continues to grow. The Open Philanthropy Project (a spin-off of GiveWell) provides grants in six key areas: potential risks of advanced artificial intelligence, biosecurity and pandemic preparedness, criminal justice reform, farm animal welfare, scientific research and effective altruism. 80,000 Hours provides career advice to young people who are looking to have the maximum positive impact on the world. Named after the number of hours in the typical career, 80,000 Hours encourages people to focus on reducing threats that could lead to humanity becoming extinct, such as nuclear security and climate change, and improving institutional decision-making.

In *The Precipice*, Toby Ord argues that the moral case for philanthropy to support research into existential risks comes from valuing future lives as highly as present lives. If humanity survives, trillions more humans may be born. Ord argues that our descendants could transcend our current limitations, exploring the frontiers of knowledge and wisdom to 'reach heights that would be forever beyond our present grasp'. Yet he estimates that the odds of a humanity-ending disaster this century are one in six – making a powerful case for devoting more resources to averting catastrophe.

Not everyone needs to specialise in calamities. For those considering more conventional careers, Giving What We Can encourages people to think about whether they can maximise their positive impact by seeking out a high-income career, and then giving a large share of their income to charity. Controversially, Giving What We Can's Aveek Bhattacharya argues: 'The marginal benefit of most direct efforts to combat poverty is small. If you don't take that charity, NGO or political job, the chances are that someone of similar talent and motivation will, and will perform the job to a similar level. On the other hand, if you were to go into a high-paying job, you would be able to earn and donate money that would have been otherwise unlikely to go near the developing world. You may even be able to pay for two or three extra people to do the work you initially wanted to do.'[30]

Effective altruism is not without its critics. GiveWell's focus on impact evaluation has been questioned by charity-ranking site Charity Navigator, whose managers have decried the effective altruism movement as 'Big Brother in the guise of defective altruism'.[31] Charity Navigator argues it is foolish to try to judge whether one charitable cause is better than another. Instead, its own rating system focuses on a charity's financial health (using metrics such as its administrative expenses) and transparency (such as whether board members are listed on the organisation's website). While this approach allows them to rate over 9000 US charities, it says little about whether the organisation is changing the world for the better. A charity might have low overheads and competent management yet deliver its programs incredibly inefficiently.

Another critique of effective altruism contends that such a hyperrational Spock-like approach risks taking the humanity out of philanthropy. Traditional charity, they argue, fosters love. Effective altruism doesn't.[32] Effective altruism's critics contend that there is a humanity to putting a few dollars into the hand of a needy person begging in the street that making an electronic bank transfer to a successful African charity cannot match. According to research by the Hudson Institute's William Schambra, only 3 per cent of donors choose an organisation based primarily on its effectiveness.[33] Most donors support organisations that serve their immediate vicinity, a philosophy Schambra calls 'philanthrolocalism'.

Commentator David Brooks maintains that the 'earning to give' model is flawed because life is not just a means to produce outcomes – it is an end in itself. Responding to utilitarian philosopher Peter Singer, Brooks argues: 'If you choose a profession that doesn't arouse your everyday passion for the sake of serving instead some abstract faraway good, you might end up as a person who values the far over the near. You might become one of those people who loves humanity in general but not the particular humans immediately around.'[34] Brooks' critique is powerful, but not fatal. He writes that, 'If your profoundest interest is dying children in Africa or Bangladesh, it's probably best to go to Africa or Bangladesh, not to Wall Street.'[35] Yet it is easy to imagine that an altruistic banker might maintain her ethics by regularly travelling to see the programs her donations support and engaging with the charities that run them.

The effective altruism movement is likely to continue to grow over coming decades, as donors increasingly look for ways to ensure their gifts do the most good. This means that Australian charities will increasingly be asked for evidence that their programs are making a difference.[36] We encourage charities to consider carrying out high-quality evaluations of their programs – not merely before/after comparisons, but rigorous evaluations with credible control groups. Several Australian non-profits, including Evidence for Learning, Sacred Heart Mission and Kids First, have carried out randomised evaluations of their programs: allowing them to provide donors with top-quality evidence of their impact.[37]

Foundations forever?

In 2014, private hospital magnate Paul Ramsay died. Ramsay was single and had no children. His will left around one-seventh of his fortune to his friends.[38] The remaining $3 billion went into the 'Paul Ramsay Foundation', making it instantly the largest foundation in Australia. Apart from a desire to create a centre for the study of 'Western civilisation' (which quickly became the topic of hot public debate), Ramsay left little indication as to what his foundation should fund. It has now opted to focus on breaking cycles of disadvantage.

Spurred by rising inequality and a spirit of generosity among Australia's elite, private foundations have grown significantly in recent decades. Measured in terms of donations, the nation's second-largest foundation is the Minderoo Foundation, whose priorities include modern slavery, cancer, oceans and Indigenous disadvantage.[39] Third-largest is the Ian Potter Foundation, which supports the arts, early childhood, the environment and medical research. The Lowy Foundation supports foreign policy research, among other activities. The Graham and Louise Tuckwell Foundation supports university scholarships.

In some cases, foundations have prompted charities and non-profits to produce more evidence of their impact and report their failures more openly. John McLeod, co-founder of JBWere's philanthropic services division, observes that 'there's more being asked of charities in terms of how successful a gift has been rather than "thank-you-and-we'll-put-a-plaque-on-the-wall"'.[40]

Foundations are especially valuable when they fund innovative and unorthodox causes. In the United States, the Bill and Melinda Gates Foundation has turbocharged malaria research and helped to shake up orthodoxies in school education. The Howard Hughes Medical Institute provides investigator grants that encourage researchers to 'take risks... even if it means uncertainty or the chance of failure'. In 2015, the Ford Foundation shifted its grant-making to focus entirely on inequality, an issue that the foundation's leadership saw as receiving too little investment from government and other philanthropists.[41] By contrast, some of Australia's largest foundations fund traditional causes, such as sandstone universities, venerable art galleries and trusted hospitals. But there are other Australian foundations supporting activities considered too controversial or risky for government to fund. For example, Barry and Joy Lambert have given money to support research into medicinal cannabis at the University of Sydney. The Scanlon Foundation funds research into racism. The Reichstein Foundation, under the banner of 'Change not Charity', aims to invest in inspirational people, projects and organisations, with the goal of addressing the causes of disadvantage, rather than merely treating the symptoms. Such foundations are less likely to fund activities that would otherwise have been supported by government or by other philanthropists.

There is a legitimate public interest in the activities of charities and foundations. According to the Australian Treasury, the tax deductibility of charitable donations reduces government revenue by almost $2 billion a year, equivalent to what the government spends on paid parental leave.[42] This has prompted a debate over whether charitable foundations should endure forever, or automatically sunset a few decades after their founders die. On one end of the spectrum, the Global Priorities Institute's Phil Trammell argues that the great virtue of waiting is that foundations can invest their assets. For example, money invested in the Australian share market was 325 times more valuable at the end of the twentieth century than it had been at the start of the century.[43] Trammell advocates 'patient philanthropy': the idea that foundations should grow their assets while awaiting the optimal moment to give money away (for example, a rural poverty foundation might wait for a severe drought).[44] Conversely, others argue that private foundations should not operate in perpetuity, but ought to shut down after a particular point in time. The most extreme expression of this view is that of Judge Richard Posner, who describes the perpetual charitable foundation as 'a completely irresponsible institution, answerable to nobody'.[45]

Scholar Rob Reich argues that setting an end date on foundations recognises that new social issues will arise which cannot be foreseen today.[46] Could we really have expected nineteenth-century philanthropists to anticipate the need to prevent nuclear war, promote online education or protect the rights of transgender people? If not, what makes us think that today's foundations will be ready to solve the challenges of the twenty-second century? Unlike the Nobel Prize, which is planned to operate in perpetuity, Bill and Melinda Gates have specified that their foundation will close twenty years after their deaths. An even more stringent approach was adopted by billionaire Chuck Feeney, whose Atlantic Philanthropies foundation closed in 2020, the year he turned eighty-nine, having given away US$8 billion. Feeney adopts a philosophy of 'giving while living', and quips, 'I want the last cheque I write to bounce.'[47]

For donors, people like Feeney, Gates, Buffett and Ramsay epitomise the principle that generous giving and good living are inseparable. As social justice campaigner Henry Spira observed in his final years, 'One wants to feel that one's life has amounted to more than just consuming products and generating garbage. I think that one likes to look back and say that one's done the best one can to make this a better place for others.'[48]

For community builders, philanthropy is often the means of turning altruistic visions into reality. If you're in the donor hunting game, we recommend the three Es of philanthropy: enthusiasm, ease and evidence. Tell an enthusiastic story to potential givers about how your work can make a positive difference. Create pathways that make it easy for people to give, such as rounding up for charity, the six-second sign-up for workplace giving, or a simple way to donate a pre-loved laptop. And develop an evidence base – ideally through randomised evaluations – to prove to effective altruists that what you're doing is truly transformative.

7

SOCIAL CONNECTIONS AND SOCIAL PURPOSE

Compared with Australians in the 1980s, the typical Australian today has half as many close friends and knows only half as many neighbours. Almost three in ten hardly ever or never catch up with friends. Half say they are lonely at least one day a week. Within a generation, the share of Australians who live alone has doubled.

Our social bonds bring pleasure in themselves, but they also have a protective dimension – helping us weather life's vicissitudes. Across nations, trust is associated with faster rates of economic growth and higher levels of wellbeing.[1] In this chapter, we explore some of the projects that are boosting trust in Australia. We dub these organisations and programs 'trust accelerators', because of their potential to create deeper community connections, while also addressing social disadvantage.

Trust accelerators

When Carla Clarence and Kerry Jones began exploring a home-sharing solution to ease housing vulnerability for older women, they struck a trust problem. Women were keen to come together and share their resources but anxious about finding the right balance between connection and privacy, social support and personal space.[2] So, explains Clarence, they asked the group to help create the solution, which became Our Place. The women were excited by what co-housing could offer them, but needed to consider potential challenges. 'What if it's not working out or someone's care needs become quite significant or you end up with a partner?' They found the best matches were based on common values rather than common interests. So good matchmaking had to wrestle with topics sometimes considered taboo, including religion and politics. Potential sharers needed to get beneath thes surface before signing the lease. Our Place is a process which quickly advances the bonds of understanding far enough for the participants to figure out if they could be themselves when living together.

Sharing a home can make a big difference to older women's emotional, financial and physical security. But a bad match can be worse than living alone. Our Place helps women feel confident they'll be sharing their space with someone they trust.

Six orange chairs

For the first few days of Orange Sky Laundry's existence, it was all about the washing machines. How many could they get? Could a washing machine function without a rigid base? Could it run off a battery? How about in a van? The challenges were wiring, water waste, physical space, alignment, stacking, heat extraction and stability. But once Nic Marchesi and Lucas Patchett solved these problems and their mobile laundry for the homeless was ready to roll, they discovered that the real genius of the Orange Sky proposition was a set of collapsible plastic chairs.

It's not like the mobile washing service isn't clever, and it's not like it doesn't work or isn't needed. It's just been eclipsed by the blazing star power of the Orange Sky social scene. Which brings us back to those plastic chairs. Co-founder Lucas Patchett sums up the approach: 'The most important things our vans carry are the six orange chairs, not the washing machines and driers. And just the feedback we started receiving about our volunteers being happy, being spritely, really pushing for those conversations. It was something that a lot of communities I think in Brisbane hadn't experienced, and it was, I think, when we started realising we were onto something a bit special with this time that we had.'[3]

Orange Sky started out as a practical project. Patchett and his friend Nic Marchesi wanted to make life more pleasant for the more than 100,000 Australians who are homeless. A free, mobile laundry, with the gear to wash and dry clothes on the spot, could serve multiple people in multiple locations – it could go where the people needed it. Marchesi and Patchett had planned the service as something they could do with their mates, to give back to the Brisbane community. From the first wash they did, they began to see they were on a different path. As Patchett recalls: 'Homelessness is a complex issue. Nic was stunned when I told him the very first person we did laundry for, Jordan, had studied the same chemical engineering course at the same uni as me. It was as if we were on the same life trajectory and here was Jordan, eight years down the track. All it had taken was two or three wrong turns. These are our homeless friends, not our customers or clients. They may be different friends to those we have a barbecue with on a Sunday, but they're really important in our lives.'[4]

Orange Sky's friends wanted to talk. As much as they appreciated the laundry service, the thing they were missing most from their lives was a sense of belonging and connection. Because a load of washing takes a while, and because the vans have a weekly routine, the service became an opportunity for unhurried, non-judgemental conversations. 'We talk about our service being a catalyst for conversation,' says Marchesi, 'and you know, really, far from the washing and the drying of the clothes, it's an opportunity to have a chat.'[5]

For Harry, an Orange Sky regular in Collingwood, the bond he formed with the volunteers and the routine of the van's visits were far more meaningful than the laundry service: 'Every time they come down here I feel good. I live alone but when I have a bad day and Orange Sky is here, well, I forget about the bad day. And they look after you.'[6]

The social dimension of Orange Sky's work is precious, because it's harder to create an experience than it is to provide a service. For some of the marginalised people Orange Sky work with, a straight offer of social support could be a turn-off. The hygiene facilities (some vans are also fitted with shower facilities) attract new clients, give cautious individuals an alibi for being there and ensure people stick around to chat. As Patchett observes: 'Once we realised the impact of those conversations, the impact that clean laundry can have on someone's life, we knew then that we had something we could take all around Australia.'[7]

Orange Sky relies on volunteers who can maintain the culture of friendship and mutual regard that has developed around the service. The vans have been progressively upgraded, and as a way of opening up their potential volunteer pool (and minimising mechanical incidents) Orange Sky developed a smartphone app that guides volunteers through the process of activating the electrics and hydraulics. It's a courtesy to the volunteers, but it also means Orange Sky can recruit on sociability rather than technical nous.

Initially, Orange Sky chose locations where other service providers, such as food vans, shelters or drop-in services, had already established a service. These are spaces where Orange Sky's friends feel safe and are comfortable, and where they feel an equal sense of ownership of the interaction. If those spaces change or new ones emerge, the service can adapt. Marchesi is proud of what they have built: 'Being on four wheels we're able to be responsive ... our service can be operating 24/7, but it can be anywhere at any time.'[8] Orange Sky now also use the open-source data from Infoxchange's support service search engine Ask Izzy to pinpoint the best spots for their vans. The data shows locations where people are searching for laundry services but not finding any. By looking at the times when searches peak, they can figure out the best time to send a van. For non-profits trying to figure out where there is most need for their service, Ask Izzy's search data can provide valuable insights.

The Orange Sky story contains several other useful lessons for social purpose organisations. Listen to your clients and let your service evolve to meet their needs. Use technology to produce output metrics – a valuable resource for managers and fundraisers. And, if possible, use technology to make volunteers' jobs easier.

From Patchett and Marchesi's initial idea – put two washing machines and two driers in the back of an old van, drive around Brisbane's parks, hostels and drop-in centres to wash and dry clothes for free – Orange Sky has grown into a rich experience for friends and volunteers alike. 'What we stumbled on was a world first,' explains Patchett, 'something that connected the community, reduced the transmission of really bad diseases but most importantly and most simply, improved the lives of others.'[9]

The name 'Orange Sky' comes from a song by British singer Alexi Murdoch, about a person who has a dream that they are standing under an orange sky. The key line of the song is 'In your love, my salvation lies'. The charity has come to see its fundamental purpose as connecting people. But they're not excessively earnest. In 2016, Patchett and Marchesi were named Young Australians of the Year. At the ceremony, they were speaking with Victoria Cross recipient Ben Roberts-Smith. On the way in, Roberts-Smith wrapped his arm around Patchett and whispered something in his ear. Feeling a bit left out, Marchesi asked what the veteran had said. Patchett replied that the words were, 'Lucas, your fly's undone, mate.'[10] He told the story at every event they spoke at over the coming month.

When Orange Sky Australia (as it's now known) was in its infancy, Marchesi and Patchett pitched for public donations with washing-related metrics. Six dollars would pay for one wash, $60 paid for one stop, $120 paid for one day and $600 paid for one week. These days, Orange Sky has a different ask: '$288 supports an entire shift of genuine conversations, clean laundry and warm showers.' Similarly, the live tally of 'Our impact this week' puts 'hours of conversation' in pole position, ahead of wash loads and warm showers. The 'hours of conversation' metric comes across at first as deliberately offbeat, but it's actually a significant indicator of the sense of belonging the service creates. Service providers with a social element to their activities should track these social impacts, regardless of whether sociability is a stated mission. It could be a quantitative measure, like meaningful conversations, or qualitative feedback from clients. What you learn might change how you work.

The social benefits that have always been a part of service provision tend to be undervalued and underrecorded. This was certainly the case for Melbourne social enterprise café STREAT, which was established to help homeless young people develop life skills and gain hospitality qualifications. In one of their regular program evaluations, the team had created a word cloud from the reports of former participants. Chief executive Bec Scott – one of the leaders we profile in Chapter 10 – noted that the dominant word wasn't 'home' or 'job', but 'belonging'. STREAT's mission had been 'stopping homelessness the delicious way', but Scott now recognised that what had mattered most to those in the program was how it felt to be welcomed into a stable place after living on the margins. Inadvertently, they'd been doing double-plus-good: providing opportunity and inclusion. STREAT changed their mission statement to include belonging, and adjusted the way they judged success.

Phone a friend

The rise in mental health problems among teenagers, accompanied by high levels of loneliness across the adult population, suggests that the typical Australian could do with a few more close friends. Loneliness develops when we have fewer social ties than we'd like. It's a hunger, not just a lack. For those who struggle most and are already lonely or isolated, helping them reconnect is urgent work. The trust and confidence we need to build new connections can be taught. These lessons are valuable for all, and vital for some.

We're all familiar with Lifeline, but did you know there's now a FriendLine service? If you're feeling a bit cut off, or just want to talk something over, you can call 1800 4 CHATS (1800 424 287). Started in 2018 by the social connection charity Friends for Good, FriendLine provides an anonymous support line for anyone in the community. FriendLine gives callers an opportunity to share their thoughts or worries and have them recognised in a casual conversation. The service is not for times of crisis – callers are referred to Lifeline or Beyond Blue if they're in distress – it's for routine support in the early stages of isolation or loneliness. Founders Patricia Lauria and Laura Rouhan first developed the service as a low-cost approach to a gap in the social support coverage being provided to isolated seniors. They were hearing that on weekends and evenings it was hard to find any kind of contact beyond the crisis lines.

During the COVID-19 lockdown, the lines were overloaded with callers of all ages coming to terms with a sudden experience of isolation. 'People have had a shock about what loneliness can feel like,' explains Lauria, 'and how it can take you by surprise if that resilience isn't there and the usual social supports go.' At the peak of virus-related anxiety, FriendLine's switchboard ran hot. Regular sufferers of loneliness and new sufferers of social isolation were all reaching out for support.

Whereas crisis counselling lines encourage an almost clinical approach, FriendLine volunteers open up. 'FriendLine volunteers talk about their own life,' says Lauria, 'as a way to help people develop the social skills they need to build friendships. The caller is not just talking but also listening and reciprocating and beginning to form those communication skills.' Through the course of repeat calls, FriendLine's clients aren't just receiving a routine pick-up, they're strengthening the skills they need to have an engaging conversation: an important step to making friends.

FriendLine's goal is to prevent chronic loneliness from progressing to serious mental ill health. Recent funding will allow them to expand capacity more than tenfold, from 5500 calls a year to 60,000 calls each year. That extra reach lets them help more Australians who are hungry for friendship.

Nourishing connections

Combining social services with friendship is a classic example of a double-plus-good program. On Sydney's Northern Beaches, Suzanna Pawley has trialled a Meal Mates program, combining Meals on Wheels with a social call. A Meals on Wheels volunteer, carefully matched to the client, brings cutlery and crockery along with the food, and stays to serve and share the meal. The Meal Mates trial showed signs that adding this social dimension could solve some routine problems experienced by the regular program: volunteer absenteeism went down, clients always answered the door, and people ate more regularly. Clients who previously wouldn't get out of bed, wouldn't get dressed or wouldn't eat began to shift back towards a sociable meal-time routine and better self-care. They reported the food tasting better when the meal was shared. Conversations relaxed the clients and they ate more. Adding the opportunity to socialise and talk gave the recipients pleasure, a bit of extra purpose and order in their lives, and a better diet.

In Chapter 3 we learnt how a fulfilling personal experience as a volunteer in an aged care home shaped Anna Donaldson's vocation and led her to set up the digital literacy and inclusion charity Lively. Donaldson saw 'young people with no experience banging their head against a wall, wondering how they get experience when no-one will give them work'. As digital natives they had skills to share, and those who had greatest need of those skills were also the population at greatest risk of isolation and loneliness. Lively's employees have two responsibilities: helping older people learn to use technology, and building a genuine, friendly relationship. But Lively aren't laissez-faire about their double-plus-good objective. Their helpers get training in both technology and sociability. 'We start with some exercises and training content to build understanding and empathy of old people's experiences,' says Donaldson. 'We break down the stereotypes and assumptions and get young people to put themselves in the position of an older person starting to lose connection and independence.' Unlike a computer program, there's no failsafe algorithm for forging human connections – but taking an intentional approach raises the odds of creating genuine bonds.

Be a friend

When he was studying in Perth to be an occupational therapist, Nick Maisey received a jarring email: 'Hi, my name's Tim ... I'm twenty-three, I like movies, the beach and I'm interested in learning to surf. I don't have any friends and I'm wondering if anyone's interested in getting to know me.'[11] The unusual message was a reminder that most lonely adults don't ask for a friend. People become unmoored from social groups, family or relationships for many different reasons. But it can be confronting to admit you have no friends. The email prompted

Maisey to throw a big barbecue at a local park, which launched the social connection charity Befriend.

Like FriendLine, Befriend puts reciprocity at the heart of its relationship-building strategies. Befriend's Community Builders initiate conversations about citizen behaviour, friendship and participation and support people who want to improve social bonds in their local community. Typically, the Community Builders cultivate local 'Hosts', and support them to set up local groups, gatherings and events. Befriend's Hosts take charge of organisation and hospitality – they make people comfortable, introduce people and act as a social lubricant until natural connections build.

Befriend experiences might be tied to a sporting fixture or festival. They include nights out, group meals, gigs and comedy shows. There are casual classes to learn a new skill in company, and routine events such as pub trivia, hobby groups, book clubs, evening picnics, or small gatherings at the beach to listen to music while the sun goes down. Befriend believes that routine is the rhythm for connection, so their activities are frequent, with invitations shared through a central members' list, Hosts' personal networks and local councils. Befriend is deliberate about establishing a welcoming atmosphere and providing gentle encouragement for everyone to contribute. These conditions allow friendships to flourish over time.

Befriend's Community Builders understand that being 'inclusive' means more than just hosting welcoming events. So they work to ensure their open invitations are reaching the people who face the steepest challenges in connecting. These are the people who most need Befriend's welcoming warmth to find their tribe. By focusing on those most in need of friends, Befriend is putting Sutton's Law of Social Capital to work.

Befriend's Community Builders are there to give support, but they're working towards the point where they can phase themselves out and a healthy network of reconnected locals will carry on supporting each other. Since 2011, Befriend's Community Builders have trained over 800 local Hosts and connected more than 12,000 people.

Maisey gave a picture of what Befriend's friendship journey can look like: 'Tom is a young man who's been used to being treated as someone who needs help and support. Tom joined Befriend and started coming along to locally hosted social gatherings promoted through our Network. The local Network deliberately communicates that openness to everyone's contribution, and over time Tom has been able to shift from being a member of the network to someone who's now a volunteer, making a more direct contribution. Now he's hosting events. He's run a bowling group and a beginners' photography group and found different ways to use his own passions as an open invitation to others to share that passion with him.' Tom has become an active citizen in his area and has found the friends he needs to live a happy, healthy and connected life.

Gather my crew

The other dog owners didn't know much about Frank, but they enjoyed seeing him and his three sausage dogs at the local park. He had a ready smile and sometimes brought along lemons from the tree outside his house. Then one day, Frank didn't show up. After a few days, some of his fellow dog walkers decided to check in on him. It turned out he'd fallen, broken his ankle and was confined to a wheelchair. He had told the community nurse that he didn't know anyone in the neighbourhood who could help him with household chores. Aleshia, a fellow dog walker, decided to coordinate a schedule, using the website Gather My Crew. The site allows someone who needs help to list the help they need, and helpers can sign up to assist. Over the next three months, the dog walking community created a roster to provide Frank with company, dog walking, shopping and meals. By the time he was out of the wheelchair, the support group had grown to twenty-seven people.

Gather My Crew was created by psychologist Susan Palmer, who had seen a gap between the needs of her cancer patients and the desire of their friends and family to assist. So she created an online tool that allowed people going through tough times to post tasks and invite friends and family to accept them via a shared calendar. Tasks might include childminding, meal preparation or transport to medical appointments.

An early user of Gather My Crew was Karen, who had lost her husband to cancer five years earlier. As the mother of two young boys, she felt scared and overwhelmed when she was diagnosed with breast cancer. As the chemotherapy began, she struggled to manage the daily tasks of looking after her family. One night, she set up an account and listed the tasks that needed doing over the following eight weeks. Then she sent an email to her mothers' group. In the morning, all the tasks had been accepted, and she had emails from people offering additional help.

Since 2017, Gather My Crew has coordinated 2000 dog walks, 5000 lifts, 7000 social visits and 14,000 meals. The platform overcomes the discomfort people often feel about asking for help and makes it possible to coordinate a large 'crew' of helpers. It represents a powerful form of CyberConnecting – employing technology to turn offers of 'let me know what I can do' into real assistance. By making it easy to ask for help and straightforward to answer the call, the platform transforms a dormant network of loose ties into the kind of all-encompassing support that characterises the most connected tribes, villages and kinship groups.

Group harmony

Brian Triglone, the founder and conductor of Alchemy Chorus, sometimes hears that dementia patients are brighter after singing. But he knows that's a short-term aspect. 'It's only part of what Alchemy is about. We're strongly focused on creating the sense of community it gives to them and their carers.' Triglone explains: 'The original idea of Alchemy Chorus was that it would target those with mild to moderate dementia living at home with a carer. Dementia can bring about a withdrawal from supportive routines and social circles. It can be awkward and embarrassing and there is a risk of social isolation. The carer, usually the husband, wife or partner, is gradually losing a lifetime partner or friend and the effect on them can be devastating. So the choir offers a way for the couple to become socially re-engaged using the medium of singing, which everyone can do and enjoy.' Rather than providing just a singalong session, Triglone conducts the weekly practice along the lines of a performing choir. Like Astrid Jorgensen's Pub Choir, performance is a key part of the Alchemy Chorus model. 'We didn't want the choir to be hidden away singing to themselves. The added dimension of performance gives the singers a tremendous boost, they're getting out and entertaining people.'

Triglone notes that while there are similar singing programs, they tend to be on site at retirement homes or nursing facilities. Alchemy Chorus operates as a performing choir, connected to the community, not as a care activity. 'The element of normality is enormously important to everyone. If it was just the people with dementia singing it could have a curiosity value, but with the different groups in the choir you can't easily tell who's got dementia; they're all there together, united in singing. They don't want to be a curiosity, they want to blend in. Our members don't want to be patronised in any way but rather to be genuinely included in the community.'

The model is lean. Alchemy Chorus is a volunteer organisation, and the musicians are also volunteers. For a typical weekly session, they have a pianist to accompany the choir, a bass player and a guitarist. Triglone conducts. At each session, Alchemy Chorus takes a $5 contribution from members, and asks for donations from the audience at their concerts. The only major expense is hiring a community hall for their Thursday-morning practice sessions. In the last year, the organisation's regular takings, plus donations from three concerts, covered operating costs and left enough for a $3000 donation to Dementia Australia, the peak body that provides support services and makes referrals to the choir.

Over three years, the choir has doubled in size – all the more impressive given that a third of its members have a degenerative, terminal illness. Weekly attendance now averages just over eighty. Alchemy Chorus has also served as a place to make new connections and friendships have formed among carers mourning the loss of a dementia-affected partner.

Alchemy is now facing an influx that is challenging them to define their purpose more clearly. Singers have started arriving with paid carers who are not there to be part of the choir. The organisation wants to support new dementia patients, but professional carers disrupt the cohesion of their mutually supporting system. It's sharpened Alchemy's focus on their highest priority, which is supporting full-time carers and building community among affected families.

Around 450,000 Australians live with dementia, with a further 1.5 million Australians involved in their care. Alchemy Chorus has found a way for couples affected by dementia to access community support and build new friendships. It occupies an unusual niche, but not a unique one. One lesson from Alchemy Chorus is what can be done when social purpose groups include carers in their activities. Think of the potential for disability support groups to include carers, children's playgroups to include parents, and aged care groups to involve adult children. And unlike past efforts to turn lead into gold, this kind of alchemy really works.

Welcome to our neighbourhood

'Brian is a lovely guy, with a great calm energy,' says Craig Wilkins, chief executive of Conservation Council South Australia and The Joinery. 'He comes in once a week and just potters around the site, seeing all the little jobs that need doing and he just jumps in and gets them done. We've gotten to the point where people who've come to the site organically now feel a real sense of ownership. He was a volunteer at the community bike shop we have on site and he just took this role on. There's no obligation. He comes when it suits him, but he feels this real belonging and just took on this role because he saw the need. People like Brian have become hugely important to The Joinery, they help set the tone. And for us, being able to take them up on that generosity is a marker of our success.'

The Joinery's Franklin Street block was once home to an Adelaide City Council bus depot. After being decommissioned, the block was mostly derelict and the council put out a call for someone to revitalise the well-located site. Conservation Council SA answered the call: 'We were fortunate,' explains Wilkins, 'right place, right time. This derelict building, and the council wanting people to jump in and do something with the space. A big, clunky old building and there was the opportunity to take it on.' First, they carried out a risk analysis – the rent would be low but if a developer came onto the scene the council could move them on with minimal notice. They would be up for the refurbishment and maintenance costs, but everything on the site would be theirs and under their sole control. They were initially given a three-year lease, and invested $120,000 on the refurbishments and technological infrastructure required in a modern co-working space. After that initial lease period, they secured another three years and have negotiated a further five years at the site, taking them through to 2025. For the moment, The Joinery's success has given it a claim on the site.

'Our vision was to create a home or hub for people who are yearning to do something around sustainability,' says Wilkins. 'But we were clear we didn't want it to be an eco-space, we wanted a community space. That was the best way to entice people in rather than being seen as an activist centre. Our mix of tenants includes [Christian aid organisation] TEAR and [refugee agency] UNHCR, so that adds in a migration lawyer, and along with the events and sustainability focus it means we've got a healthy mix of people coming through the doors, so we're not stratified.'

At the start, Conservation Council SA put out an open invitation to a range of organisations and groups in the nearby area, encouraging them to get on board and be partners in making the site work. They also hosted some existing local enterprises to provide a continuous presence on the site that would bring people through the gates from the outset. 'There was a nearby community garden that had been run by an adjacent affordable housing and homeless organisation. We encouraged them to locate on our site. We invited in a community bike workshop that was struggling to find an ongoing space. We gave them that space for free. To get the activation we were willing to give the space away.'

Creating the right mood is critical, says Wilkins. 'People say they love the vibe. On the ground floor we have the funky café, and there are couches and spaces where people can hang out. School groups come in or people drop in with their kids. That melting-pot feel is what makes it attractive as a place to be. The info centre on the ground floor has curated a really wonderful series of events tapping into different parts of the sustainability zeitgeist over the past years.'

For Wilkins, the critical element of The Joinery's success is the sense of partnership between government and the community. 'If a local government or council is willing to provide a space, that's when a community can step in and make it work. I don't think it would work if it was a council-run property. Part of our success is the community doing it themselves. So that's essential. But there's no way we could be doing this without the council providing the space; we couldn't afford this location and be able to give the space away or discount it to let the community do its work. Financially it wouldn't work if we owned the building and had to pay full commercial rates and charge full fees to cover it. The council's support means we can be generous to the community groups. We provide space for groups who wouldn't be able to afford to do their activity at full cost, and we get the value of their energy and commitment.'

Wilkins sees The Joinery as a hybrid. It's a collective space in spirit, but it's not community-owned or -governed. Rather than creating a members' committee or a body to share governance work through collective decision-making, Conservation Council SA took carriage of all the governance for the site. This frees up tenants to focus on the work that brought them to The Joinery in the first place. Wilkins explains: 'I think we've stumbled on an approach that means people can bring their best energies. A lot of the activity inside and out starts with someone saying, "I want to do this," and we say, "Fantastic, here's the space. Go for it."' The Joinery has held around 4000 events, gatherings, meetings and workshops. Members of Conservation Council SA get priority access, but the facilities and spaces are open to outside hirers.

Hubs such as The Joinery can have a direct positive effect on their immediate community (because they're interesting places to hang out) as well as increasing the productivity of co-located organisations who work there. As people who work in technology accelerators often observe, there are frequent payoffs that are real but difficult to predict or put a value on – those informal conversations and unplanned collaborations that coalesce to solve a problem. But there are also bottom-line benefits. The cost of well-located real estate and quality infrastructure are an increasing drain on the budgets of non-government organisations. Shared spaces will keep more non-profits viable and visible.

Governments have been moving towards a co-location model for frontline services for several years, and Community Hubs Australia has been successfully using existing facilities, such as local schools and community centres, as a single site offering multiple services for migrant families. This is a natural role for philanthropists who would like to strengthen the social capital ecosystem. In the United States, co-location advocates are urging foundations to look at carefully placed co-location projects as a way to increase the return on their giving. In the words of China Brotsky, Sarah Eisinger and Diane Vinokur-Kaplan, authors of *Shared Space and the New Nonprofit Workplace*, 'well-spent resources on creating nonprofit centers can replace multiple scattershot requests for capital and rent funding'.[12]

Some Australian philanthropists have already started to take on a leading role in spreading the impact of co-location. For example, Our Community founder Denis Moriarty and social investor Carol Schwartz have created a different kind of hub – Our Community House – a co-working space where up to 400 social-sector workers can set themselves up among like-minded collaborators.

For non-profits, Our Community House is the Crystal Palace of co-location. Located in North Melbourne, it is spacious and beautiful, with funky furniture and an indoor plant wall. Purchased for Our Community by Schwartz and her husband Alan, the building offers the usual benefits of shared workspace (cutting costs and boosting collaboration), but it also deliberately signals the social sector's status. It's got a different look from the local government building that became The Joinery, but both spaces show the benefits of co-location.

Conservation Council SA could have found a more modest tenancy for its own purpose, but by taking the entrepreneurial path that led to The Joinery, they've been able to support organisations that share their mission and create a community resource that has a direct positive impact on the local inhabitants. Their 'lush and productive oasis in the middle of the city' has been designed as somewhere people can 'connect and create a better future.' It's a social experience as much as a social purpose, but if either was missing, would Brian strap on his tool belt to do the rounds each week?

Striking social capital gold

When the goldrush town of Beechworth was developing as the government centre for north-eastern Victoria in the mid-1800s, one of its first needs was a place to house lawbreakers. Beechworth Gaol, which once housed Ned Kelly, was built by the town's first inmates, constructed in a panopticon design from granite that was quarried onsite. With its origins in frontier making, and its strong links to Kelly, the gaol's history is shot through with social disquiet, the dynamics of inequality and an outlaw myth that grew from the story of an energetic mind gone wrong.

Today, Old Beechworth Gaol is being reborn as the headquarters of a social project to slow the contraction of opportunity in regional areas. The Australian Centre for Rural Entrepreneurship (ACRE) sees entrepreneurial creativity as the means to regenerate regions. By igniting entrepreneurship in regional communities, ACRE aims to make them better connected and more vital – places where you *can* make a living and *want* to make a life.

In 2016, ACRE led a group of local families and established philanthropists to buy back the Old Beechworth Gaol, and revamp it into a space that offered jail tours, a café, and co-working spaces for local enterprises – from business consultants to artists. As ACRE chief executive Matt Pfahlert puts it, 'We like to think that we play a role as a bridge maker, between generations and between sectors, and we see the Old Beechworth Gaol as a wonderful canvas for this to happen.'[13]

As a long-term investment in the area's entrepreneurial culture, ACRE has also embarked on a program that encourages local school students to create social enterprises and develop citizenship skills.[14] The curriculum is licensed from Scotland's Social Enterprise Academy, illustrating the lesson that sometimes it's better to buy off the shelf than design a bespoke solution. Students meet people from the local business community, collaborate with classmates outside their friendship circles and mentor the next cohort of participants.[15] When Pfahlert appeared on radio to profile the program, one of the entrepreneurs, an eleven-year-old called Oscar, seized the opportunity to phone in and promote his drone-based imaging company. Listeners loved it.[16]

Like Conservation Council SA's role in The Joinery, ACRE's work shows how larger charities can use their standing and resources to create a community of purpose whose social impact is more than the sum of its parts. Social purpose precincts can extend those benefits to a larger number of organisations, allowing them to collaborate, share ideas and resources. To make it easy for people to engage, these precincts need to be accessible. As the real estate maxim goes, there are three things that count: location, location, location.

Conversations are the chief currency of social capital, and a shared purpose provides the foundation for conversations to begin. Conversations between organisations, sector workers, volunteers, supporters and community members are a starting point for more connected communities. They're also the basis for more productive community builders. Organisations can create new connections (FriendLine and Befriend) or fire up existing ones (Gather My Crew). By shifting their focus to meaningful conversations, Orange Sky dramatically increased the reach of their laundry service, which has significant benefits for the self-esteem and health of homeless people. Their 'meaningful interaction' metric could be a useful benchmark for other community builders too.

Just as volunteering organisations need to insulate their volunteer culture against disruptive elements, community builders must strike a balance between inclusion and the integrity of their purpose. The dynamics that allow Alchemy Chorus to rebuild experiences of community and belonging for dementia-affected couples are delicate. Protecting Alchemy's purpose creates some natural limits on the people who can be involved.

Like Orange Sky Australia and The Joinery, ACRE found an innovative solution to a pressing social problem. All three benefited from a willingness to adapt their model, to collaborate with government and other non-profits and to scale up quickly.

As with technology startups, many new social enterprises will ultimately fail, but it's vital that Australia continues encouraging fresh approaches and creative solutions. Rebuilding community cannot be the task of existing non-profits alone – it must also involve new organisations, networks and collaborations.

8

SPIRITUAL CONNECTIONS

Every week, more than two million Australian adults attend a religious service – a time to focus on the deeper meaning of life and to share the lessons of their faith. Across religions, from Christianity to Islam, Buddhism to Hinduism, the focus of worship is on the scriptures and teachings, but the value of religion goes beyond the theological. Australians who attend religious services are 10 percentage points more likely to volunteer in their communities.[1] Australians who regularly attend religious services donate $700 a year more to charity than those who do not.[2] And not all of this is religious philanthropy: regular religious attendees give $150 a year more to secular causes. Across two million attendees, that's at least $300 million more in donations.

Since the 1950s, weekly religious attendance among Australian adults has fallen from three in ten to just one in ten. Across Australia, hundreds of churches lie vacant. From a social capital perspective, the collapse of religious communities matters in its own right – but it also matters because of how it affects volunteering and philanthropy in secular organisations. One of the best predictors of giving and donating is being asked, and religious groups are particularly good at calling on their members to help others.

But while some religious communities are failing, a few are flourishing. In this chapter, we explore some of the growing spiritual movements across the country and discover some of their lessons for religious social capitalists.

Pentecostal progress

At the end of January 2020, after bushfires ravaged the east coast, members of the Bayside Church in Melbourne decided to forgo their upcoming church camp at Phillip Island. Church members would still pay for a camp, but they would give the places to firefighters and fire victims instead. Partnering with Volunteer Fire Brigades Victoria, the church offered those affected by the fires a 'Respite from Reality Retreat' over the March long weekend, covering their accommodation, meals and activities.

Bayside Church founder Rob Buckingham attributes his faith to an act of hospitality. As a teenager, he was hitchhiking around Australia when a truck in which he was a passenger collided with another truck. The occupants of the other vehicle were killed. After leaving hospital, Buckingham stayed at the home of the truck driver who survived the crash with him. The driver and his wife were Pentecostal Christians, and by the time he left their home, Buckingham was no longer an atheist. After attending Bible college, he moved to Melbourne, where he founded Bayside Church in Cheltenham, a suburb south-east of the city. For its first eighteen months, the congregation met in a funeral chapel. It then moved to a primary school, and then a secondary school, before purchasing its own premises, a printing factory. In 2000, Bayside Church had around 300 regular worshippers. By 2010, this had grown to 900. Today, the congregation numbers about 1800, spread across several services.

Theologically, Bayside is an evangelical and Pentecostal church, affiliated with the Crosslink Christian Network. At a time when traditional Christian denominations are shrinking fast, Pentecostal churches are bucking the trend. From 1986 to 2016, the share of Australians who identify with the Anglican, Lutheran or Uniting churches halved.[3] Presbyterians and Catholics are declining in number too. By contrast, Buddhism, Hinduism, Sikhism and Islam are growing rapidly. Among Christian denominations, the fastest-growing are Pentecostal churches.

Perhaps the best-known Pentecostal church in Australia is Hillsong, which has conservative views on social issues and focuses on the prosperity gospel.[4] Hillsong founder Brian Houston once wrote a book titled *You Need More Money*, and the church was dubbed by one critic an 'evangelical-industrial complex'.[5] By contrast, Bayside has been active on social justice issues; it was the first Pentecostal church in Australia to welcome gay and lesbian worshippers.[6] This is especially significant given that Christianity's stance on homosexuality is the single most common reason that people say they don't engage with the faith.[7]

After purchasing their own premises, Bayside Church began outreach work in Indonesia. This led to Rob Buckingham and his wife Christie travelling to Bali to meet convicted drug traffickers Andrew Chan and Myuran Sukumaran. Christie Buckingham became Sukumaran's spiritual adviser, and the church was active in the – ultimately unsuccessful – campaign for clemency. Bayside Church continues to campaign for an end to the death penalty.

The Bali Nine campaign is just one of the ways that Bayside Church has engaged with the public conversation. Before he was a pastor, Rob Buckingham worked as a radio host, and presented programs on the now-defunct Melbourne easy listening station 3MP and Melbourne Christian station Light FM. For a time, Bayside Media – the church's media arm – produced a weekly television talk show. Services are live-streamed, Rob Buckingham writes a weekly blog, and the couple regularly take questions on Facebook. This made the church community especially resilient when coronavirus forced the temporary cessation of religious services.

Other large Pentecostal churches, including Planetshakers in Melbourne, Influencers in Adelaide, Kingdomcity in Perth, and Hope Centre in Brisbane, are characterised by eye-catching websites. For such congregations, music is an essential aspect of their strong appeal to worshippers. Hillsong United, the umbrella organisation for the church's music empire, has sold over twenty million albums.[8] Bayside's theology has much in common with these Pentecostal megachurches, but with less focus on entertainment and more on social justice.

One reason Pentecostal churches have been successful is their focus on fresh arrivals. Just as successful retailers and restaurants consider how they will be perceived by a first-time visitor, thriving religious organisations think carefully through the experience of someone coming to worship for the first time. This involves everything from whether they can find a parking place to who will greet them at the front door. Does the building smell fresh, or old and musty? Will a surly greeter make a new visitor feel unwelcome? Researcher Fleur Creed argues that one of the explanations for the growth of Pentecostal megachurches is how they get first-timers connected: 'Newcomers are followed up on a weekly basis with phone calls, invited to join a "Connect" group (small group), of which there are many, and invited onto a service team within weeks of joining.'[9] There is a broader lesson here for all religious community builders: initial impressions count.

The School of Life

Ironically, while many Pentecostal churches are using rock anthems to turbocharge the theology, movements such as Alain de Botton's School of Life are keeping the pulpit but ditching the theology. In one talk – delivered in a style that is a cross between a sermon and a lecture – de Botton muses on the role of art in a meaningful life: 'The essays of Plato. The novels of Jane Austen. The painting of Titian and Botticelli. The poetry of Matthew Arnold ... Really what I'm trying to do with art is to invite you, all of you, to start to use art as something that can alleviate your sorrows, bring you hope, give you courage. A resource, a living resource, that's there for our hearts and not an academic or historical exercise.'[10]

Fourteen per cent of Australians describe themselves as spiritual but not religious.[11] In his book *Religion for Atheists*, de Botton argues that non-believers can enjoy more fulfilling lives if they adapt religious practices. He commends Buddhist tea ceremonies and Jewish Shabbat dinners for recognising the link between body and mind. He advocates secular pilgrimages, in which journeys aren't taken simply for 'relaxation' or 'adventure', but to deliberately build character; with destinations carefully selected for their ability to reorient our personality. De Botton also praises the approach that religion takes to moral education, contending that wisdom largely consists of applying accepted truths, rather than finding insights at the frontiers of philosophy.

As a practical philosopher, de Botton aims to turn his ideas into impact, by shaping a community that provides a source of wisdom on living well. Since its founding in 2008, de Botton's School of Life has produced dozens of videos and opened venues in eleven cities, including Sydney and Melbourne. These stores sell books and self-help paraphernalia, organise public lectures and offer classes with titles such as 'Improving Your Emotional Intelligence', and 'Philosophy Salon: Plato'. Their rapid uptake demonstrates the appetite for de Botton's spiritual-but-not-religious movement.

A similar story lies behind the Sunday Assembly movement, which invites atheists to gather together to sing, hear inspirational talks and share a cup of tea. As Kathryn Murray, one of the organisers of the Sunday Assembly in Melbourne puts it, 'Because it is a godless congregation, we don't have a doctrine to rely on, so we take reference from everything in the world. From the arts, from nature, from everything that we can get our hands on.'[12] In addition to its monthly meetings, the Sunday Assembly encourages members to donate blood, help out on Clean Up Australia Day and assist with other community events. However, the movement remains small. In the United States, the number of Sunday Assembly chapters halved in the three years to 2019, as the movement struggled to motivate members to stay engaged (an exception is Utah, where a strong Sunday Assembly movement serves as a departure lounge from Mormonism).[13] Philosophically-inspired togetherness does not seem to stir the kind of passion that underpins the world's major religions.

We've seen already from Bayside Church and other Pentecostal churches the value of using technology to strengthen rather than supplant spiritual ties. Religious bodies with thriving congregations tend to have a strong presence on the internet. To use internet initialisms, success online seems to correlate with success AFK (away from the keyboard) and IRL (in real life). For example, Alain de Botton's School of Life has a YouTube channel that has attracted millions of views. Brad Chilcott, founder of Activate Church in Adelaide, tweets about the treatment of refugees, workers' rights, economic inequality and family violence. Planetshakers allows parishioners to live-stream their four Sunday services, to donate online and to request a prayer online. Lakemba Mosque posts its Friday sermons on Facebook, complete with English subtitles and Auslan translation. Like the almighty in Hinduism, successful CyberConnecting takes many forms.

Benevolent believers

In the Melbourne suburb of Doncaster, Zulfiye Tufa joins a group of Muslim mothers each Thursday morning. They're part of Benevolence Australia, a 'semi-sacred' space for Muslims to get together for conversations, celebrations and meals. Tufa says, 'I love it. It's great. I've met so many mums. It's a social thing, but it's also really educational for me ... about how to raise my child ... I can learn from other mums.'[14] In the Islamic community, some of the strongest growth is in semi-sacred spaces such as Benevolence Australia. Founded in 2008 by Syrian-born Muslim Saara Sabbagh, the community now has over 500 members. Sabbagh explains, 'You don't have to be a practising Muslim to attend. Women don't have to wear a headscarf. Men don't have to grow a beard ... It's not your local mosque, but it's not your local café ... Our motto is "come as you are".'

Operating with the same spiritual ethos as Ta'leef Collective in the United States and Rumi's Cave in Britain, Sabbagh laughs as she says, 'To be honest, I think I started it for myself. I didn't feel a sense of belonging in my own community.' One expert in Islam points to the tendency of many mosques to have strong cultural roots – to be known as a Pakistani mosque, a Turkish mosque or an Indonesian mosque. The imams who preach at these mosques sometimes deliver their sermons in those languages. Consequently, some mosques can feel out of touch to second-generation and third-generation Muslim Australians. Furthermore, spaces like Benevolence Australia welcome discussions around difficult topics such as suicide, family violence and same-sex marriage. They provide comfortable venues and facilitate deeper engagement through spiritual retreats, support groups for converts to Islam, and outreach to the non-Muslim community through workshops on 'Understanding Islam'.

Many Australian Muslims are first- or second-generation immigrants, so providing a strong sense of identity fulfils Sutton's Law of

Social Capital: go where the need is greatest. A similar attitude characterises Uniting Church Reverend Margaret Mayman. In her leadership of Pitt Street Uniting Church in Sydney, and St Michael's Uniting Church on Collins Street, Melbourne, Mayman has deliberately taken an approach that is significantly more left-wing than many other Christian churches. Mayman has written that 'the choice for abortion can be a morally good choice'.[15] She has campaigned in favour of refugees and backed the 2019 school climate strikes. This reflects a lesson we saw in the case of philanthropy: enthusiasm counts. Mayman's approach has a sense of urgency and energy that can sometimes be lacking in more traditional churches. Comparing the drivers of membership growth in different churches, one study found that openness to innovation correlates with membership growth. Growing churches are twice as likely as shrinking churches to agree that 'this congregation is always ready to try something new'.[16]

As well as their Melbourne roots, Benevolence Australia and Bayside Church share a common characteristic: both groups are working to solve community problems. Whether it's addressing family violence or helping fire victims, successful religious institutions take a positive and engaged approach to the challenges in their neighbourhoods. This contrasts with the angrier and more resentful approach that unsuccessful religious bodies sometimes adopt. The same activist spirit characterises other strong religious communities. In Canberra's north, Kippax Uniting Church is integrated with the social services provided by UnitingCare (the church's charity arm). There, new parents can access daily playgroups and sign up for evidence-based parenting programs Newpin (New Parent and Infant Network) and HIPPY (a two-year home-based early learning and parenting program). The centre provides emergency relief packages year round, and over 500 Christmas hampers. Its Kippax Connections program helps link people to educational and work opportunities. Kippax's The Mower Shed is a social enterprise that provides gardening and mowing services, with a focus on employing those who have struggled to find other work. From social care to lawn care, Kippax's different strands of work are drawn together under a single guiding principle: 'together, create community'.

Another innovative model is the Southport Church of Christ, which works with the nearby Gold Coast University Hospital to provide accommodation for families of patients in intensive care.[17] The church community provides emotional support as well as housing: another example of hybrid vigour in action.

Church plants

Church planting is the process of establishing a new church. Pete Greenwood, who started Inner West Church in the Melbourne suburb of Kensington in 2015, describes planters as the church's 'research and development division'. Greenwood set up his church after identifying the inner-west area as one that wasn't served by many existing churches. The congregation meets in a rented hall owned by the YMCA. In response to the critique that new churches might simply be attracting worshippers from nearby, Greenwood says that he deliberately tries not to engage in 'sheep stealing'. Although some transfer of Christians from other churches is inevitable, Greenwood's goal is to focus on those who have never attended (the 'unchurched') and those who have lapsed (the 'dechurched').

According to a survey of 110 church planters, most meet in schools, halls or homes, with only a third meeting in a church building. Pastors of these churches tend to describe their worship style as contemporary, and their congregation as multi-ethnic.[18] The average new church has thirty-eight worshippers in its first year. After four years, this has grown to an average of seventy congregants (considerably fewer than in the United States, where the typical church plant has grown to

124 worshippers after four years). It takes the median new Australian church five years before it becomes financially self-sufficient.[19]

To help church planters, Australian church-planting networks have sprung up, including City to City Australia, Acts 29 Network, Geneva Push and the International Network of Churches. These networks assess potential church planters, and then provide those who pass muster with training, mentoring and even financial support.[20] These practical resources (what one network calls 'Church in a Box') are helpful, but even with this support most new churches will inevitably go the way of most small businesses.

Successful church founders tend to be those who identify a need in the community. In establishing his church in the Melbourne suburb of Werribee, Mark Tibben was driven by the fact that new churches had not kept pace with the growth of housing in the area. As he noted, 'Christian denominations and networks either haven't prioritised planting as a needed strategy for reaching the city, or have failed in efforts to do so.'[21] Tibben called his church 'Sojourners Church', in recognition of what he saw as the restless aspirations of western suburbs residents. This approach reflects a key lesson of other successful community builders: strong tribes need a shared identity. The congregation meets at function rooms attached to a football ground. Because two-fifths of the congregation are under the age of six, there is a strong focus on activities for young people, and the service aims to last no longer than an hour.

In a survey of more than 400 US churches, researchers Thom Rainer and Eric Geiger looked at the factors that differentiated vibrant, growing churches from non-growing and struggling churches.[22] They found that vibrant churches tended to be simpler. They have a straightforward ministry design, without activities that clutter their core mission. Rainer and Geiger's book *Simple Church* has much in common with Rick Warren's *The Purpose Driven Church*.[23] They argue that religious leaders can learn from successful businesses such as Apple and Google, which present a minimum of clutter to users. Warren Buffett espouses simplicity, refusing to invest in firms that are too complicated for him to understand. This minimalist philosophy, which is at the heart of religions such as Buddhism and Japanese Shinto, can help provide focus in an increasingly busy world. We've seen simplicity at work elsewhere – from parkrun's 8 a.m./Saturday/free approach to Atlassian's six-second sign-up for workplace giving. The principle applies here too. Australian churches, temples and mosques that are most vibrant have a clarity of purpose and a simplicity of execution. This may involve a purity of theology (many of the fastest-growing congregations take a more orthodox approach), but it can also involve a clarity of mission, such as serving the truly disadvantaged.

Across community life, few institutions have suffered a larger decline than religious and spiritual groups. The implications of this change are more than theological. Secular organisations benefit from the civic energy created by faith-based groups, so the waning of religious communities has sucked volunteers and donations out of other bodies too. But there are many who are successfully swimming against the tide – managing to build strong communities of faith and spirituality. The success of Pentecostals and church planters, the creation of semi-sacred spaces, and the emergence of spiritual-but-atheist communities all suggest that it is possible for spiritual and religious organisations to grow under the right conditions.

What are the key lessons from growing communities? Think about the experience of newcomers and make sure their first visit is not their last. Reach out to untapped communities – implementing Sutton's Law of Social Capital rather than 'stealing sheep' from existing faith communities. Know the neighbourhood, and work to serve its needs, through campaigning on issues of concern, providing parenting programs or offering work to the jobless. CyberConnect by using social media, podcasts and live-streaming, not as a substitute for face-to-face interactions but to strengthen the community. Keep the message and the approach as simple as possible. Don't attempt a mushy appeal to everyone, but build a keen tribe of believers with a distinctive sense of identity. Religion and spirituality have a powerful role to play in a reconnected Australia. We have faith that devout communities will continue to emerge and flourish in the decades ahead.

9

POLITICS PLEASE

In 1894, South Australian suffragettes brought the state's parliament to the brink of passing a bill to allow women the vote. At the last minute, opponents came up with a cunning strategy – they amended the bill to include what they thought was a ridiculous notion – that women would not only be able to vote but run for office. Their ploy backfired, and South Australia became the first jurisdiction to allow women full electoral equality.[1]

Australia has led the world in democratic innovation. We invented the polling booth. We created the secret ballot, which other nations sometimes call 'the Australian ballot'. We were among the first in the world to ensure that elections are run by a nonpartisan electoral commission. We pioneered compulsory voting. Australia was dubbed the democratic laboratory of the world. Yet for all this, engagement with democracy is declining.

By comparison with other countries, participation rates in Australian elections remain high. Yet in recent Australian elections, the share of people who fail to vote has doubled, as has the proportion of people who show up but cast an invalid vote. The problem is even worse in some communities – with Indigenous turnout estimated at just 52 per cent.[2] Most Australians don't trust their government. For every respondent who believes the government acts in the nation's interest, there were three who didn't. A majority believe that government is run in the interests of big business.[3] Trust in government and belief in democracy are lowest among those who have the least knowledge about politics. Fewer adults are involved in civic and political groups. Why is this?

In his book *Politics Is for Power*, political scientist Eitan Hersh argues that too many people have started treating politics as though it is a sport or a hobby.[4] Political hobbyists, he contends, spend their time following the gossip, retweeting the latest outrage and keeping score on who's up and who's down. They track the national conversation insatiably but couldn't tell you anything about the problems in their local community, much less who's trying to solve them. Hersh likens political hobbyists to sports fans, who happily shout encouragement at their team and insults at their opponents. You don't go to a sports match aiming to win over the opposing fans – the rivalry is the whole point of the game.

Politics should be different. For a start, there's no distinction between the arena and the grandstand. Every citizen is a player. If things aren't right in your community, that's not necessarily someone else's problem. It might be that you're the one to fix it. A reconnected Australia requires people to treat politics not as a spectator sport, but as a mass participation activity.

In this chapter, we'll start by looking at how citizens joined together to campaign for marriage equality, pocket parks, low-income housing, refugee rights and a more representative parliament. Then we'll look at how young unions are seeking new supporters. And finally, we turn to consider how a system-wide reform – participatory democracy – might reshape politics for the better.

Yes, yes, yes

It's easy to forget how much attitudes towards same-sex marriage have shifted in Australia during the past couple of decades. In the late 1980s and early 1990s, fully one-third of Australians thought homosexual acts in private between consenting adults should be criminalised, and three-quarters believed that gay people who contracted HIV were to blame for their condition.[5] It was only in 1997 that Tasmania repealed its anti-homosexuality laws, the last Australian jurisdiction to do so. When polls about attitudes to same-sex marriage were first conducted, in 2004, just 38 per cent of respondents supported marriage equality. Yet in 2018, several months after same-sex marriage had been legalised, 65 per cent backed it. Many pollsters describe this as the largest movement they had seen in public attitudes on any issue. What caused views to change so fast?

The campaign for marriage equality began in earnest in 2004, when the Howard government changed the law to specify that marriage could only be between a man and a woman. Rodney Croome, who had been jailed over his opposition to laws criminalising homosexuality in Tasmania, organised a national phone hook-up among activists. As its leaders, the marriage equality movement chose 23-year-old Luke Gahan and 27-year-old Geraldine Donoghue. Gahan didn't have much experience in political campaigns. Donoghue had barely any. But they were passionate and hardworking. Gahan came up with the organisation's name, Australian Marriage Equality, 'on the floor of my bedroom in my apartment in Sydney with the landline sitting on the floor, writing down possible acronyms'.[6] The group formally launched in 2005.

Over the coming years, Australian Marriage Equality set about transforming the attitudes of Australians towards same-sex marriage. They held public rallies, met with politicians and worked to engage more gay and lesbian people to join the movement. Some people in the community viewed marriage as a patriarchal institution and wanted little to do with the campaign, while others thought that access to healthcare should be the greater priority. As the campaign grew, it engaged new constituencies. An Australian chapter of Parents, Family and Friends of Lesbians and Gays – an organisation originally founded in the United States in 1972 – provided a way for the community to engage heterosexual allies, including parents and grandparents.

Conversation by conversation, support grew. By the 2010s, surveys showed that a clear majority of Australians backed the right of gay and lesbian Australians to marry. Pressure built as other nations legalised same-sex marriage: New Zealand in 2013, Britain in 2014, the United States in 2015. Yet even after Malcolm Turnbull took over from archconservative Tony Abbott as prime minister, opposition within the Liberal Party meant that the public support had to be overwhelming. The 2017 postal ballot was regarded as insulting by many, but Australian Marriage Equality built a grassroots campaign that involved more than 15,000 volunteers. Tiernan Brady, a veteran of the Irish marriage equality campaign, emphasised: 'This is a campaign about conversations: with someone you know, about someone you know.' The equality campaign knocked on over 100,000 doors and made more than one million phone calls. A 'ring your rellos' campaign encouraged young people to speak with their family about the issue, explaining why it mattered. Groups such as Blackfullas for Marriage Equality and Australian Christians for Marriage Equality were formed.

There were plenty of reasons for the 'Yes' campaign to be angry about the denial of marriage equality, but the equality campaign made a deliberate choice to keep its message positive: focused on love and symbolised by a rainbow. In November 2017, the results of the postal ballot were in. Sixty-two per cent of Australians voted in favour of same-sex marriage. When the law passed the parliament later that month, campaigners in the public galleries stood and sang together: 'We are one, but we are many / And from all the lands on earth we come /

We'll share a dream and sing with one voice / I am, you are, we are Australian.'

Political change is a team sport, not an individual enterprise. From its sparsely attended launch in Erskineville Town Hall in 2005, Australian Marriage Equality helped build a movement that, twelve years later, changed the law. We can see a similar dynamic in other campaigns too. The Green Bans that saved Sydney's Centennial Park and The Rocks. The Vietnam moratorium marches that preceded Australia's withdrawal from the Vietnam War. The 2000 Sorry Day Bridge Walk that increased pressure for an apology to the Stolen Generations. The Every Australian Counts campaign that fought for the creation of the National Disability Insurance Scheme.

Replacing hobbyism with activism may involve building your own political 'tribe'. As we saw with the example of Intrepid Landcare groups, small organisations that are deeply committed to change can make a powerful difference. In the early days of Australian Marriage Equality, the task was not merely to win over heterosexual Australia, but also to persuade gay and lesbian Australians that the issue was worth campaigning for. Another lesson is to campaign with enthusiasm. As in the case of effective philanthropic campaigns, energy and optimism can help catalyse members and build momentum for change. No matter how large the problem, it's vital to be able to paint a vision of a better world.

Grassroots action

Successful campaigns can start small and local. Ferrington Crescent is a short street of twenty-two houses in the Sydney suburb of Liverpool, with a small park in the cul-de-sac. Most of the residents own their homes and many have lived there for decades. The pocket park was rarely used. Neighbours knew each other, but rarely dropped in without a specific reason and didn't mingle in the street. When Liverpool City Council decided they were going to sell off some pocket parks, they wrote to the residents. Ferrington Crescent resident Lisa Warton explained what happened next: 'The day we got the letter, half the street came out saying, "What are we going to do about this?" ... People didn't want this to happen.' Residents decided to get active. 'We all wrote letters and then attended council. And even though there were about thirteen parks [being sold off], our park had more people objecting than all the others combined.'

Instead of selling the park, the council offered to upgrade it. Residents formed a group they called the Ferrington Collaborative. Working with council staff and the local men's shed, they redesigned it into a 'community-focused, public gathering space ... with a design akin to an extended backyard'. The experience has had many benefits. 'We're all more aware of what's going on in each other's lives,' said Warton, 'and have that experience behind us of working with local government to get an outcome for the community.' Three years on, Warton reflects, 'I'd forgotten what it was like before when I didn't know anyone. Now I've been chatting to residents on a regular basis for several years and I forget sometimes that wasn't normal before.'

And it all started with a handful of letters.

Finding common ground

Sometimes the motivation to take action comes from a much more dramatic experience. Liz Dawson was working in a women's refuge one evening when one of the women began to verbally abuse another. The culprit, who had experienced a traumatic life, was asked to move out and stay at a hotel instead. When she threatened to take her own life, the mental health workers said they could not provide accommodation. As Dawson and her colleague were trying to find a solution, the woman went outside and hung herself with a sheet. Sixty-nine-year-old Dawson cut her down with a pair of scissors. The woman survived, but it highlighted for Dawson the trauma of sleeping rough – how homelessness exacerbated physical and mental health problems.

Decades earlier, social campaigner Rosanne Haggerty had managed to persuade philanthropists and government officials in New York to fund a model of permanent supportive housing – Common Ground Community – combining counselling with secure accommodation to assist the long-term homeless. In 1993, Haggerty's team refurbished the decrepit Times Square Hotel into housing for low-income and homeless tenants. The site became both the proof of concept and the standard bearer for Common Ground. The model spread across the United States, and to Adelaide, Melbourne, Sydney, Brisbane and Hobart.[7]

Inspired by the 'housing first' approach, Dawson, a retired primary school teacher, set about campaigning for a Common Ground in Canberra. As a volunteer counsellor for the Salvation Army, she began by persuading the charity to partner in the project. Next, Dawson convinced senior businesspeople, philanthropists and public servants to serve on the board. They helped her secure a $500,000 commitment from a local foundation. The project had a clear goal, and Dawson built a tribe of supporters, one conversation at a time. She used every opportunity to talk with people about the project, from homeless people to the Governor-General, on the principle that 'if anyone offers to help, I find a way in which they can'.[8]

As the campaign for Common Ground Canberra gathered momentum, Dawson was diagnosed with terminal bowel cancer. She also contracted temporal arteritis, which led to rapid blindness. Dawson joked that 'the wonderful thing about being blind and with terminal cancer is that no-one says no to you'.

When lobbying the federal government became a priority, Dawson bought a ticket to attend a breakfast function with the housing minister,

Brendan O'Connor. In the depths of a Canberra winter, Dawson waited outside the venue in subzero temperatures for fifteen minutes so she could corner the minister for a moment. Dawson's guerrilla advocacy succeeded, and the federal government agreed to join the ACT government in funding the project.

In July 2015, Common Ground Canberra opened its doors, providing forty apartments for a mix of low-income tenants and people who had endured chronic homelessness. For some residents, it was the first place they'd ever had to call their own. One tenant, Josh Rourke, had previously been living in a tent in the backyard of a man he had met on a bus. 'Being here completely changes my moods and everything; it's a complete life-changer', he said. 'I've seen the worst of the worst and now I'm living in the best of the best.'[9] A plaque was unveiled, dedicating the building to Liz Dawson, who had died eight months earlier. Common Ground Canberra would not have happened without her clarity of purpose and tenacity. Conviction attracts collaborators, and Dawson's direct appeals turned decision-makers into allies. The formal structure Dawson put in place to anchor the project helped marshal community-sector, philanthropic and political support. Changing the trajectory of a homeless person's life is a hard challenge, but by campaigning forcefully for a proven solution with a localised scope, Dawson was able to cut through the thicket of issues that can sometimes make big problems seem impervious to grassroots action.

This is your refugee life

Before Sankar Kasynathan was a human rights campaigner, he was a refugee. In the 1980s, the Sri Lankan civil war had thrown his educated, middle-class family into chaos. Their home was raided and ransacked. Kasynathan's father, a Tamil academic, was interrogated by the police. His siblings hid in neighbouring attics while Tamil homes were targeted by arsonists. At one point, all the children were sent to stay with Sinhalese neighbours, where they would be safer, while Kasynathan's parents abandoned their home, gathered all their money and got the family out on a flight to Australia. When the family of six arrived at Melbourne airport, they were met off the plane and welcomed by an Australian family, who shared their home with the Kasynathans until they could find their own place to settle.

Three decades later, Kasynathan is drawing on his personal experience to take Amnesty International's humanitarian advocacy in a new direction. My New Neighbour is a persuasion model which centres on a staged storytelling event that can convey at close quarters the friendship and neighbourliness generated by refugee settlement in our communities.

Over the years, many people have campaigned to increase the number of refugees allowed into Australia. At the same time, conservative media outlets and opportunistic political figures have fed community anxieties and transmuted unfamiliarity into suspicion. Inevitably, the counterclaims of compassion and border protection fail to find any common ground. My New Neighbour seeks to move beyond ideological headbutting by talking directly to people about what it means to support a person who has fled persecution and is asking for understanding. My New Neighbour campaigns are intended for conservative communities. They seek to start conversations with people who don't support refugees but who might be open to changing their view. The campaign has focused on regional towns such as Shepparton and Wagga Wagga, and is working towards the kind of cross-party support that has seen Canada's private refugee sponsorship program survive for over a generation.[10]

'No-one thinks, "How can we be cruel to refugees today?"' explains Kasynathan. 'There's a goodness in our relationship with our neighbours across the country. We need to protect that from the uncertainty that comes from the unanswered questions a lot of people have about refugee resettlement.' After meeting with community leaders, church groups and local councils, My New Neighbour promotes a public event: a facilitated conversation between a refugee and someone who has helped them settle into Australia.

Kasynathan likens the format to *This Is Your Life*, an old television program that documented a guest's life, drawing on their family and friends to tell the tale. In My New Neighbour, the refugee and the person who helped them present a shared story. The audience discovers how the pair met, how they found common ground, their challenges, moments of humour and how they've shaped each other's personalities. As a result, Kasynathan says, 'instead of going to town hall events with former refugees standing up and telling their story, we have two people. A local person who can be up there alongside them and say, "I stood up and wanted to help this person settle in my neighbourhood."'

My New Neighbour events are both emotional and deliberative. People can relate to the friendship, and the events become the jumping-off point to spread the story more widely in the region through media and traditional grassroots activities such as petitions, public canvassing and telephone calls.[11] Supporters then ask the council to pass a formal motion supporting refugees. Kasynathan sees My New Neighbour as a way to systematise 'the serious grunt work that needs to happen to shift people's hearts and minds. It's not pretty and it won't happen fast. The full package is long and arduous and painful. Progress is step by step. There are no shortcuts to shifting people's attitudes.' This kind of campaigning is the very antithesis of political hobbyism.

Alongside the direct human appeal of the storytelling events, the campaign enlists local advocates who can expand My New Neighbour's access to the wider community. It might be a member of the chamber of commerce who has sway with conservative councillors, or a retired police officer who's become good mates with a refugee athlete he sees every week at parkrun. Beyond its political objective, the campaign is building trust – just as the campaign for marriage equality also served to reduce homophobia.

A migrant's place is in the House – and the Senate

In the 2013 federal election, Victorian Wesa Chau campaigned as a Labor Senate candidate. At polling booths, she found Chinese peers approaching her with some unexpectedly basic questions about voting. These were people who, like Chau, had lived in Australia most of their lives. They spoke English and had voted before, but had never seen a candidate that looked like them, so had never really felt that election campaigns were addressed to them. As a consequence, Chau has seen that even some highly educated Chinese Australians 'still don't quite understand how the system works'. 'Before that,' explains Chau, 'I knew that having representation was really important, but that showed me *why* it was important. As opposed to this concept of representation and this concept of equality, there's actually a real democratic function there as opposed to it's nice to have.' When representatives reflect the demographics of their communities, diverse interests are more likely to get considered. It can help break down concentrations of power that erode trust, asks electors to consider more points of view, and allows more segments of society to feel they have a stake in decision-making.

One way to encourage parties to choose a more diverse slate of candidates is through the kind of civic advocacy that's embodied in the Harmony Alliance. The alliance is a membership-based organisation advocating on behalf of Australian women with a refugee or migrant background. It's Sutton's Law of Social Capital in action again: the best way to boost civic engagement is to go where the need is greatest. During the 2019 election, the alliance created a campaign around civics and policy choices to give more migrant women clear reasons to vote.

The primary objective of 'Harmony Votes' was to ensure that as many as possible of the 3 million migrant women on the electoral roll got themselves to a polling place and knew what to do when they arrived.[12] Harmony Votes provides a quick guide to the three tiers of government and an overview of preferential voting and proportional representation. In short, it's a version of the Australian Electoral Commission's electoral education program, curated by multicultural women for multicultural women. As we showed in Chapter 2, people who know more about politics are more satisfied with democracy. So the Harmony Alliance's work should increase the number of migrant women who see political engagement as genuinely worth the effort.

A lesson from Harmony Votes for other campaigns is the way that it used policy issues to encourage voter turnout. Harmony Votes took values that migrant women might identify with – immigration, family violence, access to justice – and tied the prospect of reform to the act of voting. Their campaign toolkit could readily be customised to address issues and barriers faced by other groups with low voter turnout rates. The Harmony Votes campaign addressed that deficit of civic skills and engagement that Chau experienced in her run for office. Electoral participation isn't the only way to make a political contribution to civil society, but it's fundamental to democracy.

Young unions

As we have seen, union membership in Australia has been falling steadily, and young people are increasingly unlikely to join up. Young organisers are realising the union model needs to adapt to reconnect with millennials and Generation Z. Prompted by scandals about the mistreatment of young people in hospitality and retail workplaces, modern unions are adapting how they reach and inform young workers in order to create active workplace citizens. Hospo Voice and the

Young Workers Centre are reclaiming lost territory by showing young employees, often in their first job, how unions balance out the unequal power dynamic in many workplaces.

On Valentine's Day 2017, a group of young protesters gathered outside Honey Birdette's Sydney headquarters to call on the lingerie chain's customers to 'break up' with the brand. The protest was an action in a series of campaign events to protest the chain's failures to respect its young female staff or protect them from sexual harassment. The protesters, mostly former workers and young women, held placards – 'Women's safety over money, I'm a worker #NotYourHoney' – and called on Honey Birdette to improve its workplace conduct and safety procedures.[13] One poster depicted a mock break-up letter: 'Dear Queen B – it's over, you know it, I know it, it's been coming for years.'[14]

The campaign started when former Honey Birdette employee Chanelle Rogers went public with concerns about unsafe working conditions and the sexualised culture workers were expected to uphold. Rogers wrote: 'I saw workers humiliated and threatened by management because they weren't wearing perfectly applied lipstick all day, their heels weren't high enough, and because they didn't "talk the way a Honey should talk".' The campaign attracted thousands of supporters. Worksafe inspected the stores and issued fourteen improvement notices, including 'no training on how to manage difficult or threatening customers' and 'failure to provide a safe workplace'.

The Young Workers Centre was launched in 2016, at a time when more than half of the people leaving unions were in their teens or twenties. The centre was created by Victorian Trades Hall as a dedicated service to provide young people with the education, empowerment and organising tools that would help them assert their workplace rights. Their key message is clear: 'The best way to prevent your rights being exploited at work is to join a union.'

Young Workers Centre campaigns have helped employees challenge management decisions or workplace culture at Mecca Cosmetica, General Pants, Grill'd and Subway. Director Felicity Sowerbutts believes these actions show junior staff that 'there is power in workers telling their stories and sharing their experiences ... it is a brave thing to do, and the more they tell their experiences, the more progress they can make.'[15] Inexperienced young workers are routinely exploited by many different sectors because they aren't well informed, confident or organised. So the centre educates young people about their rights and helps them collaborate across workplaces. The programs present workplace rights in a life skills frame, offering the kind of advice many young people wish school had covered when they enter workforce: What can I be fired for? How do I read a payslip? How does superannuation work? What is wage theft?

The centre aims to rejuvenate union membership by giving young employees concrete reasons to join. Their campaigns emphasise the democratic and egalitarian roles unions play in the workplace, but they also show how being informed and organised can help workers hold their own. The approach is positive and enthusiastic, and the political issues are presented on a personal scale. It's warm and supportive in its advocacy for the rights of informed workers, and fierce and visible when required to assert them. The Young Workers Centre also offers young people legal support, from drafting a letter of demand for unpaid wages through to taking a case to the Fair Work Commission.

Like retail, hospitality is a major employer of young people, and these workplaces have also proven to be treacherous for uninformed employees. One survey estimated that 76 per cent of hospitality workers are underpaid. In 2018, to connect with workers who aren't easily reached by traditional organising methods, Australia's first digital union, Hospo Voice, was created. Founded by the United Workers Union (itself a recent merger of United Voice and the National Union of Workers), Hospo Voice is a CyberConnector for the union movement, with its traditions of education, empowerment and activism. Its $9.99 monthly membership has led Hospo Voice to be described as 'a new kind of union featuring powerful digital tools, a Netflix-style membership and people power'.

When the online union established itself, there was some concern that it marked a deviation from the union tradition of delegate-based engagement. But for those who are troubled by what falling youth numbers could mean for future union coverage, the approach has appeal. 'We haven't got the luxury of ... shooing them away,' acknowledges South Coast Labor Council secretary Arthur Rorris, 'we need to bring people in, and that means trying new things – particularly with young people, and particularly at a time we know wage theft is so rampant.'[16] In addition to reducing pay inequality, unions boost community cohesion. Rebuilding unions will help forge a more connected Australia.

Hospo Voice provides app-style tools to support smart workplace self-care, including Pay Checker, Rate My Boss, Record My Hours, Harassment Diary and FairPlate, a star rating tool that allows customers to check how well the management treat their staff. These give workers practical ways to strengthen their position and benchmark their situation against industry standards.

Hospo Voice doesn't have delegates who can get out to every small retail store or neighbourhood café, but its high-profile actions penetrate into the sector. They keep their campaign focus tight – combining social media and grassroots mobilisation to pressure bad bosses to do right by their staff. They're also educating hospitality workers about their workplace rights, and the power of collective action to shape a better world.

The Young Workers Centre equips employees with the kind of workplace savvy that they need to take on lousy managers. If an employer explains to a new hire that penalty rates don't apply in Perth, the worker knows they're being lied to. Hospo Voice provides support and advocacy and mobilises protests. It also offers practical tools that put junior workers in a better position to pursue a claim. These junior unions highlight the contrast between CyberConnecting and online political hobbyism. The activism that comes from these union campaigns is archetypal: affected workers calling out a problem and asserting their right to a solution. By helping some of the lowest-paid workers in Australia, these innovative unionists are implementing Sutton's Law of Social Capital: go where the need is greatest, and use the tools the job requires. Where political hobbyists are content for the medium to constrain the message, union CyberConnecting sees digital as a tool to build solidarity and reduce inequality.

Deliberative democracy

People can feel a sense of dread at being chosen for courtroom jury duty, but the chance to serve on a citizens' jury is often a welcome opportunity. 'If you receive an invitation from the Premier,' said one South Australian citizen juror, 'it's a rare thing to pick out of your post box. Nobody gets asked these things. It's a gift. You've been asked, you've been invited. Something about you was chosen. Even though it's randomly selected, you feel "oh wow, I feel so lucky."'[17] Asked to work together on issues such as reducing obesity, choosing the best infrastructure projects, or reforming third-party insurance, citizens have engaged with the process and arrived at well-considered decisions. Collective decisions feel fair. And being involved in making them can counterbalance a feeling of political powerlessness, disconnection or distrust. Deliberative interactions require courtesy, empathy, an open mind, respect, reciprocity and responsiveness. They require that people be willing to shift their opinions (though in the end they might not), and give time and consideration to opposing viewpoints.[18]

Deliberative democracy requires people to recognise an essential economic principle: most decisions involve trade-offs.

Deliberative democratic processes have been used in Australia to inform planning decisions, decide on the limits of tolerance for nuclear waste, fine-tune laws on cat and dog ownership, improve bike lane protocols, plot a ten-year trajectory for the city of Melbourne, and set a local planning frame for Adelaide's nightlife. Globally, the Belgians, Irish and Brazilians tend to lead the pack on participatory practice. But in 2011, the West Australian city of Geraldton was the 'World Winner for Community Participation and Engagement' in the United Nations International Liveable Communities Award. The award recognised Geraldton's '2029 and Beyond' project, which engaged thousands of residents in a discussion about the city's economic and environmental sustainability.

In 2011, the City of Canada Bay Council, in Sydney's inner west, sought to stimulate low levels of community engagement by allowing residents to set the entire council budget through a participatory budgeting process. Residents responded well, re-electing Angelo Tsirekas, the mayor who had led the process, with a 9 per cent swing. But the project was a pilot, supported financially by the newDemocracy Foundation, and Tsirekas acknowledged that the council would not have been able to afford the process without that private funding.[19]

In most parts of Australia, councils have the power to appoint regular citizens to committees, giving them power over tourism promotion, for example, or the management of council-owned sporting facilities.[20] Wyndham City Council, in Melbourne's outer west, has used these committees to manage several of its community centres. Yet few other Australian councils are using their ability to establish citizen member committees.[21]

That's a lost opportunity. Citizen committees have potential to play a constructive consultative role, and smart councils should take advantage of that. Councils could even try out a lottery process to select committee members who are representative of the broad community.

Innovations like these are already starting to happen elsewhere. In April 2019, a local parliament in a small region of East Belgium became the first in the world to implement a permanent mechanism for citizens to play a part in setting its deliberative agenda. A 24-member Citizens' Council (serving for eighteen months at a time) will be able to determine issues to be deliberated on by a randomly selected citizens' assembly. Assemblies will be made up of fifty or more citizens, aged over sixteen, and will have the support of a secretariat in the parliament. Some have hailed this as the first time that citizens have been given a direct and ongoing role in setting a parliament's agenda, putting them on the same level as elected politicians.[22]

By taking similar steps to support more participatory actions, Australian councils can boost trust and improve the social capital of their community. Happier communities tend to be more positive about their decision-makers. Mayor Tsirekas's 9 per cent swing suggests that voters can reward politicians who are willing to trust the electorate to shape decisions.

Deliberative democracy exercises are not without political risk. Sometimes the criticism can be fair – such as when governments run sham deliberations to justify decisions they've already made. Sometimes the criticism is unfair, as when deliberative democracy leads to politicians being accused of shirking the duties of leadership.

A key lesson is that deliberation is not just about the outcome, it's about the process. Australia's exercises in citizen deliberation have generated goodwill among participants, and increased interest in the work of government. But other jurisdictions have taken the model further. For a sense of what an ongoing deliberative practice could provide to a city's social structure, consider the participatory budgeting of Porto Alegre, a coastal city about the size of Adelaide in southern Brazil.

Porto Alegre's process works like this: district level committees hold plenary sessions to identify the priorities for their area and elect the local delegates who will advocate for those priorities at a city-wide budgeting forum. Anyone can attend the sessions and contribute, but only local residents can vote.[23] The city-wide process is carried out over several months and draws in experts to provide participants with advice on costings and the viability of the proposals. Once the budget is agreed by the participatory council and the mayor, it's passed to the elected city council to be ratified.

Porto Alegre's participatory budgeting program has been running since 1989. Since then, civic and associational life in Porto Alegre has thickened, as small interest groups spring up around the process to feed in ideas. Spending has shifted towards the neediest areas of the city, encouraging greater trust in the fairness of public funding. Around one in twelve adults plays a part in the process, though poorer and less-educated residents tend to be underrepresented.

Australian deliberative democracy specialist Wendy Russell doesn't see these kinds of consultative processes as upending the way that most government decisions are made. As she puts it, 'I see citizen juries as interventions that can provide an example of good discourse, with the hope of influencing discussion and deliberation within politics and in public debate more broadly. For that to really work, we need more people to have access and be involved, and we need to make sure they get exposure and are promoted to inform people.' One marker of success may be participants' recognition that government cannot make everyone happy. Ironically, this may make citizens a little happier with government's decisions.

Deliberative democracy goes beyond standard community engagement. As practitioner Lyn Carson observes, deliberative democracy processes 'are a way to find out how randomly selected citizens, without vested interests, think about an issue when presented with detailed information from differing viewpoints and given support to discuss it in a non-adversarial way'.[24]

In 2015, VicHealth's Citizens' Jury on Obesity explored strategies to reduce the problem of excessive body weight. After a two-day deliberation, the seventy-eight jurors presented government with twenty recommendations, including better food labelling, more water fountains, and healthier food in schools. The jury's deliberations were informed by experts, as well as by a public survey that yielded over 2000 responses, and a digital campaign that asked the public to #ShowUsYourFridge by sending a 'shelfie'.

In 2017 and 2018, the ACT government used a deliberative process to consider possible reforms to third-party car insurance. At the outset, Chief Minister Andrew Barr committed to implement whichever model came out of the citizens' jury. Around fifty jurors were randomly chosen. The jurors initially met for two weekends to define their priorities. Next, an expert, guided by a reference group, devised four models to be considered by the jury. The jurors then met again over two more weekends, finally voting in favour of a no-fault scheme. For their work over the four weekends, each juror was paid $450. The reform then passed through the ACT Legislative Assembly, taking effect in 2020.

The ACT's insurance reform is expected to save motorists over $100 on their insurance premiums, and expand coverage by 40 per cent, including accidents where no-one is at fault (such as where a driver hits a kangaroo).[25] An adviser to the process later observed: 'As an actuary and a subject matter expert I have seen many insurance scheme reforms over the last three decades. They are routinely driven by politics and strongly influenced by vested interest groups. It was remarkable to me how the deliberative democracy process used in the ACT responded to both of these problems. The commitment of government to pursue the citizens' jury recommendations was key. More impressive was the way a carefully facilitated process involving critical thinking skills went right past a series of interventions from vested interest groups.'[26]

In 2009, the newDemocracy Foundation ran a world-first 'Citizens' Parliament', to answer the question 'How can Australia's political system be strengthened to serve us better?'. There were 150 randomly selected participants: one from each federal electorate. The youngest was eighteen. The oldest was ninety. Participants gathered for a series of one-day meetings in major capital cities, then for four days in Canberra. Some found it a life-changing experience. As one Indigenous participant reflected: 'For a rare moment in my life I actually felt a part of the majority and not minority.'[27]

How do we spread those life-changing benefits to more than a few hundred people? At a larger scale, one of the most successful projects is Madrid's participatory budgeting process, Decide Madrid.[28] Established in 2015, the project was initiated in response to widespread citizen distrust in government, fuelled by high unemployment, austerity and corruption scandals. Decide Madrid allows residents to propose new spending projects up to a budget of €100 million. Through an online portal, any Madrid resident over sixteen years can propose a project, such as street furniture, bike lanes, kindergartens or cultural centres. Officials check to see that each proposed project is legal and viable. Residents then vote on their favourite projects. The Madrid city council funds the top choices. In 2018, Decide Madrid attracted 400,000 participants. Madrid's Director of Citizen Participation, Miguel Catania, believes the program has shifted public attitudes to decision-making in the city. According to Catania, Madrileños now walk around the city looking for ways they could make it better. 'They no longer feel like they are just guests in the city that somebody else designed.'[29]

There's no reason the ongoing process couldn't be replicated by an ambitious Australian city council. Indeed, in its 2018–19 budget, the Victorian government allocated $30 million for the public to spend on local infrastructure through the 'Pick My Project' initiative.[30] The one-off pilot allowed regional areas across the state to propose infrastructure projects valued between $20,000 and $200,000. If the projects were viable and legal, a profile was loaded onto an online platform for public voting. Success was then determined by where the project ranked in the overall vote. The successful projects included lighting for a hockey centre, community gardens, solar hubs, a bus for a mobile playgroup, support for homeless services and hospitality training for female migrants. But to bring about the change in attitude Madrid's Miguel Catania points to, or the kind of changes seen in Porto Alegre, these processes will need to become a regular fixture of community decision-making.

The UK hasn't led the world in deliberative democracy, but British activists have grasped the importance of public advocacy for the process. After Brexit left many Britons unsure if their democracy remains fit for purpose, public participation charity Involve launched a grassroots advocacy campaign calling on people to demand more avenues for citizen-led decision-making. The aim is to encourage citizens to channel their frustration, and become more engaged in local political activism, instead of switching off. Australians who like the idea of better citizen representation could follow Involve's lead and demand change. But it's Australia's local, state and federal governments that will need to play a significant supportive role in meeting that demand.

When it comes to the health of Australia's democracy, there's bad news and good news. The bad news is that, on many metrics, the political engagement of Australians has waned over the past generation. The good news is Australia has all the ingredients we need for a democratic renewal. In this chapter, we've emphasised what we see as the two main aspects of this. One is that it's vital to move beyond political hobbyism and join others to work for change. That can be something as substantial as winning a vote for marriage equality, reducing chronic homelessness, changing attitudes to refugees or encouraging more ethnic diversity in our parliamentary candidates. But it can also involve attending your local council meeting to give your views on the local pocket park, organising a group of people to see your state representative about putting traffic lights on a busy intersection, or joining with others in your workplace to demand a fair day's pay for a fair day's work.

The other aspect of political renewal is participatory democracy – a mode of engagement that can lead to better decisions, to more understanding of the political process and to greater support for the final outcomes. As we have documented, disenchantment with democracy is greatest among those who have the lowest levels of political knowledge. Addressing this isn't just about the quality of civics education in schools – it's also about providing lifelong opportunities for people to get involved.

In June 2020, as protests over the killing of George Floyd roiled hundreds of US cities, Barack Obama wrote an essay directed to those who sought to reform the criminal justice system.[31] It was the former president's recipe for how to bring about change. Obama rejected the view that only protests could bring about reform and that voting was a waste of time. Instead, he argued that while protests put 'a spotlight on injustice', eventual change depends on electing responsive government officials. Obama also pointed out that while much of the focus was at the national level, policing practices are mostly a state and local matter. Yet voter turnout in local elections can be pitifully low, meaning that races are sometimes won and lost by a few hundred votes. Finally, he urged the need for reformers to link broad injustices to particular demands: 'The more specific we can make demands for criminal justice and police reform, the harder it will be for elected officials to just offer lip service to the cause and then fall back into business as usual once protests have gone away.'

Whether you want to end racial injustice, curtail family violence or address global warming, creating political change can seem daunting. But ultimately, these issues will not be solved by shouting at the television or using social media to share the latest outrage. As with successful campaigns of the past, reform requires activists to build an enthusiastic tribe. At the same time, governments should create structures that make politics more porous. The challenges of populism and disenchantment are visible in many nations around the world. If there's a country that can show others how to create a more connected democracy, why shouldn't it be the nation once dubbed the democratic laboratory of the world?

10

LEADERSHIP LESSONS

Humans are inherently social. We draw our identities from our families, sporting teams, workplaces, neighbourhoods and nations. Most of the lasting achievements of our species have come from people working together, sharing their brains and brawn. By definition, building community cannot be a solo pursuit.

Yet as we contemplate the momentous task of reconnecting Australia, the stories of community leaders can help inspire us. They are a reminder that connecting people is a challenge, fundraising can be tough and setbacks are surmountable. In this chapter, we profile four social entrepreneurs – global poverty campaigner Matt Napier, donation-enabler Juliette Wright, Indigenous mentor Jack Manning Bancroft and social enterprise builder Bec Scott. We identify common traits across their diverse stories and draw out shared lessons for anyone seeking to be an effective community leader.

Pain

'One afternoon, I walked into the caravan, and said to my wife Wendy, "I'm done, I can't go on." I took off my shoes and they were soaked in blood and I just sat on the bed there for a minute and thought and thought about life. And I thought that there were so many people around the world in wheelchairs who would give anything to get blisters on their feet from walking too far. There are so many people who are blind and would love to see the scenery that I've seen. I've still got three meals a day and a roof over my head. So in the whole scheme of things I'm not doing too bad. About two minutes later I put my shoes back on, grabbed some water and walked on.'[1]

It was 2013, and 36-year-old Matt Napier was walking 4500 kilometres from Perth to Sydney, bouncing an Aussie Rules ball as he went. His 'Global Poverty Walk' took almost five months, and saw him face temperatures up to 45 degrees Celsius. His sunburn got infected, and there were days when he drank ten litres of water.

Napier hadn't always been into extreme endurance for a charitable cause. When his school held a walkathon, he recalls being one of the last kids to finish. But when he travelled to Nepal in his late twenties – his first overseas trip – he saw extreme poverty firsthand. 'Children as young as four and five begging on the streets with no food and no school to go to.' On the flight home, Napier recalls, 'I thought to myself, why should I be so lucky to come back to my privileged life in Australia and leave those poor people behind when the only difference was the country they were born into?'

With the fearlessness of Bear Grylls and the ethics of Peter Singer, Napier decided in 2016 to walk across Africa, trekking 2300 kilometres from Walvis Bay in Namibia to Maputo in Mozambique. Where he had walked across Australia bouncing an Aussie Rules ball, he would now walk across Africa kicking a soccer ball. There was one more twist. To highlight the impact of poverty, Napier decided that he would do the walk while spending less than US$1.50 a day on food. That pretty much guaranteed he would be constantly hungry, 'my stomach eating away at itself in ways it never has before'. On some mornings, he would walk 15 kilometres before breakfast. Then he would eat some porridge. Lunch consisted of two-minute noodles or a sandwich. Afternoon tea was a handful of nuts or a piece of fruit. Dinner was pasta with some sauce and basic vegetables. By the time the two-month trek was over, Napier had lost 15 kilograms.

His walk not only raised tens of thousands of dollars for anti-poverty charities, it helped inspire others. When Napier arrived in Botswana, the customs officer said, 'Ah, Matt Napier, I have been waiting for you!' and eight customs officials joined him for the first seven kilometres of his walk into Botswana, where loudspeakers at the next town called locals to attend an official welcome to the hard-walking Australian. It was a pleasant contrast to his experience a few days later, when he entered a 10-kilometre stretch of road known as the 'danger zone' due to the risk of lions.

As he met local communities, Napier distributed soccer balls to schools and sporting groups. Money to buy the balls came from funds raised by Mac Millar, a Queensland boy then aged just thirteen, who had been shocked by the fact that children in developing nations often can't afford a simple soccer ball, and so made it his mission to help get balls to children in disadvantaged communities around the world. Over the course of the journey, Napier distributed nearly 200 soccer balls.

When you change a person's life, you sleep easier that night, Napier says. He and Wendy aim to live a simple life, giving away half their income. They recently founded Towards a Better World, a charity that provides farming skills to South Sudanese refugees who have fled into neighbouring Uganda. The inspiration comes from those they have encountered. Napier reflects on the experience of meeting a woman in

Mozambique, at the end of his 2016 trek across the continent. 'She was living in a tin shed not much bigger than 2 metres long and 2 metres wide. She had four children; the first had passed away from a preventable illness, her second child had HIV/AIDS, her third child and only son had a mental illness and had to sleep under a tarpaulin next to her tin shed, and her fourth child was the victim of a hit and run and was paralysed from the waist down.' She received around $9 a month from the government – when it could afford to pay her. Before the conversation, Napier had been 'pretty content' and anticipated going back to a normal life. After meeting her, he thought, 'No, I can't do that.'

Matt Napier's story illustrates how the most severe needs of others outside our own neighbourhoods can inspire action. Economic growth is fundamental to human flourishing. But as a slogan from the 1968 protests put it, 'Nobody ever fell in love with the growth rate.'[2] Instead, what drives social justice campaigners like Napier are memories of children in Nepal and a mother in Mozambique. A sincere connection with the most disadvantaged can fuel leaders to keep going. It can turn a person from a schoolkid who struggled to finish the walkathon to a man who puts shoes back on his blister-battered feet and keeps walking to help end poverty.

Purpose

The first donation, in 2010, was a microwave oven for a man who had recently lost his wife and was unable to cook. Nine years later, on Valentine's Day 2019, the millionth donation came through. It was a wheelie walker for a rehabilitation centre in south-east Queensland.

A kind of Tinder for donations, GIVIT is an online platform for people who want to donate household objects, from laptops and washing machines to bicycles and trampolines. But while Tinder aims to get people together, GIVIT donors rarely meet the recipients of their generosity. When a match is made, charities or GIVIT vans pick up the items and take them to the person in need. Crucially, the pick-up only happens when a donor and recipient are linked, so donations don't gather dust and GIVIT doesn't pay for expensive warehouses.

GIVIT was hatched out of frustration. When her second child was born, generous friends gave Brisbane naturopath Juliette Wright far more clothes than the infant could possibly wear. But when she tried to pass them on to someone in need, Wright discovered that there was no obvious donation channel for new items (most charities focused on used clothing). She developed GIVIT at her kitchen table, supporting fifteen charities. Wright recalls when GIVIT's first match, the microwave oven, came through, and 'the joy when that first donation was made by a stranger'.[3]

The items allocated through GIVIT can make a real difference. Wright recalls one of the site's early donations. A single mother was staying in temporary accommodation that wasn't near public transport. She needed a bicycle to get her child to daycare and herself to a part-time job. A donor provided not only a bicycle but also a child bike trailer, two helmets and safety vests. Elsewhere, donated soccer boots helped a young refugee join his local team. A sewing machine provided a creative outlet to a woman with mental health issues. A boxing bag provided an outlet for the energies of frustrated teens.

At the time of writing, the GIVIT website included requests for a ride-on lawnmower for a Queensland farmer who lost everything in a fire, shampoo for a Perth organisation running centres to help children with incarcerated parents, a chicken coop for a facility that supports Canberra teenagers with mental illness, and a freezer for a small school in regional New South Wales providing healthy meals to their students.

Less than a year after GIVIT launched, floods hit Queensland, turning three-quarters of the state's local government areas into disaster zones. Premier Anna Bligh asked GIVIT to handle in-kind donations, and Wright found herself answering 3000 to 4000 emails a day. Over a three-week period, GIVIT coordinated more than 30,000 donations, including a teddy bear from a young child.

Not everything was suitable. One man wanted to donate his broken swimming pool, Wright recalls. 'I had to tell him that no-one wanted to see another broken body of water.'[4] He wasn't the only one to misjudge the needs of the 200,000 people affected. As Wright reflects, 'In our day-to-day giving, the quality that comes through GIVIT is about 95 per cent – so we only reject about 5 per cent of donations. But in a disaster, only 25 per cent of the stuff that goes through the website is quality.' In a disaster, she notes, donors think, 'Oh, people have lost everything, they'll take anything … If only people could get their Christmas heart on during a disaster.'[5] The discovery that some donations do more harm than good led GIVIT to change its rules, so it only accepts new or as-new items.

Another challenge that GIVIT faces is not to undercut local retailers. In the 2011 floods, a donation of 5000 pairs of gumboots had to be spread across the state, to ensure that local stores weren't harmed. Flood the market with as-new items and the grocery store might suddenly discover its customers disappearing. Philanthropy isn't as simple as it first seems.

The floods also taught Wright the importance of knowing her emotional limits. A tour of Grantham was so draining that it consigned her to bed for two days. When she meets vulnerable people, she often needs 'a day of quiet to recover and have a good cry … I feel it is so unfair that people should suffer'. Wright acknowledges, 'I am best inspiring people to give to the homeless person, not counselling them.'

This approach reflects the economic principle of comparative advantage: focus on the things you're best at and leave the rest to other people. Just as Foodbank doesn't distribute gumboots, Juliette Wright's

GIVIT rarely distributes food. The success of both organisations is partly due to the fact that they understand their strengths and the strengths of others.

Wright's story also draws attention to another aspect of comparative advantage: setting limits on what an organisation will do can be empowering. In our conversations with social service organisations, we'll often ask them what they *don't* do. Organisations that try to do everything risk achieving nothing. Non-profits that know where they fit in the larger picture are more likely to become truly great in their chosen area. Specialisation lets organisations grow stronger.

Even after setting limits, Wright still found running GIVIT emotionally taxing. In mid-2015, GIVIT came to the brink of collapse, as she struggled to find sponsors and secure long-term grants. Today, those structural issues have been addressed and Wright is more reflective about her role at GIVIT. As the child of workaholic parents (her mother was a nurse and her father a doctor), she recognises the risk of burnout. At the end of 2019, Wright took three months' leave from the charity, to enjoy her children, her garden and her slow roasts. The break was partly because she felt her reputation was intertwined with GIVIT's, in ways that were unhealthy for both her and the organisation. It also helped her relax, and changed her ethos from the macro to the micro: 'I no longer want to resource all impoverished people in Australia ... now all I want to do is make a difference to one person every day.'

'GIVIT has been the most challenging thing I have ever done,' Wright says.[6] But there are unexpected rewards. GIVIT provided equipment to help a remote Indigenous school establish its first football team. GIVIT delivered a washing machine to a mother of three just before Christmas. A Brisbane social worker told Wright that every homeless person in the city had probably received something through GIVIT. 'Imagine being able to say that in Sydney or Ballarat,' she muses.[7]

Passion

The boy was ten years old. At age seven, he had seen his father stab his mother. When a dance teacher came to his school in Glebe, the boy enjoyed the class, then slipped out to break into the instructor's car and steal his GPS. He was smart and charming, but it was clear that he was on a path to join his older brothers in jail. After Jack Manning Bancroft met him, he went away thinking, 'How does a ten-year-old know how to break into a car?'[8] Bancroft vowed that he'd 'run through walls' to stop Indigenous boys throwing their lives away in this way.

Growing up, Bancroft got used to people telling him he was too light-skinned to be Indigenous. His father, Ned Manning, was a non-Indigenous actor, writer and teacher. His mother, Bronwyn Bancroft, was an Aboriginal painter from Baryulgil in north-eastern New South Wales. When people told Jack Bancroft he was one-quarter Aboriginal, he'd joke that it must be his right leg, which explained his footballing success. Afterwards, he looked on being fair-skinned and Indigenous as 'being like an undercover cop' – taking pride in your identity, while being able to eavesdrop when someone tells a racist joke.[9]

When he finished high school, Bancroft won a scholarship to attend Sydney University's St Paul's College, Australia's oldest residential college. Surrounded by students from affluent backgrounds, he bristled. 'To say I had a bit of a chip on my shoulder about privilege was probably an understatement,' he recalls. 'It was more like a potato farm.'[10] Bancroft swiftly found that the scholarship exposed his insecurities: 'anger towards privilege, thinking I wasn't smart enough, and my identity'.[11] He felt like a fraud, he doubted himself, and he felt frustrated at pretentious classmates who didn't seem to recognise how lucky they were. Nevertheless, as he outlines in his autobiography, *The Mentor*, Sydney University allowed Bancroft the space to unfurl himself. He enjoyed philosophy classes, played cricket, organised social events and spent time at the Koori Centre, where he built strong friendships with people who made him feel 'like my Aboriginality was legit'.[12]

In 2005, Bancroft launched the Australian Indigenous Mentoring Experience. He quips that he added the last word to the name so that 'if we stuffed something up, we could call it an experience'.[13] The pilot program was run in Alexandria Park Community School near Redfern, where school officials had said they could trial the mentoring experience on a Friday, because that was the hardest day to get students to attend. The Year 9 students weren't immediately receptive. One put his hand up and said, 'You just feel sorry for us cos we're black, hey?'[14] Bancroft replied that he simply wanted the student to be the best he could be, adding that the mentors would benefit too – because some had never met Aboriginal people before. On the first day of the program, mentors and mentees were matched up and began answering 'get to know you' questions. Once the program was underway, it didn't take long before school attendance on Friday was higher than on other days. More of the students stayed on to Year 10 than in previous years. Some finished Year 12.

Bancroft's passion keeps bringing him back to Indigenous children. Like the seventeen-year-old unable to spell his own name, who hoped for a professional football career but was more likely to end up in a cycle of poverty and crime. Or Alicia and Emily Johnson, two sisters at Dulwich High School who came from a family where no-one had ever attended university. Bancroft recalls that AIME pushed them – hard – to raise their aspirations. In 2010, Alicia became the first Indigenous school captain in Dulwich High's 115-year history. The next year, Emily became the second. Both went on to enrol in university. More than thirty AIME participants have become school captains – many of them the first Indigenous school captain in their school's history.

Bancroft is still a young man, but he reflects on some of the lessons he has learnt through AIME. He has changed his attitude towards the privileged people he met at St Paul's College. Since he started the organisation, hundreds of St Paul's students have mentored with AIME, fundraised for AIME or promoted AIME. He now reflects that 'it's exactly the same to have low expectations of Indigenous kids as it is to have low expectations of rich people ... If you expect the worst of people, you better believe they'll deliver it in spades. But if you open your heart and expect the best, they will deliver.'[15] In his book, Bancroft thanks the students and staff at St Paul's 'for proving me wrong by showing me that, if given the chance, we all want to see change.'[16]

'Almost every single thing that I have done for the first time, I've stuffed up,' Bancroft admits.[17] He recounts the story of having to fire his little sister, Ella, four days before Christmas – watching tears stream down her face, and knowing that he should have made the decision much sooner. Bancroft quotes one of his mentors, Geoff Morgan, who says that if a staff member is a square peg in a round hole, it's 'better to bid adieu sooner rather than later'.[18] He concludes, 'When it doesn't work, end it. Fire fast and early. Let each other be free to find true happiness in the world and in doing so, you'll avoid having to fire your sister four days before Christmas.'[19]

Partnerships

When she was sixteen years old, Bec Scott's family lived in Vanuatu. Her father was working on international aid projects, and one night the family found themselves staying on the island of Epi, in a grass and bamboo hut. They had been due to take a boat trip to another island, but the seas were too rough, so the boatman put them up in his home. Scott slept in the girls' room. When they were due to leave the next morning, one of the boatman's daughters, a sixteen-year-old called Merilyn, offered Scott one of her dresses. Scott was astonished. 'She only had two but she kept insisting I take one. That level of generosity was just astounding to me, a stranger was willing to give me half of everything they owned. With that phenomenal level of generosity something shifted in my mind. I started thinking about attachment to things, what gives people happiness, and being in the service of others.'[20]

When she finished high school, Scott wasn't sure what path to pursue. So she let luck chart her path, flipping a coin to determine whether to become a scientist or an artist. Science won, but the two passions merged after graduation when Scott got a job working as part of a travelling science circus, in which she played the part of 'The Slime Queen'. A decade with the CSIRO followed.

In the mid-2000s, Scott was visiting Hanoi on annual leave when she walked into KOTO, a café founded by Vietnamese-Australian social entrepreneur Jimmy Pham. Pham had created the café – the name stands for 'Know One Teach One' – to provide street kids with skills and stable jobs. To Scott, it was an epiphany. She phoned her partner – psychologist Kate Barelle – and told her that she wanted to work at KOTO. Then she quit her job at the CSIRO and volunteered for two years in Hanoi.

In 2010, Barelle and Scott decided to take the KOTO model to Melbourne. They founded STREAT, a social enterprise that trains young people in hospitality. The venture began with a pair of coffee carts in Federation Square, where they braved the sun and rain for six months before securing an indoor location in Melbourne Central. They tried crowdfunding, and sold a cookbook to raise money – but the breakthrough came when Geoff Harris, founder of Flight Centre, purchased a property in Cromwell Street, Collingwood, and gave it to STREAT for fifty years. The building is unique – opened in 1869 as the Bath and Bristol Hotel, it was shut down for violating Sunday liquor laws. The premises went on to serve as a painter's studio, massage parlour and – most recently – a brothel.[21] As STREAT's headquarters, the Cromwell Street building is a café, bakery, roastery, training academy and catering company.

STREAT aims to recruit young people in crisis and provide them with six months' employment, after which they transition to a partner employer. That period is critical, says Scott. 'If we can get you stable and into the workforce for a year, everything changes for you.' For young people who have been sleeping rough, STREAT aims to provide a warm welcome. Scott reflects on the fact that when her graduates were asked what mattered most to them, 'they were talking about what it feels to be welcomed into a place after having been marginalised for a long period of time, they talked about what it was like being in a building where they wouldn't have been allowed before, about being out of prison and knowing you weren't going back in the next twelve months'.

Supporting the transition from homelessness to stable employment is particularly challenging in a competitive industry like hospitality. Scott points out wryly that the typical Melbourne café 'doesn't have psychologists and youth workers – it doesn't say: "if you've been in prison or are homeless or have mental health challenges, we want you!"' Nonetheless, she has managed to find commercial partners. STREAT runs cafés for ANZ, AMP, the Royal Automobile Club of Victoria and RMIT University. This not only allows them to train more young people, but to be more financially self-sufficient. A decade after starting the enterprise, Scott estimates that about 85 per cent of the business is self-funded, which lets her 'start to breathe – not just chasing money to survive another year'. Internal funding, Scott argues, also 'allows you to try some different stuff and try things government hasn't been brave enough to fund'. From a stable financial base, innovation can thrive.

Ultimately, it's innovation that most excites Scott. The common theme of her various 'career hooks', she says, is 'how alive I've always felt at the interface between disciplines. My world has never been filled with binary choices, but rather a colourful spectrum of possibilities'.[22] When engaging with large firms, Scott looks to expand beyond catering: 'Once we're inside a corporate, we can pretty quickly go in all directions: corporate giving, volunteering, Christmas merchandise, invite us to strategy planning. By bringing us inside, they're insourcing their conscience.' A similar philosophy applies to startups. Over the decade, Scott estimates that STREAT has assisted around 200 social enterprises, about ten of which have been founded by STREAT staff.

In the first few years after founding STREAT, Scott recalls accompanying a group of nine new staff members to their first day of hospitality training, at an institute on La Trobe Street. One young man looked shaky, and Scott tried to reassure him not to be nervous on his first day of TAFE training. He explained that he felt overwhelmed because the training centre was across the road from Flagstaff Gardens. 'That used to be where I slept,' he told Scott.[23]

Matt Napier, Juliette Wright, Jack Manning Bancroft and Bec Scott are remarkable in their own special ways, but as leaders of social ventures, they share four common traits.

First, pain. Napier hopes he will never again experience the pain that comes from walking 15 kilometres each day before breakfast. But the experience, he tells us, has made him more compassionate, and more grateful for what he has. For Bancroft, growing AIME meant firing his younger sister. They're not unique. Plenty of other social entrepreneurs have told us about the sacrifices they've made to achieve their goals. Community building is rarely painless.

Second, purpose. These successful social entrepreneurs all have a guiding mission. Napier wants to end global poverty. Scott wants to end homelessness. Wright wants to take GIVIT national, and promote a culture of philanthropy among young people through the GIVIT Schools program. Bancroft wants to reach out to the 160,000 young Indigenous people who do not currently have access to a mentor, and build AIME into 'one of the coolest brands on the planet', rivalling Red Bull and Nike, so that 'instead of kids wanting to buy soft drinks or sneakers, they want to be mentors and build better human relationships'.[24]

Third, passion. On her desk, Juliette Wright has the quote: 'What would you do if you knew you could not fail?'[25] Bec Scott's desk has a sign that says: 'Please be aware that when you say "No, that's not possible", I hear you say "Yes, let's get creative!"'[26] Like other successful entrepreneurs, they live their cause day and night. Bancroft advises those who lack a burning passion not to start a social enterprise. 'Don't do it unless you have to because it sucks. This ain't a glorious pursuit. It's really, really hard.'[27] But even a burning passion can burn out. Proper reflection – like Wright's three-month break – is essential to effective leadership.

Fourth, partnerships. For all their passion, Napier, Wright, Bancroft and Scott don't see themselves as lone wolves. That should come as a relief, because it would be a strange civic resurgence that relied on isolated individuals. Instead, these leaders recognise their comparative advantages and see themselves as part of a larger ecosystem. By partnering with a teenage social entrepreneur, Napier distributed more soccer balls in Africa than he could have done alone. STREAT looks to multiply its points of connection with large corporations, and mentor startup social enterprises. Bancroft emphasises the role of partners within his own organisation, warning that passion and vision 'means nothing if you run off alone'. He stresses the value of distilling emotion and vision into a path: 'A position description offers light. As do manuals. Training videos. Values. Internal newsletters. Monthly updates. Staff retreats. Distilling your mission into a single sentence. It's worth getting right, or at least trying to.'[28]

RECONNECTING AUSTRALIA

The village of Homewood, 35 kilometres south of Chicago, is regarded as one of the most liveable neighbourhoods in the area. The racially diverse, middle-income community hosts an annual chocolate festival, inviting locals: 'Bakers Kneaded – Enter the Chocolate Fest Bake-Off'. One day, a team of research assistants from the University of Chicago approached commuters at the Homewood train station as they waited for the express train to Chicago. The investigators asked a straightforward question: imagine that someone wanted you to get on the train and converse with the person next to you. Would that make the trip more or less positive? Overwhelmingly, commuters said that if they had to talk with a stranger, it would make for a more miserable trip. Next, the research team approached a different group of people and randomly asked some of them to actually chat with the person next to them on the train. These commuters were given a giftcard and asked to fill in a survey about their experiences. Other commuters were simply asked to fill out the survey and not to do anything different on their trip. The results were not what people had anticipated. Commuters who had been asked to interact with another person on the train enjoyed the trip more. Psychologists Nicholas Epley and Juliana Schroeder titled the resulting study 'Mistakenly Seeking Solitude'.[1]

So fundamental is society, Aristotle claimed, that it preceded the individual. But we humans sometimes need a gentle nudge to put down our devices and engage with other people. When it happens, we are often surprised to learn how interesting other people are and how much we enjoy those social interactions. Even if you consider yourself a total hedonist, caring only about your own happiness, you should probably spend more time chatting with strangers.

Australia today faces a community crisis. Australians are less likely to join community organisations, to know our friends and neighbours, to attend a religious service, to play sport or even to participate in a government survey. On average, Australians are more socially isolated, less engaged in a common civic community and more disconnected than ever before. The mental wellbeing of young Australians, especially girls, has worsened considerably since the iPhone was launched in 2007.

Yet across the county, there are social entrepreneurs who are bucking the trend. On Saturday mornings, parkrun brings thousands together to share in the common pleasure of a five-kilometre run. Kids Giving Back aims to build a culture of philanthropy in the next generation. On the streets, Orange Sky Australia uses a mobile laundromat to facilitate connecting conversations. In the spiritual realm, evangelical Bible study groups and Muslim conversation groups continue to grow. In an era when many feel overwhelmed by social media, tools like Screen Time and techniques like digital sabbaticals are helping reclaim real life from devices.

When the coronavirus lockdown began, much of the community activity was spontaneous. Neighbourhoods organised local groups at a street and suburb level to support people who are elderly or socially isolated by offering to do their shopping, walk their dog or just check in with a regular phone call. Schools organised students to write thank-you notes to doctors and nurses, and letters to nursing homes where residents might be feeling lonely.

Across Australia, teddy bears appeared in people's windows as part of the 'Going on a Bear Hunt' initiative to keep children active. In the City of Melton, residents went further, with a new group coordinating people to knit 'Trauma Teddies' for the Red Cross to supply to children who've experienced distress. As Easter approached, the teddies shared window space with Easter egg colouring pages, taped up for neighbourhood egg hunts. Turning a street-facing window into a checkpoint on a treasure hunt was a way families and young children could share a common experience.

The emergence of mutual aid groups marked a sense of common purpose. A survey in April 2020 found that while Australians felt more confused, bored, angry, lonely, anxious and fearful during the lockdown, they were also more likely to feel a sense of solidarity.[2] Another study found that people were more likely to regard other Australians as trustworthy in April than they had been in February.[3]

The same pattern emerged in Britain, where more than a thousand mutual aid groups sprang up. 'I've lived in Lancaster Gate for two years,' explained Nicola Spurr, a mutual aid organiser in London, 'and I've never really spoken to my neighbours. London can be a bit like that, it can be a lonely place. But we saw this huge outpouring of solidarity and neighbourliness straight away.'[4] In Spurr's area, there were dieticians, therapists and dementia specialists offering their services free of charge. Her comments point to a potential payoff beyond the current crisis: these interactions have broken the ice and may create opportunities for future community-building efforts.

In Rio de Janeiro's favelas, residents responded to the government's laissez-faire attitude to public health by organising localised information campaigns. Health messages were posted on painted banners and messages were broadcast from megaphones mounted on cars which drove around the area. Resident groups ran community donation campaigns to fund food and hygiene kits for the poor and the homeless and installed public sinks to encourage handwashing. The response went beyond kindness and support, with resident groups issuing a manifesto setting out the policy responses they expected from city officials.[5]

All these actions were confirmations of resilience and solidarity, but they also acted like a psychic tonic. They inspired, boosted morale and challenged people to find their own ways to connect with those around them. They showed that it would still be possible to give care and regard – in that casual, neighbourly way – and that the tribal connections that run in the background of our routine lives could remain strong.

In Australia, perhaps the most remarkable phenomenon of spontaneous mutual aid was Catherine Barrett's group, The Kindness Pandemic. As the first COVID-19 cases were being confirmed, people hoarded toilet paper and hand sanitiser, and panic-bought staple foods. Media outlets covered angry arguments in supermarkets, but not the more frequent acts of generosity. Feeling that the crisis held real possibilities to shift towards a more supportive and connected society, Barrett decided to do 'something small to create change', and set up a Facebook group that asks its members to share the good things they are doing to help others out. 'The next morning after I set it up there were 1000 people, and I knew then that it was something.'[6]

If Australia ever has to provide a national character reference, we couldn't do better than the Kindness Pandemic page. One person bought coffee for everyone in the Centrelink line. Another purchased chocolate bars for the staff at their local supermarket to enjoy on their break. Children painted small stones to make a rainbow in a public park. An Uber driver refunded the fare of a passenger who had depleted her savings travelling regularly to see her sick mother in hospital. A shopper paid for the groceries of the person in front of him when she didn't have enough money. Neighbours stocked street libraries with free rolls of toilet paper. Six weeks after its launch, the page featured thousands of stories and had attracted more than half a million members.

The Kindness Pandemic loosely organised its content around campaigns that ran for a week or two. Some were simple, such as their 'Thank a Postie' campaign. Others aimed to build connections, such as their 'Love Stories' campaign, which invited preschoolers to write messages of support to older generations, then facilitated intergenerational penpal connections. Kindness Pandemic organisers drew on the network to identify problems that were going unnoticed, such as the cancellation of prenatal classes leaving expecting mothers feeling underprepared. Members also posted local tasks that called for targeted kindness.

Barrett sees kindness as an active virtue, and worked with her team to translate the surge of engagement into making a lasting impact. With the aid of volunteer management platform Be Collective, they set up a standalone website to handle the volume of activity and as a landing point for 'how to' guides that encourage new groups to form, providing information to help them start out on a good footing. One rule is 'don't do it on your own', because you'll help more people if you're connected to other like-minded groups.

The Kindness Pandemic generated spinoffs. An outdoor advertising firm offered to put some of the messages on its billboards. One read: 'Our favourite florist kindly delivered my anniversary bouquet for free after I was laid off.' A Kindness Pandemic pledge campaign asks community leaders what acts of kindness they'll continue. It's a reminder of the value of CyberConnecting – using a Facebook campaign as the starting point, not the end goal.

There's a great deal for community builders to learn from the vigorous, spontaneous growth of informal support groups during the pandemic. But there are good lessons too from the collapse of formal volunteering that followed the onset of physical distancing. In Chapter 3 we saw that the coronavirus lockdown caused two-thirds of volunteers to cut back on their helping activity.[7] The immediate effect of this was to place pressure on voluntary services, from suicide support helplines to meal deliveries. But another impact was on the volunteers themselves. Compared with those who were able to keep volunteering, those who had to stop volunteering were lonelier and less happy. While this is not necessarily causal, it does point to the possibility that helping others provides psychological protection against distress.

In Chapter 7, we discussed the friend-building work of Suzanna Pawley, who runs the Benevolent Society's Meals on Wheels service on Sydney's Northern Beaches. When the lockdown began, Pawley found that the hardest part of adapting the service to physical distancing measures was managing the impact on longstanding volunteers. 'We had 120 drivers before the restrictions came in,' Pawley said, 'and within a matter of weeks that dwindled to thirty.' Eventually anyone over sixty-five had to be stood down. One driver was in tears. 'That was so hard,' Pawley explained, 'because a lot of our volunteers rely on that work to build up the identity of who they are. We were taking that away and it was really traumatic – people were frustrated and angry, there was the fear and that was manifesting in different ways.'

Meanwhile, others stepped up. In the Wollongong suburb of Warilla, Sharyn Bourne 'inherited' her parents' Meals on Wheels role: 'Mum and Dad are volunteers who are now in isolation because of their age, so when I was stood down at work I took over their run.'[8] A few minutes up the coast in Port Kembla, 29-year-old Naomi Thomson made the same decision: 'Something in me went, "I could be a part of that and make sure people feel [looked after]."'[9]

Seeing an opportunity to build something fresh in the face of adversity, former Socceroo Craig Foster established the Play for Lives campaign, under the tagline 'Australia's volunteers are being sidelined.

It's time for our sportspeople to sub in.' Athletes couldn't play for points, so they should play for lives. Play for Lives partnered with Aussie rules players, netballers, baseballers, cricketers, basketballers and footballers. The Play for Lives website matched athletic volunteers to charities that needed help with tasks such as delivering medications, packing food hampers and driving cancer patients to appointments. While the campaign was promoted nationally by the Red Cross and Football Federation Australia, sportspeople tended to mobilise in their local area. Foster saw this as especially important for professional players, who he felt had become detached from the communities that provided their fan bases. His goal in creating Play for Lives wasn't just to fill a short-term need, but also to make a lasting difference. Foster observed, 'I think it's also almost a historic opportunity for sport to recalibrate our relationship with all of society and to better understand vulnerable communities who were perhaps invisible to professional athletes and professional sport.'[10]

The first half of 2020 was a time of uncertainty and disruption; a reminder of how debilitating isolation and loneliness can be. At the same time, spontaneous surges of care and support spread out across our networks of weak ties. Australians evidently have a healthy appetite, and plenty of energy, for the work of reconnecting. The Kindness Pandemic, Play for Lives, informal support groups, and fill-in volunteering are examples that remind us of the altruism and community talents that Australia can draw upon to become a more connected nation. But it won't happen by accident, and no-one wants to rely on a deadly virus as a way of building community. Instead, a reconnected Australia requires blending enthusiasm and innovation to create institutions and cultures that foster community connections.

In each chapter, we've sought not just to tell stories, but to draw out lessons for community builders. Look to serve multiple objectives: to be double-plus-good. Rigorously evaluate your impact and use that evidence to attract new donors. Use technology for CyberConnecting – augmenting interpersonal connections, not supplanting them. You can't hurry love, but you can accelerate trust – friendship and new connections need a basis of trust, and that can be actively built. Abide by Sutton's Law of Social Capital: focusing on disadvantaged communities, where the need is often greatest. Have a simple purpose to your organisation and a clarity of mission. Follow the principle of hybrid vigour and expand the gene pool of your partners and supporters – you'll be stronger for their different skills, insights and connections. Make it as easy as possible for people to join, volunteer and donate. Exhibit the enthusiasm that has been claimed to be worth twenty-five IQ points. Invite people to be a part of your community and welcome them if they come. Eschew political hobbyism in favour of working with others to solve problems. Whether your purpose is exercise, environmentalism or evangelism, build a tribe by creating a clear identity. Know your neighbourhood and work to serve its needs – then look to link up with others doing likewise. Recognise the role of passion, purpose, pain and partnerships in effective community leadership.

There are many threads that governments could tie together to help communities reconnect, especially in disadvantaged neighbourhoods. Like any other kind of capital, social capital isn't evenly shared, and the less you start out with, the harder it can be to accumulate what you need. To surmount the obstacles of isolation and loneliness, Australia will need new policy solutions that range across housing, healthcare, education, homelessness, digital infrastructure, business practice, urban planning and transport. Where local communities decide to form cooperatives and collectives, government regulations should encourage these new forms of innovation.

The problem is big, but the solutions can be simple. As a starting point, you could host an end-of-year catch-up with your neighbours. Events like these are easy to arrange and provide a chance for adults to chat about sport, movies and upcoming holidays, while the kids gorge on chips and cake. If you're looking to organise a gathering for those in your apartment block or street, there are plenty of useful resources at NeighbourhoodConnect.org.au and NeighbourDay.org. In Western Australia, some councils even reimburse the costs of organising street parties, up to a maximum of $100 (alcohol is not funded).[11]

A more connected community will be a happier community. When he orders a coffee, community campaigner Peter Kenyon routinely asks the barista to add an additional coffee onto his bill and later give it to someone who cannot afford one. This unusual coffee habit helps build a stronger sense of community. Just imagine how much fun it would be to live in a nation with tens of thousands more Peter Kenyons.

For that matter, imagine what a day in a Reconnected Australia might look like.

In the morning, you might start the day by meeting up with the neighbourhood walking group, an eclectic bunch that get together to share stories and get their steps up. On days when you're feeling more energetic, there's also the local cycling, CrossFit and running groups. Each of them exploits the principle that coaches have used for years: we're more likely to exercise when we know there's someone waiting for us. Those who have a bit more time make their way afterwards to the local café for a cuppa. Others say goodbye and head to work.

During their commute, people look for opportunities to engage with others. Unlike Disconnected Australia, in which many people favoured driving, public transport is seen as the classy way to get around. British prime minister Margaret Thatcher is reputed to have once said that a man who catches buses past the age of twenty-six is a failure. In a Reconnected Australia, the opposite is true – as people look to get out of their cars and onto public transport. And the experience is different too – as well as 'quiet carriages', some train networks now feature 'chatty carriages', in which friendly conversation is encouraged. Some commuters still pop in their earbuds or scroll the social media feeds, but it's rarer now, as people recognise what they might miss out on in the real world if they disappear into the virtual void.

On the road, private transport and public transport are starting to meld. In a Reconnected Australia, ride-sharing has become much cheaper, as two or three passengers often share the cost of a pooled trip. Some people still have private cars, but the growth of driverless cars is making them increasingly rare. At first, the experience of sharing a trip with a stranger was confronting, but then something interesting happened: the average person became noticeably better at striking up an easy conversation with a new person. Just as exercise strengthens our muscles, so too socialising turned out to be mostly practice. There's a kind of social flywheel at work, with each connection powering the next.

In a Reconnected Australia, almost everyone thinks nothing of introducing themselves to a stranger and sharing a few common insights. The result has been a noticeable decline in political polarisation, since it's hard to hate someone who barracks for the same football team, lives in the same suburb, enjoys the same music, but just happens to vote for a different political party. Social commentators have also remarked on its effect in other settings. As teenagers have grown more social, their mental wellbeing has improved.

Part of the explanation seems to have been that adolescents are provided with more opportunities to connect in an outdoors setting. A Dutch scouting tradition known as 'dropping' has been adopted by many Australian families.[12] Adapted from military exercises, groups of three to five adolescents are dropped in a bush area, where they are expected to find their way back to a base camp using only a primitive

GPS device. The journey starts late in the evening and sometimes doesn't end until the early hours of the morning. Adults trail the children at a distance, observing but not helping. The children bond with one another and expand their sense of self-reliance.

Drawing on traditional Indigenous rites of passage, most families now mark the transition to adulthood by taking their children on a bush camp, with others of the same gender. So a thirteen-year-old girl and her mother may join a dozen others in a 'Pathways to Womanhood' retreat, while a teenage boy and his father may attend a 'Making of Men' camp.[13] These programs provide a chance to unplug from devices and plug into the wisdom of others who can share their experiences of what it means to be an adult.

Among people of all ages, a common revelation is that parties are simply more fun than they used to be. 'I never knew there were so many fascinating people around,' one person told their local newspaper. 'I guess we were all just as interesting back in the day when we spent all our time scrolling through Facebook – but we never seemed very good at sharing our own insights. It was more like "check out this video!", and then we'd go back to staring at our screens.' Young people don't feel they need alcohol to converse, so they're less likely to drink to excess.

How's work? Well, it hasn't stopped being hard. Retail workers still experience rude customers. Junior lawyers are still stressed. Teachers still don't get as much respect as they deserve. Many startup businesses still fail. Firefighters, police officers and miners still risk injury. More people enjoy their jobs than in the past, but almost everyone would prefer being on holiday to going to work. Yet in a Reconnected Australia, there's a greater sense of common purpose in many workplaces. When union membership rates started to rise, business leaders feared that it would harm productivity. The opposite turned out to be true. As automation reshaped workplaces, managers discovered that a culture of constructive problem-solving allowed them to make the best use of artificial intelligence, industrial robots and mobile technology. Where Disconnected Australia used to rank poorly on measures of management quality and worker happiness, both metrics have now soared. Among the most productive workplaces are those owned by their employees or their customers. Plenty of firms now have employee share-ownership schemes, so workers get a slice of the profits. It's increased growth and reduced discontent. People like capitalism more when it delivers them some capital.

Even in regular companies, greater trust has made employees more willing to share their profit-boosting ideas. Putting an employee representative on the board – once a radical Germanic idea – has become the new fad among effective firms. When people ask how Australia got out of the productivity slump of the 2010s, the most common answer is 'we learnt to trust one another again'. Productivity has translated into such strong wage gains that there is an active discussion about whether ongoing pay increases are the best way of improving wellbeing. Across the ideological spectrum, there is discussion about whether to increase the standard amount of annual leave from four weeks to six weeks.

Another reason that a Reconnected Australia is more prosperous is that social ties have made it easier to do handshake deals and encouraged diverse companies to collaborate. As Nobel laureate Kenneth Arrow once observed, 'Virtually every commercial transaction has within it an element of trust.'[14] Like the New York diamond dealers, Australian businesses have found that a stronger community is good for the bottom line. People are more trusting, and more trustworthy. That means startup entrepreneurs find it easier to attract potential investors, and established businesses are less worried about getting ripped off in their next transaction. The link between strong social ties and a well-functioning economy surprised those on the right who subscribed to the Gordon Gekko 'greed is good' philosophy.

It also surprised those on the left who had been saying that social isolation was an inevitable consequence of capitalism and competition. Contrary to both views, it turns out that markets work best when people trust others. And when markets are working well, they create the economic conditions that allow civic society to thrive. It's easier to think about the needs of others when your own household income is growing.

After work, a Reconnected Australia really comes into its own. As they develop more medium-density housing around transport nodes, urban leaders have been touting the benefits of a 'thirty-minute city', in which people across the city can access the places they need within half an hour.[15] With the gift of time, people are more fulfilled and happier than they were in a Disconnected Australia. Traditional groups such as cricket teams, scouting organisations and Rotary Clubs have seen a resurgence, but the most exciting developments have been in the creation of new civic communities. Just as the collapse of civic community killed organisations, the rebirth of social capital has encouraged vigorous new strains of community-focused startups.

Who would have thought, in a Disconnected Australia, that there would be a local community dedicated to telling the world's greatest stories? That fathers' groups would become as popular as mothers' groups? That cinemas would host movie discussion groups just like libraries host book groups? Once a culture of leaving turned into a culture of joining, social entrepreneurs began creating an abundance of new organisations. Communities pitch in to sponsor refugees, with the government guaranteeing that if locals can meet the costs of resettling a new family, their settlement will be in addition to the national quota.[16] The sharing economy has expanded to encompass items that people use only occasionally. On weekends when people want to use a campervan, power saw, kayak or trailer, many choose to go online and find a neighbour willing to rent it out for a small fee.

In a Disconnected Australia, at-risk youngsters once turned to street gangs for a sense of identity. Now there are much more exciting options to be found with sporting clubs, adventure expeditions and mentors. Who would hang around trying to shoplift trinkets in a banal shopping centre when you could be part of something bigger than yourself? In a Reconnected Australia, people recognise that the wellbeing of the kids in the neighbourhood is a shared responsibility. If a primary schooler can't afford tap dancing shoes, communities pitch in. If a teen can't get to basketball practice, the school finds a way to make it work. Affluent parents see themselves as having a role in helping raise disadvantaged children in the community. As a volunteer sporting coach, an informal careers counsellor or a friendly neighbour, parents provide a literal social safety net for vulnerable children in the community. As New Jersey senator Cory Booker puts it, it takes a 'conspiracy of love' to raise children well. Adults now take pride in saying that they look out for the disadvantaged children in their community 'as though they were my own nieces and nephews'.

A Reconnected Australia turns out to look a whole lot different than a Disconnected Australia. Most people live within ten minutes' walk of a public park, and most suburbs have good footpaths to get there. Major public parks are better designed – from adventure playgrounds to encourage risk-taking by children to funky sculptures and hedge mazes to entertain adults. Separated bicycle paths alongside major roads have allowed more people to combine exercising and commuting. In hillier areas, e-bikes give a gentle assistance uphill, making cycling accessible to more people. Quirky motorways and expansive public squares are among the shifts away from drab uniformity and towards engaging urban design.

When you walk into a modern office building, the stairways are prominent, with the lift wells tucked away in the corner.[17] The result is more people using the stairs and more serendipitous interactions.

Designers are experimenting with bringing facilities together – like early childhood centres on school campuses and aged care centres on university campuses. With COVID-19 cured, many nursing homes allow university students to live rent-free, in exchange for being 'good neighbours' to the residents.[18] Urban mixed-use developments have moved on from the old-fashioned 'ten apartments above a café' model to apartment buildings located next to train stations, co-located with supermarkets, gyms, movie theatres and medical centres.

Among the strongest predictors of healthy ageing are strong communities and active living, so one of the things people noted as Australia became more reconnected was the rise in longevity. As community grew stronger, Australian lifespans approached those in places like Italy's Sardinia and Japan's Okinawa, where strong social connections and regular exercise had produced the world's longest life expectancy.[19] A Reconnected Australia not only has more centenarians, it also boasts lower rates of dementia and other incapacitating conditions. People aren't merely living more days, they're enjoying better days.

One thing that hasn't changed is that people are often dissatisfied with government decisions. But rather than kvetching from the couch, they respond by seeking out elected officials and putting their views to them. To resist unfairness and insist on reform, citizens form neighbourhood groups, draft petitions and organise protests. This hasn't just made politicians more responsive; it's led governments to use deliberative forums *before* they write new laws. When parliament enacted the ethical principles governing self-driving cars, deliberative democracy was crucial in ensuring that the law reflected the nation's values. There is now talk of an annual 'Deliberation Day', when people engage in structured debates about the main issues facing the country.[20]

Finally, a Reconnected Australia turns out to be more egalitarian. People no longer talk about those on welfare as 'bludgers' or 'leaners', for one simple reason: they're more likely to know someone who's been there. Instead, there's widespread recognition that bad luck could strike any of us and that the social safety net is there for all. In a Disconnected Australia, people would mouth the platitude that society is judged by how it treats its most vulnerable. In a Reconnected Australia, our institutions put that value into action. When people talk about why it's necessary for philanthropists, governments and neighbours to do more to help the most disadvantaged, they'll often say, 'Because we're all in this together.' It's a connected 'we' society, not a self-centred 'me' society.

Does a Reconnected Australia sound like the kind of place you'd like to live? If so, then it's our job to help create it. Whether you're a volunteer or a donor, a policymaker or a charity leader, each of us has a part to play in Australia's civic renaissance. In this book, we've suggested some ideas, but we're keen to hear yours. If you're doing innovative things to build community, drop us a note and let us know how others can follow in your footsteps. Together, we can get Australia reconnected.

ACKNOWLEDGEMENTS

Our thanks to those parliamentarians and former parliamentarians who co-hosted 'Reconnected' forums with us, including Anne Aly, Terri Butler, Sharon Claydon, Julie Collins, Milton Dick, Don Farrell, Patrick Gorman, Luke Gosling, Ross Hart, Julian Hill, Justine Keay, Matt Keogh, Peter Khalil, Susan Lamb, Sue Lines, Emma McBride, Brian Mitchell, Claire Moore, Julie Owens, Graham Perrett, Tanya Plibersek, Louise Pratt, Amanda Rishworth and Tony Zappia. We are grateful to Martin O'Shannessy, who added questions on friends and neighbours to a 2018 OmniPoll survey, and to Gary Morgan and Julian McCrann, who provided us with Roy Morgan data on sporting participation for 2001 to 2019. Thanks to the community builders and experts who shared their insights and stories, including Michael Albert, Jack Manning Bancroft, David Barda, Catherine Barrett, Elaine Bensted, Michael Bernard, Nicholas Biddle, Jess Bloomfield, Danae Bosler, Matthew Boyd, Rob Buckingham, Mark Campbell, Wesa Chau, Brad Chilcott, Carla Clarence, Libby Coker, Tim Costello, Matt Crawley, Fleur Creed, Peter Dawson, Bev Debrincat, Robert Dixon, Anna Donaldson, John Dryzek,

Naomi Edwards, Karyn Freeman, Tracy Gillard, Ellie Gillet, Alice Glenn, Daniel Gobena, Liam Golding, Murray Goot, Pete Greenwood, Nathan Hagarty, Leigh Hambly, Bruce Hammond, Phil Harrison, Luke Hilakari, Kirsten Holmes, Leigh Hubbard, Kerry Jones, Astrid Jorgensen, Lavanya Kala, Shankar Kasynathan, Andrew Katay, Peter Kenyon, Catherine King, Sebastian Kocar, Adam McKay, Patricia Lauria, Victor Lee, Barbara Leigh, Tim Leigh, Nick Maisey, Nic Marchesi, Estelle Marine, Leigh McLaughlin, Barbara Mifsud, Liz Migliorini, Julie Molloy, Matt Napier, Clayton Neil, Tim Oberg, Rob Oerlemans, Evelyn O'Loughlin, Toby Ord, Jan Ormerod, Karlya Parnell, Alison Parsons, Lucas Patchett, Suzanna Pawley, Nick Pearce, Matt Pfahlert, Robert Putnam, Liz Rhodes, Tonia Ries, Genevieve Roberts, Wendy Russell, Matt Ryan, Saara Sabbagh, Bec Scott, Krystian Seibert, Marlee Silva, Marielle Smith, Jonathan Srikanthan, Anne Stanley, Rhiannon Stephens, Ted Sussex, Melanie Tate, Fiona Telford, Neha Teli, Jeremy Tobias, Michael Traill, Brian Triglone, Maia Tua-Davidson, Iain Walker, Lisa Warton, Grant Westthrop, Robert Wiblin, Sarah Wickham, Craig Wilkins, Sonia Williams, Juliette Wright, Sarah Xu and all their collaborators. We are grateful to the splendid team at Black Inc., including Lauren Carta, Marilyn de Castro, Chris Feik, Kirstie Innes-Will and Kate Nash. Andrew dedicates this book to his four beloved community-builders: Gweneth, Sebastian, Theodore and Zachary. Nick dedicates this book to Penny and Edie, who make friends wherever they go.

ENDNOTES

If not directly referenced, quotations are from interviews with the authors.

1. SOCIAL CAPITAL

1   For an engaging account of these events, see Nicholas A. Christakis, *Blueprint: The Evolutionary Origins of a Good Society*, Hachette, London, 2019.
2   Thomas Musgrave, *Castaway on the Auckland Isles*, Lockwood and Co., London, 1866, p. 31.
3   This account draws on Barak D. Richman, 'How community institutions create economic advantage: Jewish diamond merchants in New York', *Law and Social Inquiry*, vol. 31, no. 2, 2006, pp. 383–420.
4   Marcel Proust, 'Regrets: Daydreams in the color of time' in *Pleasures and Days and 'Memory': Short Stories by Marcel Proust*, Dover Publications, New York, 2014, p. 229.
5   Xianbi Huang, Mark Western, Yanjie Bian, Yaojun Li, Rochelle Côté and Yangtao Huang, 'Social networks and subjective wellbeing in Australia: New evidence from a national survey', *Sociology*, vol. 53, no. 2, 2019, pp. 401–21.
6   Xianbi Huang and Mark Western, 'Social capital and life satisfaction in Australia', in Yaojun Li (ed.), *Handbook of Research Methods and Applications in Social Capital*, Edward Elgar, Cheltenham UK, 2015, pp. 225–41.
7   Mark S. Granovetter, 'The strength of weak ties', *American Journal of Sociology*, vol. 78, no. 6, 1973, pp. 1360–80.
8   Julianne Holt-Lunstad, Timothy B. Smith and J. Bradley Layton, 'Social relationships and mortality risk: A meta-analytic review', *PLoS Medicine*, vol. 7, no. 7, 2010. Australian research also confirms that informal social connectedness and civic engagement are associated with better health, with the relationship being strongest for mental health: Helen Louise Berry and Jennifer A. Welsh, 'Social capital and health in Australia: An overview from the Household, Income and Labour Dynamics in Australia Survey', *Social Science and Medicine*, vol. 70, no. 4, 2010, pp. 588–96.

9 Laura Coll-Planas, Fredrica Nyqvist, Teresa Puig, Gerard Urrútia, Ivan Solà and Rosa Monteserín, 'Social capital interventions targeting older people and their impact on health: A systematic review', *Journal of Epidemiology and Community Health*, vol. 71, no. 7, 2017, pp. 663–72.
10 Stephen Post, 'It's good to be good: 2011 fifth annual scientific report on health, happiness and helping others', *International Journal of Person Centred Medicine*, vol. 1, no. 4, 2011, pp. 814–29.
11 Stephen Post, 'Rx It's good to be good (G2BG) 2017 commentary: Prescribing volunteerism for health, happiness, resilience, and longevity', *American Journal of Health Promotion*, vol. 31, no. 2, 2017, pp. 164–72. Post quotes Proverbs 11:15, 'those who refresh others will be refreshed'.
12 Joanne Fritz, '15 unexpected benefits of volunteering that will inspire you', *The Balance*, 24 June 2019.
13 Hannah M.C. Schreier, Kimberly A. Schonert-Reichl and Edith Chen, 'Effect of volunteering on risk factors for cardiovascular disease in adolescents: A randomized controlled trial', *JAMA Pediatrics*, vol. 167, no. 4, 2013, pp. 327–32.
14 Kristin Layous, S. Katherine Nelson, Eva Oberle, Kimberly A. Schonert-Reichl and Sonja Lyubomirsky, 'Kindness counts: Prompting prosocial behavior in preadolescents boosts peer acceptance and well-being', *PloS One*, vol. 7, no. 12, 2012. Students in the control group were asked to keep track of three places they visited that week.
15 Marilyn Price-Mitchell, 'Acts of kindness: Key to happiness for children & teens', *Psychology Today*, 2 January 2013.
16 Andrew Leigh, 'Does equality lead to fraternity?', *Economics Letters*, vol. 93, no. 1, 2006, pp. 121–5.
17 Friendship estimates from 1985 to 2004 are reported in Miller McPherson, Lynn Smith-Lovin and Matthew E. Brashears, 'Social isolation in America: Changes in core discussion networks over two decades', *American Sociological Review*, vol. 71, June 2006, pp. 353–75 (see also: Claude Fischer, 'The 2004 GSS finding of shrunken social networks: An artifact?', *American Sociological Review*, vol. 74, August 2009, pp. 657–69; Miller McPherson, Lynn Smith-Lovin and Matthew E. Brashears, 'Models and marginals: Using survey evidence to study social networks', *American Sociological Review*, vol. 74, August 2009, pp. 670–81). Figures on trust and confidence in institutions from 1972 to 2012 are reported in Jean M. Twenge, W. Keith Campbell and Nathan T. Carter, 'Declines in trust in others and confidence in institutions among American adults and late adolescents, 1972–2012', *Psychological Science*, vol. 25, no. 10, 2014, pp. 1914–23.
18 See, for example, Organisation for Economic Co-operation and Development, *The Well-being of Nations: The Role of Human and Social Capital*, Paris, OECD, 2001; Robert Putnam (ed.), *Democracies in Flux: The Evolution of Social Capital in Contemporary Society*, Oxford University Press, New York, 2002; Andrew Leigh, 'Trends in social capital' in Karen Christensen and David Levinson (eds), *Encyclopedia of Community: From the Village to the Virtual World*, Sage, Thousand Oaks, CA, 2003.
19 Quoted in Dietlind Stolle and Marc Hooghe, 'Inaccurate, exceptional, one-sided or irrelevant? The debate about the alleged decline of social capital and civic engagement in Western societies', *British Journal of Political Science*, vol. 35, no. 1, 2005, pp. 149–67. We are grateful to David Barda and his colleagues at the Australia Forum for drawing our attention to this quote.

2. DISSECTING THE DISCONNECTION DISASTER

1   The figures in this paragraph are from Australian Bureau of Statistics, *General Social Survey, Summary Results, Australia, 2014*, Cat. No. 4159.0, ABS, Canberra, 2015, Table 1.1.
2   The Australian Bureau of Statistics gives respondents the following examples of social groups: 'Sport or physical recreation group, Arts or heritage group, Religious or spiritual group or organisation, Craft or practical hobby group, Adult education, other recreation or special interest group, Ethnic/multicultural club, Social clubs providing restaurants or bars, Other social groups'.
3   The Australian Bureau of Statistics gives respondents the following examples of community support groups: 'Service clubs, Welfare organisations, Education and training, Parenting / children / youth, Health promotion and support, Emergency Services, International aid and development, Other community support groups'.
4   *Disconnected* has a small error on this point. The text on page 16 should read: 'By the late 2000s, only 2 per cent of boys were Scouts' (rather than 'girls were Scouts').
5   Essential Media Survey, conducted on 22 November 2016. Respondents answering 'don't know' have been omitted. If 'don't know' respondents are included, the share agreeing with each of these statements is as follows: 'I just don't like joining groups' 46 per cent; 'I find it impossible to give my time to things outside of work and home' 51 per cent; 'There are fewer people available to be part of local groups' 47 per cent; 'The decline in membership of organisations is not a positive development' 64 per cent; 'People just aren't interested in joining things anymore' 60 per cent.
6   The issue is discussed in Australian Bureau of Statistics, *A Comparison of Volunteering Rates from the 2006 Census of Population and Housing and the 2006 General Social Survey*, ABS, Canberra, 2012. Part of the problem arises because the Census asks the respondent to answer on behalf of other adults in the household, and the ABS notes that people are much less likely to say that another adult in the household is a volunteer than they are to self-identify as a volunteer. This helps explain why the Census volunteering rates are lower than those in the General Social Survey. The Census reports a volunteering rate of 20.1 per cent in 2006, 17.8 per cent in 2011 and 19.0 per cent in 2016.
7   Figures on volunteer firefighters are reported in Productivity Commission, *Report on Government Services: Emergency Management*, Productivity Commission, Canberra, 2020. We report 2009–10 figures as 2010, and so on. Volunteering rates are as a share of the population aged eighteen and over.
8   Robert D. Putnam and David E. Campbell, *American Grace: How Religion Divides and Unites Us*, Simon & Schuster, New York, 2012, p. 444.
9   Putnam and Campbell, *American Grace*, p. 473.
10 Putnam and Campbell, *American Grace*, p. 477.
11 Jonathan H.W. Tan and Claudia Vogel, 'Religion and trust: An experimental study', *Journal of Economic Psychology*, vol. 29, no. 6, 2008, pp. 832–48.
12 Alain de Botton, *Religion for Atheists: A Non-Believer's Guide to the Uses of Religion*, Penguin, London, 2012, p. 63.
13 The 1904–05 New South Wales Year Book reports that 385,627 people aged fifteen or over attended a weekly religious service. We estimate that the 1904 NSW population aged fifteen or over was 935,292, an attendance rate of 41 per cent for those aged fifteen and over (William Hall, *The Official Year Book of New South Wales,*

Government Printer, Sydney, 1906, pp. 572–3, 603, 633). It seems reasonable to assume that the attendance rate for those aged eighteen and over was also around four in ten. Wayne Hudson estimates that at the time of Federation, half the adult population attended church every Sunday: Wayne Hudson, *Australian Religious Thought*, Monash University Publishing, Melbourne, 2016.

14 The data in Figure 5 are drawn from the Australian Election Study. Estimates from the Household Income and Labor Dynamics in Australia survey paint a similar picture. In the HILDA survey, weekly religious attendance fell from 10.9 per cent in 2010 to 10.5 per cent in 2014, while monthly religious attendance fell from 16.2 per cent to 15.7 per cent.

15 Peter Wilkinson, 'Who goes to Mass in Australia in the 21st century?', *The Swag*, vol. 21, no. 3, 2013; 'Mass attendance', *Pastoral Research Online*, National Centre for Pastoral Research, Issue 44, 2019. Mass attendance figures for 2001 onwards are average weekly attendances, based on a count taken over four Sundays in May.

16 In 1954, there were 2,060,986 Catholics and 1,525,129 worshippers. In 2016, there were 5,291,817 Catholics and 623,356 worshippers.

17 Peter Wilkinson, *Catholic Parish Ministry in Australia: The Crisis Deepens*, Catholics for Ministry & Women and the Australian Church, Canberra, 2012, p. 16.

18 Robert Dixon, Stephen Reid and Marilyn Chee, *Mass Attendance in Australia: A Critical Moment. A Report Based on the National Count of Attendance, the National Church Life Survey and the Australian Census*, Australian Catholic Bishops Conference Pastoral Research Office, Fitzroy, 2013.

19 Quoted in Christopher Akehurst, 'The decline of the suburban church', *Quadrant*, 22 December 2013.

20 Quoted in Akehurst, 'The decline of the suburban church'.

21 1967 and 2008 figures are for Melbourne (the 2008 figure for Sydney was almost exactly the same, at 31 per cent). These numbers are sourced from Andrew Markus, Nicky Jacobs and Tanya Aronov, *Report Series on the Gen08 Survey: Preliminary Findings, Melbourne and Sydney*, Report 1, Australian Centre for Jewish Civilisation, Monash University, Melbourne, 2009, p. 37. The 2017 figure is the average for Sydney and Melbourne, from David Graham and Andrew Markus, *Gen17 Australian Jewish Community Survey*, Australian Centre for Jewish Civilisation, Monash University, Melbourne, 2018, p. 21.

22 Husnia Underabi, *Mosques of Sydney and New South Wales*, Charles Sturt University, Islamic Sciences and Research Academy and University of Western Sydney, Sydney, 2014, pp. 24, 28.

23 'It is evident, then, that a city is not a community of place; nor established for the sake of mutual safety or traffic with each other; but that these things are the necessary consequences of a city, although they may all exist where there is no city: but a city is a society of people joining together with their families and their children to live agreeably for the sake of having their lives as happy and as independent as possible: and for this purpose it is necessary that they should live in one place and intermarry with each other: hence in all cities there are family-meetings, clubs, sacrifices, and public entertainments to promote friendship; for a love of sociability is friendship itself; so that the end then for which a city is established is, that the inhabitants of it may live happy, and these things are conducive to that end: for it is a community of families and villages for the sake of a perfect independent life; that is,

as we have already said, for the sake of living well and happily.' Aristotle, *A Treatise on Government*, translated by William Ellis, J.M. Dent & Sons, London, Ch. 9, 1912.

24 The true/false questions (and the share who answered them correctly) were: 'Australia became a federation in 1901' (77 per cent); 'The Constitution can only be changed by the High Court' (35 per cent), 'The Senate election is based on proportional representation' (48%), 'No-one may stand for Federal parliament unless they pay a deposit' (17 per cent), and 'The longest time allowed between Federal elections for the House of Representatives is four years' (26 per cent). Respondents could answer true, false or don't know. We did not use a sixth question, 'There are seventy-five members of the House of Representatives' (43 per cent), because the number of members of the House increased from seventy-five to seventy-six at the election, potentially creating confusion as to whether the question pertained to the size of the House before or after the election.

25 This chart combines data from ANU polls 1 to 28, weighted to better reflect the Australian population. Respondents were asked 'Are you satisfied or dissatisfied with the way the country is heading?', with five possible responses: 'Very satisfied', 'Satisfied', 'Neither satisfied nor dissatisfied', 'Dissatisfied', and 'Very dissatisfied'. In surveys 26 to 28, the 'Neither satisfied nor dissatisfied' option was hidden, and only revealed if the respondent attempted to skip the question. Hence the share of people nominating that middle category response is significantly lower in those surveys. We therefore chart the share who answer 'Very satisfied' or 'Satisfied', as a share of those who answer 'Very satisfied', 'Satisfied', 'Dissatisfied' or 'Very dissatisfied'.

26 Figures are from the Australian Constitutional Values Surveys, 2008, 2012, 2014, 2017, and the Global Corruption Barometer Survey 2018, as reported in Griffith University and Transparency International Australia, *Global Corruption Barometer Survey Results*, Media Release, 20 August 2018. Results exclude those who answered 'don't know'.

27 Figures are from the Global Corruption Barometer Surveys in 2016 and 2018, as reported in Griffith University and Transparency International Australia, *Global Corruption Barometer Survey Results*. Results exclude those who answered 'don't know'.

28 From 1973 to 2018, confidence in Congress dropped from 23 per cent to 6 per cent, while confidence in the executive branch dropped from 29 per cent to 12 per cent: United States General Social Survey Data Explorer, available at gssdataexplorer.norc.org.

29 Edelman splits the population into the 'mass population' (84 per cent) and the 'informed public' (16 per cent). The informed public are classified as those who are aged twenty-five to sixty-four, university-educated, are in the top quarter of household income for their age group, and report significant media consumption and engagement in public policy and business news. See Edelman, *Edelman Trust Barometer: Global Report*, Edelman, New York, 2019.

30 Cathy Alexander, 'The party's over: which clubs have the most members?', *Crikey*, 18 July 2013; Troy Bramston, 'Members fleeing Labor Party', *The Australian*, 17 April 2018, p. 1.

31 Alexander, 'The party's over'.

32 Australian Bureau of Statistics, *General Social Survey, Summary Results, Australia, 2014*, Cat. No. 4159.0, ABS, Canberra, 2015, Table 1.1. The Australian Bureau of Statistics gives respondents the following examples of civic or political groups:

'Trade union, professional/technical association, Political party, Civic group or organisation, Environmental or animal welfare group, Human and civil rights group, Body corporate or tenants' association, Consumer organisation, Other civic or political organisation'.

33 We came across Liz Low's book via a delightful column: Tony Wright, 'A poddy calf summons memories of a free-range childhood', *The Sydney Morning Herald*, 28 February 2019.

34 David Derbyshire, 'How children lost the right to roam in four generations', *Daily Mail*, 15 June 2007. The article gives two contradictory dates for when the great-grandparent was aged eight: 1919 and 1926. We use 1926, which would be consistent with 1919 being his approximate birth year.

35 Helen Woolley and Elizabeth Griffin, 'Decreasing experiences of home range, outdoor spaces, activities and companions: Changes across three generations in Sheffield in north England', *Children's Geographies*, vol. 13. no. 6, 2015, pp. 677–91; Christine Tandy, 'Children's diminishing play space: A study of intergenerational change in children's use of their neighbourhoods', *Australian Geographical Studies*, vol. 37, no. 2, 1999, pp. 154–64.

36 Australian Bureau of Statistics, *National Health Survey: First Results, 2017–18*, Cat. No. 4364.0, ABS, Canberra, 2018; Australian Institute of Health and Welfare, *A Picture of Overweight and Obesity in Australia 2017*, Cat. No. PHE 216, AIHW, Canberra, 2017.

37 Brooklyn J. Fraser, Leigh Blizzard, Grant R. Tomkinson, Kate Lycett, Melissa Wake, David Burgner, Sarath Ranganathan et al., 'The great leap backward: Changes in the jumping performance of Australian children aged 11–12 years between 1985 and 2015', *Journal of Sports Sciences*, vol. 37, no. 7, 2019, pp. 748–54.

38 The data are drawn from the Roy Morgan Single Source survey, and cover fiscal years, so what we refer to as 2001 are surveys spanning July 2000 to June 2001 (similarly, what we refer to as 2001–02 is from July 2000 to June 2002). Roy Morgan's data also includes 2000, but reported participation rates for most sports in that year are considerably lower than in the following year. After consultation with Roy Morgan, we opted to drop that year from our analysis. We also drop sports that were not included in Roy Morgan's surveys in 2001–02 and 2018–19.

39 Specifically, we classify a sport as growing or shrinking only if the regression line is significantly distinguishable from zero at the 95 per cent level of statistical significance.

40 On the popularity ranking of club sports, see AusPlay, *Participation Data for the Sport Sector: Summary of Key National Findings, October 2015 to September 2016 Data*, Australian Sports Commission, Canberra, 2016, p. 17. On trends in golf club membership, see Golf Australia, *Golf Club Participation Report*, Golf Australia, 2018, p. 14. Note that the AusPlay snapshot reports a higher level of participation than the Golf Australia time series, since the former includes non-member players.

41 Jessie Davies and Jennifer Browning, 'Golf club closures loom as memberships plummet to lowest level in 20 years', *ABC News Western Plains*, 10 August 2019. Note that the pattern of decline does not hold across all club sports. For example, surf life-saving membership rates have held remarkably steady. Since 1960, around two in 1000 people aged over fifteen have been members of surf life-saving clubs.

42 Australian Bureau of Statistics, *National Health Survey: First Results, 2017–18*, Cat. No. 4364.0, ABS, Canberra, 2018.

43 David Brooks, *The Road to Character*, Penguin, New York, 2015.
44 The question was asked in the US General Social Survey, worded as follows: 'From time to time, most people discuss important matters with other people. Looking back over the last six months – who are the people with whom you discussed matters important to you? Just tell me their first names or initials.'
45 McPherson, Smith-Lovin and Brashears, 'Models and marginals'.
46 The share of respondents who said that they had face-to-face contact with family or friends living outside the household in the previous week fell from 79 to 73 per cent. The share who said they had family or friends living outside the household to confide in fell from 96 to 92 per cent. See Australian Bureau of Statistics, *General Social Survey: Summary Results, Australia, 2014*, Cat. No. 4159.0, ABS, Canberra, 2015, Table 1.
47 Ninety per cent of Australians have met their neighbours, while 54 per cent do not know their names: Timothy Sharp, *The Connection Gap: A Research Study Exploring the State of Australia's Neighbourly Relations and Social Connections*, Happiness Institute, Sydney, 2019.
48 Sixty per cent of us say we'd like to get to know our neighbours better: Sharp, *The Connection Gap*.
49 Sharp, *The Connection Gap*.
50 Michelle Lim, 'One in four Australians are lonely, which affects their physical and mental health', *The Conversation*, 9 November 2018. Specifically, 50.5 per cent say that they feel lonely for at least one day in a week, while 27.6 per cent feel lonely for three or more days.
51 Ken Wyatt, 'Australia's New Age of Opportunity', Speech to the National Press Club, Canberra, 25 October 2017. Wyatt acknowledged that he was drawing on anecdotes rather than hard data.
52 Eric Klinenberg, *Heat Wave: A Social Autopsy of Disaster in Chicago*, 2nd edn, University of Chicago Press, Chicago, 2015.
53 Eric Klinenberg, *Going Solo: The Extraordinary Rise and Surprising Appeal of Living Alone*, Penguin, New York, 2013, p. 100.
54 Stephen J. Dubner, 'Is There Really a "Loneliness Epidemic"?' (Episode 407), *Freakonomics* podcast, 26 February 2020.
55 Specifically, the age adjustment shows what the suicide rate would have been if the age structure in the population was the same as it was in 2001.
56 Good2Give and Charities Aid Foundation, *Australia Giving 2019*, Sydney and London, 2019.
57 Good2Give and Charities Aid Foundation, *Australia Giving 2019*.
58 Not all sectors have seen a rise in real per-capita donations. Adjusting for inflation, total public donations to overseas aid charities were around $1.01 billion in both 2008 and 2018, suggesting a significant fall on a per-capita basis: Terence Wood, 'The ongoing slide in donations to Australian NGOs', DevPolicy Blog, 25 November 2019.
59 Samuel Johnson, quoted in Kevin Nguyen, 'Street fundraisers raised more than $120 million for Australian charities in 2018, report reveals', *ABC* (online), 4 January 2019; Mary Ward, 'I watched chuggers to see who they approached. I wasn't surprised', *The Sydney Morning Herald*, 8 August 2018.
60 Kevin Nguyen, 'Street fundraisers raised more than $120 million for Australian charities in 2018, report reveals', *ABC* (online), 4 January 2019.
61 Nguyen, 'Street fundraisers'.

62 Lorna Knowles, '"Charity muggers" win first round in Appco class action over alleged exploitation', ABC Investigations, 18 May 2018.
63 'Bans on paying for human blood distort a vital global market', *The Economist*, 10 May 2018. See also Robert Slonim, 'How Australia can fix the market for plasma and save millions', *The Conversation*, 2 September 2018.
64 Jacob L. Vigdor, 'Community composition and collective action: Analyzing initial mail response to the 2000 census', *Review of Economics and Statistics*, vol. 86, no. 1, 2004, pp. 303–12.
65 Household expenditure survey response rates fell from around 80 per cent in the early 1990s to the low 70 per cent range in the 2000s: see Figure 9.2 in Garry Barrett, Peter Levell and Kevin Milligan, 'A comparison of micro and macro expenditure measures across countries using differing survey methods' in Christopher D. Carroll, Thomas F. Crossley, and John Sabelhaus (eds), *Improving the Measurement of Consumer Expenditures*, Studies in Income and Wealth, vol. 74, University of Chicago Press, Chicago, 2015, pp. 263–86.
66 In *The Upswing*, Putnam and Garrett use the Google Ngrams database. However, because there is no separate Ngrams corpus of Australian books (and Ngrams cannot be searched for books that contain multiple words), we instead carry out repeated queries of Google Books. We search for the words 'Australia' and 'we', and 'Australia' and 'me', with content restricted to books (i.e. not including magazines and newspapers). Google reports the number of results of such searches to the nearest 1000, in the form 'About 1,210,000 results'. When the searches are repeated, they can sometimes differ, though only typically by +/-1000. For each decade, we sum the number of 'we' searches and divide it by the number of 'me' searches.
67 Cindy Shannon, Mark Brough, David Jenkins, Chelsea Bond & Julian Hunt, *Strong in the City: A Multi-strategy Indigenous Health Promotion Project*, Final Report, Indigenous Health Division, University of Queensland, Brisbane, 2003, quoted in Mark Brough, Graham Henderson, Rosemary Foster and Heather Douglas, 'Social capital and Aboriginal and Torres Strait Islander health—problems and possibilities' in Ian Anderson, Fran Baum & Michael Bentley (eds), *Beyond Bandaids: Exploring the Underlying Social Determinants of Aboriginal Health. Papers from the Social Determinants of Aboriginal Health Workshop*, Adelaide, Cooperative Research Centre for Aboriginal Health, Darwin, 2004, pp. 191–207.
68 See Diane Smith and Linda Roach, 'Indigenous voluntary work: NATSIS empirical evidence, policy relevance and future data issues', in Jon Altman & John Taylor (eds), *The National Aboriginal and Torres Strait Islander Survey: Findings and Future Prospects*, CAEPR Research Monograph, ANU, vol. 11, 1996, pp. 65–76 (higher levels of volunteering among Indigenous people in national surveys); Marisa Gilles, Ann Larson, Peter Howard and Belynda Wheatland, *Health, Trust and Social Capital in a Rural Town*, Combined Universities Centre for Rural Health, Geraldton, 2004 (lower levels of trust among Indigenous people in a rural Western Australian town). Both are quoted in Brough, Henderson, Foster and Douglas, 'Social capital and Aboriginal and Torres Strait Islander health'.
69 Australian Electoral Commission, *Voter Turnout: 2016 House of Representatives and Senate Elections*, AEC, Canberra, 2017, p. 15.
70 Australian Bureau of Statistics, *National Aboriginal and Torres Strait Islander Social Survey, Australia, 2014–15*, Cat No. 4714.0, ABS, Canberra, Table 1.3, 2015.

71 Mandy Yap and Eunice Yu, *Community Wellbeing from the Ground Up: A Yawuru Example*, Bankwest Curtin Economics Centre Research Report 3/16, Curtin University, 2016, p. 57.

3. VOLUNTEERING

1. Nicholas Biddle and Matthew Gray, *The Experience of Volunteers During the Early Stages of the COVID-19 Pandemic*, Centre for Social Research and Methods, Australian National University, Canberra, 2020.
2. Royce Kurmelovs, 'Winds fan flames as blazes destroy properties in Lithgow – as it happened', *Guardian Live Blog*, 21 December 2019 at 2.05 pm.
3. Michelle Brown, 'Plea for people to stop donating goods directly to "overwhelmed" fire-affected communities', ABC (online), 7 January 2020.
4. Aitor Calo-Blanco, Jaromír Kovářík, Friederike Mengel and José Gabriel Romero, 'Natural disasters and indicators of social cohesion', *PLoS One*, vol. 12, no. 6, June 2017, pp. 1–13.
5. Calo-Blanco, Kovářík, Mengel and Romero ('Natural disasters') suggest it takes around thirteen years for the positive effects to fade.
6. Thomas Sander and Robert Putnam, 'Walking the civic talk after Sept. 11', *Christian Science Monitor*, 19 February 2002.
7. Thomas Sander and Robert Putnam, 'Still bowling alone? The post-9/11 split', *Journal of Democracy* vol. 21, no. 1, 2010, pp. 9–16.
8. Daniel Aldrich and Emi Kyota, 'Creating community resilience through elder-led physical and social infrastructure', *Disaster Medicine and Public Health Preparedness*, vol. 11, no. 1, February 2017, pp. 120–6; Keiko Iwasaki, Yasuyuki Sawada and Daniel P. Aldrich, 'Social capital as a shield against anxiety among displaced residents from Fukushima', *Natural Hazards*, vol. 89, no. 1, October 2017, pp. 405–21.
9. 'Bellingen Shire Coronavirus Pandemic Response Group', Bellingen Shire Council, 2020.
10. 'Flood victim joins volunteer community', *Emergency Volunteering* (website), 10 June 2011, archived at Trove on 20 February 2017.
11. 'Flood victim joins volunteer community', *Emergency Volunteering*.
12. EV CREW is itself largely dependent on volunteers. Paid Volunteering Queensland staff are supported by around 800 volunteers who have been trained to operate and support the EV CREW system.
13. Personal conversation with Communiteer co-founder Victor Lee, 3 January 2020.
14. 'Honour Board – Top 20 volunteers for All Time', volunteer.ala.org.au.
15. DigiVol Newsletter, May 2020.
16. Future rewards for online volunteers could include virtual tours behind the scenes at the museum and webinars from natural history and museum experts. Streamed training sessions and video tutorials could also help to replicate a face-to-face experience.
17. DigiVol Newsletter, May 2020.
18. *The Guardian* gave the site a boost by developing an interactive widget, encouraging readers to become citizen scientists. Just search 'The Guardian people powered' to find it.
19. Seamus Doherty, 'Citizen science engagement and the great electronic age!', Australian Citizen Science Association website, 3 August 2018.

20 Richenda Vermeulen, 'Your culture is at the heart of telling great volunteer stories', Probono Australia website, 16 May 2017.
21 Jeni Warburton, Melanie Oppenheimer and Gianni Zappala, 'Marginalizing Australia's volunteers: The need for socially inclusive practices in the non-profit sector', *Australian Journal on Volunteering*, vol. 9, no. 1, 2004; Lorraine Kerr, Harry Savelsberg, Syd Sparrow and Deirdre Tedmanson, 'Experiences and perceptions of volunteering in Indigenous and non-English speaking background communities', A joint project of the Department of State Aboriginal Affairs, the South Australian Multicultural and Ethnic Affairs Commission, Volunteering SA, the Unaipon School University of South Australia and the Social Policy Research Group (University of South Australia), May 2001.
22 NRMA, 'Welcome to Lightning Ridge', NRMA website, accessed 10 July 2020.
23 LBG Corporate Citizenship and Volunteering Australia, *Corporate Volunteering in Australia: A Snapshot*, Volunteering Australia, accessed 10 July 2020.
24 'Best workplaces to give back 2019', GoodCompany website, accessed 10 July 2020.
25 Maggie Coggan, 'Top companies stay competitive by giving back', ProBono Australia website, 7 August 2019.
26 NRMA, 'DriveTime Program', NRMA website, accessed 20 July 2020.
27 Conversation with Kirsten Holmes; Kirsten Holmes, Amanda Davies, Leonie A. Lockstone-Binney, Mary O'Halloran and Faith Ong, *The Social and Economic Sustainability of WA's Rural Volunteer Workforce*, BCEC Research Report No. 22/19, Bankwest Curtin Economics Centre, February 2019.
28 The league has since adapted their rules so that boundary umpires are only required in the top divisions, reducing the strain on clubs to supply volunteers.
29 Leigh McLaughlin, personal communication, 18 May 2017.
30 *'Weavers'* is available as an open-source model (weavers.tacsi.org.au).

4. CYBERCONNECTING

1 Tom Cowie, '"We gotta protect what's right": Cherry Bar to ban phones at live gigs', *The Age*, 20 February 2018.
2 Catherine Hanrahan, 'More people now meet their partner online than through friends or work combined', *ABC News* (online), 26 November 2019.
3 Fourteen per cent of Australians smoke, while 20 per cent fall into the 'problematic' category for their mobile phone use, and 42 per cent say they use their mobile phone too much: Elizabeth Greenhalgh, Megan Bayly and Margaret Winstanley, 'Prevalence of smoking' in Michelle Scollo and Margaret Winstanley (eds), *Tobacco in Australia: Facts and Issues*, Cancer Council Victoria, Melbourne, 2019; Oscar Oviedo-Trespalacios, Sonali Nandavar, James David Albert Newton, Daniel Demant and James G. Phillips, 'Problematic use of mobile phones in Australia ... is it getting worse?' *Frontiers in Psychiatry*, vol. 10, no. 105, 2019; Deloitte, *Mobile Consumer Survey 2019 – The Australian Cut*, Deloitte, Sydney, 2019, p. 17.
4 Eilene Zimmerman, 'The lawyer, the addict', *The New York Times*, 16 July 2017, p. BU1. See also Eilene Zimmerman, *Smacked: A Story of White-Collar Ambition, Addiction, and Tragedy*, Penguin Random House, New York, 2020, p. 154.
5 Deloitte, *Mobile Consumer Survey 2017*.
6 Jerry Watkins, *Digital News Report: Australia 2017*, News & Media Research Centre, University of Canberra, 2017, pp. 75–6.

7   David Batty, 'One in six mobile phones contain E-coli', *The Guardian*, 14 October 2011.
8   Centre for Accident Research and Road Safety, 'Mobile phone use and distraction', Fact Sheet, Queensland University of Technology, Kelvin Grove, September 2015.
9   Sarah M. Simmons, Jeff K. Caird, Alicia Ta, Franci Sterzer and Brent E. Hagel, 'Plight of the distracted pedestrian: A research synthesis and meta-analysis of mobile phone use on crossing behaviour', *Injury Prevention*, vol. 26, no. 2, 2020, pp. 170–6.
10 Deloitte, *Mobile Consumer Survey 2017*.
11 Bray Stoneham, 'This is how long the average Australian spends using their phone every year', *Men's Health*, 7 February 2017.
12 Richard de Visser, Juliet Richters, Chris Rissel, Paul Badcock, Judy Simpson, Anthony Smith and Andrew Grulich, 'Change and stasis in sexual health and relationships: comparisons between the First and Second Australian Studies of Health and Relationships', *Sexual Health*, vol. 11, no. 5, 2014, pp. 505–9.
13 Krystal Steinmetz, 'A third of Americans would rather give up sex than cellphones', *Money Talks*, 28 January 2015.
14 Casey Schwartz, 'Finding it hard to focus? Maybe it's not your fault', *The New York Times*, 14 August 2018.
15 John Brandon, 'The surprising reason millennials check their phones 150 times a day', *Inc.com*, 17 April 2017.
16 Deloitte, *Mobile Consumer Survey 2017*; 'How much time do people spend on their mobile phones in 2017?', *Hackernoon.com*, 9 May 2017.
17 'How much time … ?', *Hackernoon.com*.
18 Chiara Zaffino and Victoria Quested, 'Perth man was dead for 12 minutes before mobile phone app saved his life', *10 Daily*, 19 November 2018.
19 Deloitte, *Mobile Consumer Survey 2017*.
20 The images can be viewed at www.removed.social.
21 Sarah Maslin Nirnov, 'Pope says no phones in church. Parishioners keep scrolling', *The New York Times*, 12 November 2017.
22 Manoel Horta Ribeiro, Raphael Ottoni, Robert West, Virgílio A.F. Almeida and Wagner Meira Jr., 'Auditing radicalization pathways on YouTube' in *Proceedings of the 2020 Conference on Fairness, Accountability, and Transparency*, 2020, pp. 131–41.
23 Quoted in Frank Bruni, 'How Facebook warps our worlds', *The New York Times*, 21 May 2016.
24 From 2015 to 2019, Facebook use fell among under-25s, but rose for older age groups: 'Teenage wasteland', *The Economist*, 20 July 2019, p. 69.
25 Sherry Turkle, *Reclaiming Conversation: The Power of Talk in a Digital Age*, Penguin, New York, quoted in Jacob Weisberg, 'We are hopelessly hooked', *New York Review of Books*, 25 February 2016.
26 'Remembrance of posts past', *The Economist*, 2 February 2019, pp. 29–30. The survey covered those aged thirteen to seventeen.
27 James Tozer, 'Leisure time', *1843 Magazine*, April/May 2017.
28 Evidence against the proposition that devices are to blame comes from a randomised experiment in which some Californian students were given computers to use at home. The study found that those who received the free computers were more likely to have used social networking sites, but no less likely to have interacted with their

friends in person. However, the study has two limitations: it looked only at effects over a six- to nine-month period, and only at computer use (most young people access social networks via mobile devices). See Robert W. Fairlie and Ariel Kalil, 'The effects of computers on children's social development and school participation: Evidence from a randomized control experiment', *Economics of Education Review*, vol. 57(C), 2017, pp. 10–19.

29 M&M Global Staff, 'Netflix: Sleep is our biggest competitor, not HBO or Amazon', M&M Global, 19 April 2017.

30 The statistics in these paragraphs are from Jean Twenge, 'Have smartphones destroyed a generation?' *The Atlantic*, September 2017.

31 For a contrary view, see Amy Orben and Andrew K. Przybylski, 'The association between adolescent well-being and digital technology use', *Nature Human Behaviour*, vol. 3, no. 2, 2019, pp. 173–82.

32 Australian Institute of Family Studies, *Young People Living with Their Parents*, AIFS, Melbourne, 2019.

33 Jennifer Baxter and Diana Warren, 'Teen employment experiences', *The Longitudinal Study of Australian Children Annual Statistical Report 2016,* Australian Institute of Family Studies, Melbourne, 2017; Chris Loader, 'Update on Australian transport trends', 30 December 2019, chartingtransport.com.

34 Michael E. Bernard and Andrew Stephanou, 'Ecological levels of social and emotional wellbeing of young people', *Child Indicators Research*, vol. 11, no. 2, 2018, pp. 661–79; You Can Do It Education, *Report on 15-Years of Research Sheds New Light on the Social-Emotional Wellbeing (SEWB) of Australian Children and Adolescents*, You Can Do It Education, Melbourne. The survey commenced in 2003, with an even lower stress level of 29 per cent.

35 Sabine Hall, Joann Fildes, Brianna Perrens, Jacquelin Plummer, Erin Carlisle, Nicole Cockayne and Aliza Werner-Seidler, *Can We Talk? Seven Year Youth Mental Health Report – 2012–2018,* Mission Australia, Sydney, 2019.

36 Greg Lukianoff and Jonathan Haidt, 'The Coddling of the Australian Mind', Google Document, available at thecoddling.com, 2020.

37 Roger Wilkins, Inga Laß, Peter Butterworth and Esperanza Vera-Toscano, *The Household, Income and Labour Dynamics in Australia Survey: Selected Findings from Waves 1 to 17*, Melbourne Institute: Applied Economic & Social Research, University of Melbourne, 2019, p. 127.

38 Jeffrey E. Brand, Jan Jervis, Patrice M. Huggins and Tyler W. Wilson, *Digital Australia 2020*, IGEA, Eveleigh, 2019, pp. 18, 23.

39 Mark Aguiar, Mark Bils, Kerwin Charles and Erik Hurst, 'Leisure Luxuries and the Labor Supply of Young Men', *Journal of Political Economy*, forthcoming 2020.

40 Ryan Avent, 'Escape to another world', *1843 Magazine*, April/May 2017.

41 Michele J. Fleming, Shane Greentree, Dayana Cocotti-Muller, Kristy A. Elias and Sarah Morrison, 'Safety in cyberspace: Adolescents' safety and exposure online', *Youth and Society*, vol. 38, no. 2, 2006, pp. 135–54.

42 Reality and Risk Project, 'Things to know about porn and young people', itstimewetalked.com.au, accessed 20 July 2020.

43 David Corlett and Maree Crabbe, 'Aggressive and debasing: The real issues in porn debates', *The Conversation*, 21 August 2013.

44 Oviedo-Trespalacios et al., 'Problematic use of mobile phones in Australia'.

45 Nick Vega, 'I just lost a 159-day Snapchat streak and I couldn't be happier', *Business Insider Australia*, 13 August 2017.
46 James Fallows, 'The binge breaker', *The Atlantic*, 18 November 2016.
47 Andrew Sullivan, 'I used to be a human being', *New York Magazine*, 19 September 2016.
48 Sullivan, 'I used to be a human being'.
49 Laura Marulanda & Thomas William Jackson, 'Effects of e-mail addiction and interruptions on employees', *Journal of Systems and Information Technology*, vol. 14, no. 1, 2012, pp. 82–94.
50 Adam Popescu, 'Simple ways to be better at remembering', Smarter Living, *The New York Times*, 19 October 2017.
51 Kostadin Kushlev and Elizabeth Dunn, 'Checking email less frequently reduces stress', *Computers in Human Behavior*, vol. 43, 2015, pp. 220–8.
52 Kim McMurtry, 'Managing email overload in the workplace', *Performance Improvement*, vol. 53, no. 7, 2014, pp. 31–7.
53 Steve Whittaker, Tara Matthews, Julian Cerruti, Hernan Badenes and John Tang, 'Am I wasting my time organizing email? A study of email refinding', *Proceedings of the 2011 Annual Conference on Human Factors in Computing Systems*, Vancouver, May 2011, pp. 3449–58.
54 Amy Gallo, 'Stop email overload', *Harvard Business Review*, 21 February 2012.
55 Pavithra Mohan, 'How the most productive CEOs keep email in check', *Fast Company*, 22 April 2017.
56 Chuck Klosterman, 'My zombie, myself: Why modern life feels rather undead', *The New York Times*, 3 December 2010.
57 Cal Newport, 'Is email making professors stupid?' *Chronicle of Higher Education*, 12 February 2019.
58 Gloria Mark, Stephen Voida and Armand Cardello, 'A pace not dictated by electrons: An empirical study of work without email' in *Proceedings of the SIGCHI Conference on Human Factors in Computing Systems*, May 2012, ACM, pp. 555–64.
59 Quoted in Jessica Stillman, 'This company banned internal email for a week (and loved it)', *Inc*, 30 November 2015.
60 danah boyd, 'How to take an email sabbatical', 7 July 2011, available at danah.org.
61 Paul Lewis, '"Our minds can be hijacked": the tech insiders who fear a smartphone dystopia', *The Guardian*, 6 October 2017.
62 Lewis, '"Our minds can be hijacked"'.
63 Cal Newport, 'Steve Jobs never wanted us to use our iPhones like this', *The New York Times*, 25 January 2019.
64 Morten Tromholt, 'The Facebook experiment: Quitting Facebook leads to higher levels of well-being', *Cyberpsychology, Behavior, and Social Networking*, vol. 19, no. 11, 2016, pp. 661–6.
65 Hunt Allcott, Luca Braghieri, Sarah Eichmeyer and Matthew Gentzkow, 'The Welfare Effects of Social Media', working paper, Stanford University, 2019.
66 Alissa J. Rubin and Elian Peltier, 'France bans smartphones in schools through 9th Grade. Will it help students?', *The New York Times*, 20 September 2018.
67 Rubin and Peltier, 'France bans smartphones'.
68 Henrietta Cook, 'Noise levels dialled up as school's total phone ban gets kids talking', *The Age*, 20 February 2018.

69 Sarah Keoghan, '"Engage with your kids or just stay home": Restaurant owner bans iPhone and iPad use', *The Sydney Morning Herald*, 20 February 2019.
70 Keoghan, '"Engage with your kids"'.
71 Ironically, some diners post pictures of the boxes on Instagram. See Claire Ballentine, 'Could you make it through dinner without checking your phone?', *The New York Times*, 14 July 2018.
72 Sullivan, 'I used to be a human being'.
73 The eight design principles are available at humanetech.com.
74 The examples in this paragraph are drawn from a plethora of entertaining stories compiled in Kevin C. Pyle and Scott Cunningham, *Bad for You: Exposing the War on Fun!* Henry Holt, New York, 2014, pp. 82–3.
75 Melinda Gates, 'Melinda Gates: I spent my career in technology. I wasn't prepared for its effect on my kids', *Washington Post*, 24 August 2017.
76 Nick Bilton, 'Steve Jobs was a low-tech parent', *The New York Times*, 11 September 2014, p. E2.
77 Samuel Gibbs, 'Apple's Tim Cook: "I don't want my nephew on a social network"', *The Guardian*, 19 January 2018.
78 Bilton, 'Steve Jobs was a low-tech parent'.
79 Newport, 'Is email making professors stupid?'.
80 Olivia Solon, 'Tim Berners-Lee on the future of the web: "The system is failing"', *The Guardian*, 16 November 2017.
81 Mike Allen, 'Sean Parker unloads on Facebook: "God only knows what it's doing to our children's brains"', *Axios*, 9 November 2017.
82 Casey Newton, 'The person behind the like button says software is wasting our time', *The Verge*, 28 March 2018.
83 Roger McNamee, 'I invested early in Google and Facebook. Now they terrify me', *USA Today*, 8 August 2017. See also Alex Hern, 'Interview: Roger McNamee: "It's bigger than Facebook. This is a problem with the entire industry"', *The Guardian*, 17 February 2019; Brian Barth, 'Big tech's big defector', *The New Yorker*, 25 November 2019.
84 Nellie Bowles, 'A dark consensus about screens and kids begins to emerge in Silicon Valley', *The New York Times*, 26 October 2018. It should be noted that there is little correlation between poor child wellbeing and high levels of screen use, holding constant family demographics: Andrew K. Przybylski and Netta Weinstein, 'Digital screen time limits and young children's psychological well-being: Evidence from a population-based study', *Child Development*, vol. 90, no. 1, 2019, e56–e65.
85 Chris Anderson's twelve rules are: '1) No phones until the summer before High School; 2) No screens in bedrooms (we let them use smart speakers for music); 3) All screens in public spaces (living room, kitchen, etc); 4) Network-level content blocking (OpenDNS and Google OnHub filters to block most inappropriate content). Google Safe Search on house-wide; 5) Screen Time Schedules, enforced by Google Wifi; 6) No iPads (they're gaming crack). Only Chromebooks for schoolwork; 7) Kids under 12 have to use YouTube Kids and Netflix Kids; 8) Absolutely no phones at the table; 9) We'll ask you to do your chores once. If they're not done, Dad whips out his Google Wifi app and you're off screens for 24 hours; 11) If you want a new gaming PC, you have to build it yourself from parts to get the Dad 50% subsidy; 12) No social media (Instagram/Snap, etc) until 13.': Chris Anderson, 'My 12 Rules for Kids and Screens', *Medium*, 28 October 2018.

86 The authors are as guilty of this as anyone. See Andrew Leigh and Robert D. Atkinson, *Clear Thinking on the Digital Divide*, Progressive Policy Institute, Washington DC, 2001.
87 Ross Douthat, 'The virtues of reality', *The New York Times*, 21 August 2016, p. SR11.
88 Dopamine Labs rebranded as Boundless Mind, before being acquired in 2019 by Arianna Huffington's Thrive Global, with the aim of using neuroscience to address social problems such as chronic diseases and mental health.
89 In the UK, the CHD Living group of care homes has signed up 28,000 virtual volunteers to assist with its 'Adopt a Grandparent' program.
90 Mark Zuckerberg, 'Building global community', Facebook, 18 February 2017.
91 Zuckerberg, 'Building global community'.
92 Jil Hogan, 'New community initiative Say Hello Kingston helping lonely locals connect', *Canberra Times*, 26 July 2016.
93 Sue Halpern, 'How campaigns are using marketing, manipulation, and "psychographic targeting" to win elections—and weaken democracy', *The New Republic*, 18 October 2018.
94 Brandon Isleib, 'On coping with creativity (cont.)', *Letter*, vol. 347, no. 5, 2 January 2020, available at letter.wiki.

5. GETTING ACTIVE

1 Parnell is part of Northside Community Service's Community Engagement team. Along with her colleagues Lisa Navarro-Bustos and Winston Seah, she has been working to strengthen the new communities in and near Moncrieff. When the Northside team consulted with residents about what services might help them feel more grounded as a community in Moncrieff, Parnell found she was hearing one question more often than any other: how do I get my kid involved in local sport?
2 High-income families are those with gross (before tax) household income of $175,000 or more per annum. Low-income families are defined as those with gross (before tax) household income of less than $55,000 per annum. See *AusPlay Focus: Children's Participation in Organised Physical Activity Outside of School Hours*, Australian Sports Commission, April 2018.
3 The quote was first reported in 1952. In his 1976 autobiography, Sutton denied having said it. However, Garson O'Toole argues that he probably did so. See Garson O'Toole, 'I rob banks because that's where the money is', *Quote Investigator*, 10 February 2013.
4 Quoted in 'Looking for love? Plant a tree', *Farm Online National*, 14 February 2012.
5 Quoted in Lyric Anderson, 'Conservation Volunteers Australia welcomes new project officer Ellie Gillett to Muswellbrook', *The Muswellbrook Chronicle*, 1 December 2017.
6 Quoted in Joseph Matthews, Michael Tait and Bibi van der Zee, 'Ideal fit: How GoodGym is combining exercise with good deeds – video', *The Guardian*, 26 June 2014.
7 'Michael and Sheila' and 'Clara and Victoria', GoodGym website.
8 'Paul and Beth', GoodGym website.
9 Our profile of Paul Sinton-Hewitt draws on three excellent profiles: 'The parkrun Story – Paul Sinton-Hewitt', *Strava Stories*, 27 November 2014; 'Paul Sinton Hewitt – parkrun', *runbundle*, April 2017; Aditya Chakrabortty, 'Forget profit. It's love and fun that drive innovations like parkrun', *The Guardian*, 29 August 2018.

10   Chakrabortty, 'Forget profit'.
11   'Paul Sinton Hewitt – parkrun', *runbundle*.
12   Lindsey J. Reece, Helen Quirk, Chrissie Wellington, Steve J. Haake and Fiona Wilson, 'Bright spots, physical activity investments that work: parkrun; a global initiative striving for healthier and happier communities', *British Journal of Sports Medicine*, vol. 53, no. 6, March 2019, pp. 326–7.
13   Joanne Pascoe and Michael Howes, 'A growing movement: Motivations for joining community gardens', *WIT Transactions on Ecology and the Environment*, vol. 226, 2017, pp. 381–9.
14   Kirsten Holmes, Amanda Davies, Leonie A. Lockstone-Binney, Mary O'Halloran and Faith Ong, 'The Social and Economic Sustainability of WA's Rural Volunteer Workforce', BCEC Research Report No. 22/19, Bankwest Curtin Economics Centre, February 2019. Holmes notes that alongside town members' subjective evaluation of a thriving volunteering culture, surveys were showing up to 40 per cent of local organisations couldn't fill all their volunteering roles. The garden's popularity may have come at the expense of other volunteering organisations.
15   Ellen Teig, Joy Amulya, Lisa Bardwell, Michael Buchenau, Julie A. Marshall and Jill S. Litt, 'Collective efficacy in Denver, Colorado: Strengthening neighborhoods and health through community gardens', *Health Place*, vol. 15, no. 4, December 2009, pp. 1115–22.
16   Jonathan Kingsley and Mardie Townsend, '"Dig in" to social capital: Community gardens as mechanisms for growing urban social connectedness', *Urban Policy and Research*, vol. 4, no. 24, pp. 525–37, December 2006.
17   For background, see vegout.org.au.
18   James Norman, 'Community gardens in Melbourne: Five of the best', *The Guardian*, 6 March 2014.
19   Brigid Andersen, 'Community gardens leave little time to veg out', *ABC News* (online), 22 March 2010.
20   Keith Miller and Gardening Matters, *Community Garden Social Impact Assessment Toolkit*, Neighborhood Partnerships for Community Research Report #1349, Centre for Urban and Regional Affairs, University of Minnesota, 2012.
21   In 2018, Melbourne was ranked third in the world as a food ShareCity (Sydney came in fifth).
22   Ferne Edwards and Anna Davies, 'Food sharing with a 21st-century twist – and Melbourne's a world leader', *The Conversation*, 30 May 2018.
23   Keith Miller and Gardening Matters, *Social Capital and Community Gardens: A Literature Review*, Neighborhood Partnerships for Community Research Report #1348, Centre for Urban and Regional Affairs, University of Minnesota, 2012.
24   Bridget Foley, Amy Jo Vassallo and Lindsey J. Reece, 'Lights out, let's dance! An investigation into participation in No Lights, No Lycra and its association with health and wellbeing', *BMC Sports Science, Medicine and Rehabilitation*, vol. 11, no. 11, 2019, pp. 1–8.
25   Eiluned Pearce, Jacques Launay and Robin I. M. Dunbar, 'The ice-breaker effect: Singing mediates fast social bonding', *Royal Society Open Science*, vol. 2, no. 10, 1 October 2015.

6. FOSTERING PHILANTHROPHY

1 This account has been widely reported, including in a major biography (Kenne Fant, *Alfred Nobel: A Biography*, Arcade Publishing, New York, 2006) and in Alfred Nobel's *Encyclopædia Britannica* entry. However, some historians have questioned its veracity, pointing out that no record remains of the obituary – see, for example, 'Is there any record of the premature obituary of Alfred Nobel?', History – Stack Exchange, 2018; Colin Schultz, 'Blame sloppy journalism for the Nobel prizes', Smithsonian.com, 9 October 2013.
2 See Steven Pinker, *The Better Angels of Our Nature: Why Violence Has Declined*, Viking Books, New York, 2011; Hans Rosling (with Anna Rosling Rönnlund and Ola Rosling), *Factfulness: Ten Reasons We're Wrong About the World — and Why Things Are Better Than You Think*, Flatiron Books, New York, 2018.
3 Kevin Kelly, '68 bits of unsolicited advice', kk.org, 28 April 2020.
4 Lara Aknin, Christopher Barrington-Leigh, Elizabeth Dunn, John Helliwell, Justine Burns, Robert Biswas-Diener, Imelda Kemeza, Paul Nyende, Claire E. Ashton-James and Michael I. Norton, 'Prosocial spending and well-being: Cross-cultural evidence for a psychological universal', *Journal of Personality and Social Psychology*, vol. 104, no. 4, 2013, pp. 635–52.
5 Elizabeth W. Dunn, Lara B. Aknin and Michael I. Norton, 'Spending money on others promotes happiness', *Science*, 319, 2008, pp. 1687–8.
6 Lara B. Aknin, J. Kiley Hamlin and Elizabeth W. Dunn, 'Giving leads to happiness in young children', *PLoS ONE*, vol. 7, no. 6, 2012, e39211.
7 Ashley V. Whillans, Elizabeth W. Dunn, Gillian M. Sandstrom, Sally S. Dickerson and Kenneth M. Madden, 'Is spending money on others good for your heart?' *Health Psychology*, vol. 35, 2016, pp. 574–83. Philanthropic examples are drawn from Elizabeth Dunn and Ashley Whillans, 'Give, if you know what's good for you', *The New York Times*, 25 December 2015, A27.
8 Lara B. Atkin, Elizabeth W. Dunn, Ashley V. Whillans, Adam M. Grant and Michael I. Norton, 'Making a difference matters: Impact unlocks the emotional benefits of prosocial spending', *Journal of Economic Behavior & Organization*, vol. 88, 2013, pp. 90–5.
9 Elizabeth Dunn, 'Helping others makes us happier – but it matters how we do it', TED Talk, April 2019.
10 The notion of a philanthropic campaign akin to the Slip! Slop! Slap! advertisements was originally suggested by John McLeod, *The Support Report: The Changing Shape of Giving and the Significant Implications for Recipients*, JBWere, Melbourne, 2018, p. 38.
11 On skin cancer education, see Jenny Morris and Mark Elwood, 'Sun exposure modification programmes and their evaluation: A review of the literature', *Health Promotion International*, vol. 11, no. 4, 1996, pp. 321–32. On HIV/AIDS education programs, see Malcolm Maclachlan et al., 'Transactional analysis of communication styles in HIV/AIDS advertisements', *Journal of Health Psychology*, vol. 2, no. 1, 1997, pp. 67–74. Fewer evaluations exist in the case of Australian family violence education programs.
12 'Governor general launches My Giving Moment campaign', News Release, 4 November 2013, Government of Canada, Ottawa.
13 Philanthropy Australia, *Policy Priorities for a More Giving Australia*, Philanthropy Australia, Melbourne, 2019.

14 Warren Buffett, 'My philanthropic pledge', 16 June 2010. Wealth estimate from Forbes.com real time net worth (as at 5 June 2020).
15 Peter Singer, *The Life You Can Save: How to Do Your Part to End World Poverty*, Random House, New York, 2009, p. 222.
16 James Boyd and Lee Partridge, *Collective Giving and Its Role in Australian Philanthropy*, report prepared by Creative Partnerships Australia for the Department of Social Services to assist the work of the Prime Minister's Community Business Partnership, 2017.
17 This account draws on our conversations with Jonathan Srikanthan, and his blog post 'Workplace hacking (giving) at Atlassian', philanthropy.org.au, 28 July 2015.
18 See heartsandmindsinvestments.com.au/site/charities.
19 See Louise Walsh, 'Lower-cost investing with attractive returns and social payout', *ASX Newsletter*, November 2017.
20 Good2Give, 'How a digital transformation helped Good2Give succeed', Good2Give blog post, 28 August 2019.
21 Beverley Head, 'Disrupt yourself', *AICD Company Director Magazine*, September 2019, pp. 46–9.
22 William MacAskill, quoted in Dylan Matthews, 'You have $8 billion. You want to do as much good as possible. What do you do?', *Vox*, 16 October 2018.
23 William MacAskill, 'Effective altruism: Introduction', *Essays in Philosophy*, vol. 18, no. 1, 2013.
24 William MacAskill, 'The history of the term "effective altruism"', *Effective Altruism Forum*, 11 March 2014.
25 'Young duo to "clear" the way for charitable giving', *Bryant Park Project*, NPR, 24 December 2007.
26 Nico Pitney, 'That time a hedge funder quit his job and then raised $60 million for charity', *Huffington Post*, 27 March 2015 (updated 7 December 2017).
27 GiveWell, *GiveWell Metrics Report – 2018 Annual Review*, GiveWell, Oakland, CA, 2019, p. 2. GiveWell estimates that it moved US$141 million to its recommended charities, which equates to around A$200 million.
28 Catherine Cheney, 'GiveWell is exploring giving opportunities that are more difficult to measure', *Devex*, 24 May 2019.
29 See also Elie Hassenfeld, 'How GiveWell's research is evolving', GiveWell blog, 7 January 2019; Robert Wiblin and Keiran Harris, 'Finding the best charity requires estimating the unknowable. Here's how GiveWell tries to do that, according to researcher James Snowden', *80,000 Hours*, 16 July 2018.
30 Aveek Bhattacharya and Puneet Dhaliwal, 'Debate: Helping the poor ... by getting rich: Ingenious or delusional?', *Ceasefire*, 24 November 2011.
31 Ken Berger and Robert M. Penna, 'The elitist philanthropy of so-called effective altruism', *Stanford Social Innovation Review*, 25 November 2013.
32 Jeremy Beer, 'Traditional charity fosters love. Effective altruism doesn't', *Washington Post*, 11 September 2015.
33 William A. Schambra, 'The coming showdown between philanthrolocalism and effective altruism', *Philanthropy Daily*, 22 May 2014
34 David Brooks, 'The way to produce a person', *The New York Times*, 4 June 2013, p. A25.
35 Brooks, 'The way to produce a person'.

36 In Australia, the Good Cause Co. analyses charities' public records, and delivers its recommendations on whether or not organisations deserve more donations. However, its analysis is severely limited by the lack of public information about the direct impact of charities' programs.
37 Andrew Leigh, *Randomistas: How Radical Researchers Changed Our World*, Black Inc., Melbourne, 2018.
38 Jordan Baker, 'The $3.5 billion will, the instant millionaires ... and what was left out', *The Sydney Morning Herald*, 10 May 2019.
39 This ranking is based on Philippa Coates, 'Australia's 50 biggest givers', *AFR Magazine*, 3 May 2019.
40 Quoted in Anne Hyland, 'Philanthropy 50', *AFR Magazine*, May 2017, pp. 32–6.
41 Alex Daniels, 'Ford shifts grant making to focus entirely on inequality', *Chronicle of Philanthropy*, 11 June 2015.
42 Australian Treasury, '2018 Tax Benchmarks and Variations Statement', Treasury, Canberra, 2019, p. 45, 90, 92; Australian Treasury, *Budget Statement 5: Expenses and Net Capital Investment*, Treasury, Canberra, 2019, p. 5-25.
43 Share market returns from Matthew Butlin, Robert Dixon and Peter Lloyd, 'Statistical appendix: Selected data series, 1800–2010', in Simon Ville and Glenn Withers (eds), *The Cambridge Economic History of Australia*, Cambridge University Press, Melbourne, 2015, Table A6, pp. 585–8.
44 'How becoming a patient philanthropist could allow you to do far more good', *80,000 Hours* podcast, 17 March 2020.
45 Quoted in Rob Reich, 'What are foundations for?', *Boston Review*, 1 March 2013.
46 Russ Roberts interviewing Rob Reich on 'Foundations and Philanthropy', *EconTalk*, 4 September 2017.
47 Cahal Milmo, 'Secretive ex-billionaire Chuck Feeney gives away the last of his fortune to educate Northern Irish children', *The Independent*, 17 September 2014.
48 Quoted in Singer, *The Life You Can Save*, p. 223.

7. SOCIAL CONNECTIONS AND SOCIAL PURPOSE

1 Yann Algan and Pierre Cahuc, 'Trust, growth, and well-being: New evidence and policy implications' in *Handbook of Economic Growth*, vol. 2, Elsevier, Amsterdam, 2014, pp. 49–120.
2 Brendan Crabb, 'Australian Centre for Social Innovation and IRT Group involved in trial of over-55s homesharing service in Wollongong', *Illawarra Mercury*, 28 February 2019.
3 Advance Queensland, 'Orange Sky Laundry: Our homegrown mobile laundry service for the homeless', YouTube, 26 April 2016.
4 Helen Chryssides, 'Two of us: Lucas Patchett and Nicholas Marchesi', *The Sydney Morning Herald*, 19 May 2016.
5 Advance Queensland, 'Orange Sky Laundry'.
6 Orange Sky, 'Harry – Friend of Orange Sky', YouTube, 28 March 2019.
7 Orange Sky Australia, 'Orange Sky Origin Story', Vimeo.com.
8 Advance Queensland, 'Orange Sky Laundry'.
9 Orange Sky Australia, 'Orange Sky Origin Story'.
10 Chryssides, 'Two of us'.

11 Emma Young, 'How Nick Maisey's charity Befriend is making Perth a nicer place to live', *WAToday*, 4 February 2016.
12 China Brotsky, Sarah M. Eisinger and Diane Vinokur-Kaplan (eds), *Shared Space and the New Nonprofit Workplace*, Oxford University Press, Oxford, 2019, p. 322.
13 'How do you make the change that you want to see in the world', acre.org.au, 27 March 2019.
14 Jon Faine, 'Social enterprise talkback forum', *The Conversation Hour*, ABC Radio Melbourne, 22 August 2019.
15 Michelle Anderson and Adrian Bevis, *Evaluation Report: Social Enterprise in Schools Pilot Program in North East Victoria, Australia*, prepared for the Australian Centre for Rural Entrepreneurship (ACRE), April 2017.
16 Anderson and Bevis, *Evaluation Report*.

8. SPIRITUAL CONNECTIONS

1 Claudia Mollidor, Nicole Hancock and Miriam Pepper, 'Volunteering, religiosity and well-being: Interrelationships among Australian churchgoers', *Mental Health, Religion and Culture*, vol. 18, no. 1, 2015, pp. 20–32.
2 Mark Lyons and Ian Nivison-Smith, 'Religion and giving in Australia', *Australian Journal of Social Issues*, vol. 41, no. 4, 2006, pp. 419–36.
3 Australian Bureau of Statistics, *Census of Population and Housing: Reflecting Australia – Stories from the Census, 2016*, Cat. No. 2071.0, ABS, Canberra, 2017.
4 Greg Bearup, 'The Lord's profits', *Sydney Morning Herald*, 30 January 2003.
5 Chris Rosebrough, quoted in Deborah Snow, 'Inside the Hillsong Church's money-making machine', *Good Weekend*, 13 November 2015.
6 Rob Buckingham, 'Real Christianity Part 2 – Real Christianity Is Accepting', available at baysidechurch.com.au.
7 Mark McCrindle, 'Faith and Belief in Australia', McCrindle Research, Sydney, 2017.
8 Joe Coscarelli, 'A pop-music documentarian casts a secular lens on an evangelical band', *The New York Times*, 15 September 2016, p. C1.
9 Email from Fleur Creed, 1 October 2019.
10 Alain de Botton, 'Art as Therapy', YouTube, 3 December 2013.
11 McCrindle, 'Faith and Belief in Australia'.
12 Quoted in Caroline Winter, 'Sunday Assembly atheist church comes to Australia', *ABC News* (online), 9 November 2013.
13 Faith Hill, 'They tried to start a church without God. For a while, it worked', *The Atlantic*, 21 July 2019.
14 Benevolence Australia, 'Grow With Us', YouTube, 6 October 2017.
15 Margaret Mayman, 'As a Uniting church minister I think abortion can be a morally good choice', *The Guardian*, 12 August 2019.
16 Ruth Powell, John Bellamy, Sam Sterland, Kathy Jacka, Miriam Pepper and Michael Brady, *Enriching Church Life*, 2nd edn, NCLS Research, North Sydney, 2012, pp. 44–7.
17 We are grateful to Fleur Creed for drawing our attention to this example.
18 LifeWay Research, Support, Experience and Intentionality: 2015–16 Australian Church Planting Study', Nashville, TN.
19 LifeWay Research, 'Support, Experience and Intentionality'.

20 For example, City to City provides church planters with $60,000 over their first three years; see Siobhan Hegarty, 'The couple who planted a church and the suburb that grew it', ABC Radio National, 27 August 2018.
21 Mark Tibben, 'What does contextual ministry to the western suburbs of Melbourne look like?', City to City website, 5 August 2019.
22 Thom S. Rainer and Eric Geiger, *Simple Church: Returning to God's Process for Making Disciples*, B&H Books, Nashville, TN, 2011.
23 Rick Warren, *The Purpose Driven Church*, Zondervan, Grand Rapids, MI, 1995.

9. POLITICS PLEASE

1 This story is recounted in Judith Brett, *From Secret Ballot to Democracy Sausage: How Australia Got Compulsory Voting*, Text Publishing, Melbourne, 2019.
2 AEC, *Voter Turnout*, p. 15.
3 Sarah Cameron and Ian McAllister, *The 2019 Australian Federal Election: Results from the Australian Election Study*, School of Politics and International Relations, ANU College of Arts and Social Sciences, December 2019.
4 Eitan Hersh, *Politics Is for Power: How to Move Beyond Political Hobbyism, Take Action, and Make Real Change*, Simon & Schuster, New York, 2020.
5 These surveys are from 1989 and 1993, respectively. See Melissa Bull, Susan Pinto and Paul Wilson, 'Homosexual law reform in Australia', *Trends and Issues in Crime and Criminal Justice No. 29*, Australian Institute of Criminology, Canberra, 1991; Shaun Wilson, 'Gay, lesbian, bisexual and transgender identification and attitudes to same-sex relationships in Australia and the United States', *People and Place*, vol. 12, no. 4, 2004, pp. 12–21.
6 Quoted in Shirleene Robinson and Alex Greenwich, *Yes, Yes, Yes: Australia's Journey to Marriage Equality*, NewSouth Books, Sydney, 2018.
7 In 2015, Common Ground in the United States changed its name to Breaking Ground. The organisation is still called Common Ground in Australia.
8 Liz Dawson, *Where Is My Left Eyebrow? Losing My Sight Overnight*, Halstead Press, Canberra, 2014, p. 71.
9 Clare Colley, 'From living in a tent to something quite awesome', *Canberra Times*, 4 July 2015, p. 2.
10 Canada's Private Sponsorship of Refugees program has been running for forty years and has resettled over 288,000 people. Unlike Australia's private refugee sponsorship program, refugees that are settled through Canada's private sponsorship program come in addition to the government quota.
11 The My New Neighbour toolkit (which can be downloaded at the campaign website) provides phase by phase guidance on recruiting local community allies, a council motion template, direct canvassing materials, and media tips for broadcasting endorsements from specific supporters. Of course, the central persuasion piece is the stories event, so there's a guide for staging that too.
12 Harmony Votes is an initiative of the Harmony Alliance: Migrant and Refugee Women for Change, Australia's national migrant and refugee women's coalition, in partnership with the National Ethnic and Multicultural Broadcasters' Council.
13 Osman Faruqi, 'These women are using Valentine's Day to fight against sexual harassment in the worplace', *Junkee*, 14 February 2017.

14 Gina McColl, 'Honey Birdette former staff in new campaign over alleged harassment, exploitation', *The Sydney Morning Herald*, 14 February 2017.
15 Steffanie Tan, 'Mecca is investigating claims of widespread internal bullying made by ex-employees', *Pedestrian*, 19 November 2019.
16 Ben Langford, '"Wage theft" approach winning results for hospitality workers, Hospo Voice says', *Illawarra Mercury*, 31 October 2019.
17 The Australian Centre for Social Innovation, *Verdicts on the Jury – Views of Jurors, Bureaucrats and Experts on South Australia's First Citizens' Jury*, prepared for newDemocracy Foundation, 2014, p. 17.
18 John Dryzek, 'The forum, the system, and the polity: Three varieties of democratic theory', *Political Theory*, 45, 2016, pp. 1–27.
19 Nivek Thompson, 'Participatory budgeting – the Australian way', *Journal of Public Deliberation*, vol. 8, no. 2, Article 5, 2012.
20 Anne Bolitho, 'The role and future of citizen committees in Australian local government', Australian Centre of Excellence for Local Government, University of Technology, Sydney, 2013.
21 Relevant provisions allowing committees with citizen membership include section 86 of the Victorian *Local Government Act 1989*, section 355 of the NSW *Local Government Act 1993*, sections 49 to 53 of the NT *Local Government Act 2012*, section 42 of the SA *Local Government Act 1999*, section 24 of the Tasmanian *Local Government Act 1993* and section 5.9 of the WA *Local Government Act 1995*. See Anne Bolitho, *The Role and Future of Citizen Committees in Australian Local Government*, Australian Centre of Excellence for Local Government, University of Technology, Sydney, 2013, p. 5.
22 Luca Belgiorno-Nettis, 'An innovative step toward truly empowered citizen governance', *The Mandarin*, 6 March 2019.
23 Erik Olin Wright. *Envisioning Real Utopias*, Verso, London, 2010, pp. 155–60.
24 Lyn Carson, 'Dilemmas, disasters and deliberative democracy: Getting the public back into policy', *Griffith Review*, no. 32, Winter 2011, pp. 25–32.
25 Elise Scott, 'Canberra's first citizens jury on compulsory third party insurance selects most radical option', *ABC News* (online), 29 March 2018.
26 Quoted in 'Citizens' jury on compulsory third party insurance: Australian Capital Territory', available at democracyco.com.au.
27 John Dryzek, *The Australian Citizens' Parliament: A World First*, Papers on Parliament No. 51, Parliamentary Library, Canberra, June 2009.
28 For guidelines on Decide Madrid, see decide.madrid.es. For background on the process, see the case study at involve.org.uk.
29 Sarah Wray, 'Harnessing human smarts: Meet Madrid's Director of Citizen Participation', SmartCitiesWorld.net, 5 November 2018.
30 In South Australia, the Weatherill government ran a similar public participation project called 'Fund My Idea' under the yourSAy initiative. Fund My Idea distributed $550,000 to projects up to $50,000.
31 Barack Obama, 'How to make this moment the turning point for real change', *Medium*, 2 June 2020.

10. LEADERSHIP LESSONS

1. Matt Napier's quotes are from 'Matt Napier on kicking a soccer ball across Africa (Ep. 14)', *The Good Life: Andrew Leigh in Conversation* podcast, 22 December 2016, and from his two websites, walktoabetterworld.com and mattnapier.com.au. Podcast quotes have been edited for clarity.
2. 'Esther Duflo on management, growth, and research in action (Ep. 82)', *Conversations with Tyler* podcast, 18 December 2019.
3. 'GIVIT has one million reasons to celebrate', Media release, GIVIT, 4 March 2019.
4. Jessica Hinchliffe, '2011 Brisbane floods: Juliette Wright, founder of GIVIT, reflects on generosity in wake of disaster', ABC Radio Brisbane, 11 January 2016
5. Leanne Edmistone, 'Giving her all', *QWeekend, The Courier-Mail*, 12–13 August 2017, pp. 11–14.
6. Edmistone, 'Giving her all'.
7. Edmistone, 'Giving her all'.
8. Jack Manning Bancroft, *The Mentor*, Australian Indigenous Mentoring Experience, Sydney, 2017, p. 112.
9. 'Turning the Tables', *Australian Story*, ABC TV, 28 May 2012.
10. Manning Bancroft, *The Mentor*, p. 23.
11. Manning Bancroft, *The Mentor*, p. 28.
12. Manning Bancroft, *The Mentor*, p. 52.
13. 'Turning the Tables'.
14. Manning Bancroft, *The Mentor*, p. 82.
15. Manning Bancroft, *The Mentor*, p. 70.
16. Manning Bancroft, *The Mentor*, p. 73.
17. Manning Bancroft, *The Mentor*, p. 193.
18. Manning Bancroft, *The Mentor*, p. 169.
19. Manning Bancroft, *The Mentor*, p. 189.
20. Interview with Bec Scott, Blank Pages and Empty Spaces website, undated.
21. Hudson Brown, 'STREAT: Goodness in every drop', Assemble Papers, 2 June 2017.
22. 'Hi, I'm Bec Scott', streat.com.au.
23. Michael Short, 'Full transcript: Rebecca Scott', *The Sydney Morning Herald*, 26 November 2012.
24. Manning Bancroft, *The Mentor*, p. 258.
25. Edmistone, 'Giving her all'.
26. 'Hi, I'm Bec Scott', streat.com.au.
27. Dave Williams, 'Aiming high – what it takes', Social Ventures Australia (website), 30 May 2018.
28. Manning Bancroft, *The Mentor*, p. 211.

11. RECONNECTING AUSTRALIA

1. Nicholas Epley and Juliana Schroeder, 'Mistakenly seeking solitude', *Journal of Experimental Psychology: General*, vol. 143, no. 5, 2014, pp. 1980–99.
2. Matt Liddy, Catherine Hanrahan and Joshua Byrd, 'How Australians feel about the coronavirus crisis and Scott Morrison's response', *ABC News* (online), 28 April 2020.
3. Biddle and Gray, *The Experience of Volunteers*.
4. Paul Lynch and Anna Khoo, 'Coronavirus: Volunteers flock to join community

5   support groups', *BBC News* (online), 22 March 2020.
5   Luisa Fenizola, 'How favela residents and organizations are acting and demanding action ahead of covid-19', *The Rio Times*, 2 April 2020.
6   All quotes from Catherine Barrett sourced from Fidji Simo's Facebook Live post, 'Live with Dr. Catherine Barrett, founder of the Facebook group The Kindness Pandemic', Facebook video, 17 April 2020.
7   Biddle and Gray, *The Experience of Volunteers*.
8   Timothy Fernandez, 'Meals on Wheels picks up volunteers from those who lost their jobs due to COVID-19 pandemic', *ABC Illawarra*, 28 April 2020.
9   Fernandez, 'Meals on Wheels'.
10 Anna Harrington, 'Foster: There might be a better way for sport to operate', ftbl.com.au, 18 April 2020.
11 These include the Augusta Margaret River Shire, the City of Vincent and the City of Melville.
12 For a fascinating discussion of the Dutch dropping rite, see Ellen Barry, 'In Dutch summer, a child can be left behind', *The New York Times*, 22 July 2019, p. A1.
13 Existing programs of this kind include Radiant Woman, Pathways into Womanhood, Teens to Queens, Step into Womanhood, Pathways to Manhood, Men of Honour, Journey to Manhood, the Making of Men Camp, Step into Manhood and the KI Men's Weekend.
14 Kenneth Arrow, 'Gifts and exchanges', *Philosophy and Public Affairs*, vol. 1, no. 4, 1972, pp. 343–62.
15 For a thoughtful discussion of this concept, see Peter Newman, '"The 30-minute city": How do we put the political rhetoric into practice?', *The Conversation*, 18 March 2016.
16 Since 1979, Canada's private refugee sponsorship scheme has allowed individuals and groups to add to the refugee intake. Australia's current refugee scheme does not operate in the same manner.
17 One of our favourite examples of stair-focused architecture is Seattle's Bullitt Center.
18 'Club 18-108: A Dutch care home experiments with housing students with the old', *The Economist*, 8 August 2019.
19 Dan Buettner, *The Blue Zones: Lessons for Living Longer from the People Who've Lived the Longest*, National Geographic Society, Washington DC, 2009.
20 This proposal is detailed in Bruce Ackerman and James Fishkin, *Deliberation Day*, Yale University Press, New Haven, 2004.

INDEX

80,000 Hours 149
3000acres 129

Accenture 79
Ackerman, Bruce 268
Activate Church (Brad Chilcott) 182
Acts 29 Network 186
Adelaide City Council 169
Adelaide Zoo 83
after-school sport 112–13
Against Malaria Foundation 148
aged care residents 39, 86–7
'Agents for Change' (Kids in Philanthropy) 141
Ainsworth, Leonard 142
Airbnb Open Homes 108
Airtasker 63
Akehurst, Christopher 22, 248
Albert, Michael 75–6
Alchemy Chorus (Brian Triglone) 167–8, 175
Alexandria Park Community School Redfern 221
altruism 10, 142, 154, 233 *see also* effective altruism
AMP 224
Anderson, Chris (*Wired*) 106, 258–9
Android

9 Pie 102
Night Light 102
touchscreen phones 96
Anglican church 22
Antarctic Diaries 66
ANUpoll (Australian National University) 26
ANZ 224
Apex 15
app gaming developers 67
Apple 93, 187
Architects Assist 80
Ardoch 78
Aristotle 22, 228, 248–9
Aronov, Tanya 248
Arrow, Kenneth (Nobel laureate) 238
artificial intelligence 105
Athletics Australia 16, 17
Atlantic Philanthropies foundation (Chuck Feeney) 154
Atlas of Living Australia 65
Atlassian 10, 143–4, 187, 262
Aurous 107
AusPlay 250, 259
Aussie Broadband 143
Australian Bureau of Statistics 8, 18, 45, 247, 249, 250, 251, 253, 264
Australian Catholic University 21–2

INDEX

Australian Census 18, 45, 247
Australian Centre for Rural Entrepreneurship (ACRE) 173–5, 264
Australian Centre for Social Innovation 87, 266
Australian Christians for Marriage Equality 192
Australian Citizen Science Association 67, 254
Australian City Farms 129
Australian Conservation Foundation 15–16
Australian Constitutional Value Surveys 249
Australian Election Study 24–5, 248, 265
Australian Electoral Commission 200, 248, 253
Australian Indigenous Mentoring Experience 221–2, 225–6, 267
Australian Institute of Architects 80
Australian Institute of Family Studies 256
Australian Literacy and Numeracy Foundation 109
Australian Lychee Growers Association 14
Australian Marriage Equality 191–3, 199
Australian Museum 65–7
Australian National University polls 26, 249
Australian Treasury 153

baby boomers 95
'back seat generation' 29
Bacon, Francis 67
Bali Nine 179
Bancroft, Bronwyn 220
Barda, David 246
Barelle, Kate 223
Barr, Andrew (ACT Chief Minister) 208
Barrett, Catherine (Kindness Pandemic) 230–1, 268
Barrett, Heidi (No Lights No Lycra) 130–1
Barry and Joy Lambert 152–3
Bayside Church 178–80, 182, 184
Bayside Media (Bayside Church) 179–80, 182
BeCollective 79–80
Beechworth Bakery (Tom O'Toole) 107

Befriend (Community Builders; Hosts; Networks) 164–5, 174
Bellingen Shire Pandemic Response Group 56–7, 253
Benevolence Australia 183–4, 264
Bensted, Elaine (Zoos SA CEO) 83–4
Berners-Lee, Tim (World Wide Web) 105, 258
Besley, Dean 57
Beyond Blue 161
Bhattacharya, Aveek (Giving What We Can) 149–50
Bible study groups 20, 228
Biddle, Nicholas 253, 268
Bill and Melinda Gates Foundation 142, 152, 154
Binnion, Pitsa (McKinnon Secondary principal) 103
biophilia (Edward O. Wilson) 129
Bistecca restaurant Sydney 103
Black Dog Institute 145
Blackfullas for Marriage Equality 192
Blakely, Susan 142
Bligh, Anna (fmr Qld Premier) 218
Blogger 105
blood donation 44–5
Bloomberg, Michael 142
Booker, Cory 240
Borg, Sarah 58
Boswell, Kim (Landcare for Singles) 114
Bourne, Sharyn 232
Bowling Alone (Robert Putnam) 7–8, 32
boyd, danah (Microsoft) 101, 257
Boyd, Matthew (Vollie) 63–4
Brady, Tiernan 192
Brashears, Matthew E. 246, 251
Brett, Judith 265
Brexit 210
Brooks, David (eulogy and résumé virtues) 35, 150–1, 251
Brotsky, China (*Shared Space and the New Nonprofit Workplace*) 172
Buckingham, Christie (Bayside Church) 179
Buckingham, Rob (Bayside Church) 178–9
Buddhist prayer group 20

INDEX

Buettner, Dan 268
Buffett, Warren 142, 154, 187, 262
Bullitt Center, Seattle 268
bushfires in 2019–20 54–5, 80

CallHub 108
Calo-Blanco, Aitor (economist) 55–6
Cambridge Analytica 102
Campbell, David (political scientist) 19, 20, 247
Campbell, Mark (BeCollective) 80
Carson, Ian and Simone (SecondBite) 145
Carson, Lyn 207–8
Catania, Miguel (Citizen Participation) 209–10
Catholic Church 21–2, 248
Catholic Women's League 16
Center for Humane Technology app designers 104
Center for Pesticide Suicide Prevention 148–9
Chan, Andrew (Bali Nine) 179
Chan, Priscilla 142
'Change not Charity' (Reichstein Foundation) 153
charitable foundations 151–3
charitable foundations (perpetual) 153–4
charities (online campaigns) 43, 50, 145–7, 216–19, 225
charities (street charity 'chuggers') 43, 50
Charities Aid Foundation (Good2Give) 146, 251
Charity Navigator 150
Chee, Marilyn 248
Cherry Bar (James Young) 91
Chilcott, Brad (Activate Church) 182
children 29–30, 49
Chile earthquake study 55–6
Christakis, Nicholas A. 245
Chua, Wesa 199–200
'Church in a Box' 186
church planter 185–7
church-planting networks 186
citizen committees 205–6, 266
Citizen Participation Madrid 209
citizen science 67–8
'Citizens' Parliament' 209

City of Canada Bay Council 205–6
City to City Australia 186, 265
civic engagement 7–8, 14, 18, 22–3, 27, 37–8, 40, 48–9, 199, 228, 239
Clarence, Carla (Our Place) 155–6
Clean Up Australia Day 20, 182
'clicktivism' 108
Coast Care (Landcare) 116
Coleman, James (sociologist) 7
Common Ground Canberra 195–6
Common Ground Community 195, 265
Communiteer 63, 79
community and social groups 14–18
Community Builders 107
Community Garden Social Impact Assessment Toolkit 129
Community Gardens Network 129
Community Hubs Australia 172
community resilience 56–7
Connect4Good 83
Conservation Council SA and The Joinery 169–75
Conservation Volunteers Australia 118–19
Conservation Volunteers UK 118
Convertibility Calculator 61–2, 70–1, 86, 88
Cook, Tim (Apple) 105
Cooke, Olive 42
Corlett, David 98
coronavirus shutdown 2020 9–10, 26, 228
Couch Choir 134
COVID-19 9, 53, 56, 65, 96, 107, 134, 139, 230
Covington, Alison (Good360) 146
Cowan, Nelson 99–100
Crabbe, Maree 98
Creed, Fleur 264
Croome, Rodney 191
Crosslink Christian Network 179
crowdfunding 223
crowdsourcing 65, 67
CSIRO 66, 223
Cultivating Community 127–8, 135
Cunningham, Scott 258
Curtin University 60, 70, 126
CyberConnecting 99–101, 106–7, 166, 182, 188, 203–4, 231, 234

271

INDEX

Dagnaud, Monique (sociologist) 103
Dalgarno, Captain George (Invercauld) 3
Darwinian rationalisation 55
daswandh (Sikh giving) 143
Dawson, Liz (Common Ground Canberra) 194–6, 265
de Botton, Alain 20, 181–2, 247, 264
de Condorcet, Nicolas 8
Deaf Liaison Officers 73
Deaf Society 73
Decide Madrid 209
'Deliberation Day' 240
deliberative democracy 190, 204–8, 210–11, 241
Dementia Australia 168
democracy 22–5, 49, 189–90, 199–200, 210 *see also* citizen committees; deliberative democracy
Democracy Works 108
digital connections 68–70, 91–3, 95–8, 105–6, 108–9, 162, 203–4, 208, 228
digital connections apps 9, 102–4, 108, 146
'digital detox' 13
DigiVol 66, 253, 254
Directory of Australian Associations 14–15
Disconnected (Andrew Leigh) 8–9, 14, 30, 35, 246, 247
disconnected Australia 235, 238–40, 242
Dixon, Robert 248
Do Something Near You 62
Doherty, Seamus 68
Donaldson, Anna (Lively) 86–7, 163
Donoghue, Geraldine 191
Dopamine Labs 106, 259
double-plus-good 57, 76, 115, 135, 160, 162–3, 233
DriveTime program 80
Dubner, Stephen J. 251
Dulwich Hill High School 221
Dunkelman, Marc (*The Vanishing Neighbour*) 94
Dunn, Elizabeth (researcher) 140–1
Dutch dropping rite 268

Eaglehawk Girl (Liz Lowe) 29
Edelman 249

Edwards, Naomi (Intrepid Landcare) 115, 117–18
effective altruism 147–51, 154
Eisinger, Sarah (*Shared Space and the New Nonprofit Workplace*) 172
electoral voting 8, 14, 23–5, 49, 189
emergencies 54–6
Emergency Volunteering Community Response to Extreme Weather system (EV CREW) 59–60, 87–88, 253
Engage (Ardoch) 78
episodic volunteering 64, 82
Epley, Nicholas (social psychologist) 227
Essential Media Survey 247
ethnic clubs 15
Every Australian Counts campaign 193
everydayhero 146
Evidence for Learning 151
Eyal, Nir (*Hooked: How to Build Habit-Forming Products*) 102

Facebook 54, 57, 64, 93, 95–6, 100–3, 105–8, 180, 182, 230–1, 237, 255
FaceTime 9
FairPlate (Hospo Voice) 203
FairShare 145–6
Family by Family 86
family violence campaigns 141, 262
FareShare 129
federal government trust levels 26–7, 49, 190
Feeney, Chuck (Atlantic Philanthropies) 154
Feng, Vincent (Communiteer) 63
Ferrington Collective 194
Fire & Rescue NSW 73
Fishkin, James 268
Fitzroy Crossing tournament; celebration of culture 75
Flemons, Paul (Australian Museum) 65
Flight Centre (Geoff Harris) 223
Flipd app 104
Florey Institute 145
Floyd, George 211
Foodbank (Jeanne Rockey) 145, 218
foodbanks 2
food swaps 129, 260

INDEX

Football Federation Australia 233
Ford Foundation 152
Forrest, Andrew 142
Forrest, Nicola 142
Foster, Craig (Play for Lives campaign) 232
Frankie and Benny's restaurants UK 103
Free Food night 72
Freedom app 104
'free-range' children's play 29, 49
Friendline (Friends for Good) 161-2, 164, 174
friendship 5-6, 8, 14, 35-6, 50, 124, 162-4
Fund My Idea 266
fundraising laws 43-4
Future Generation 145

Gahan, Luke 191
Garnduwa 75-6
Garrett, Shaylyn (*The Upswing*) 7, 47
Gates, Bill 105, 154
Gates, Melinda 105, 258
Gather My Crew (Susan Palmer) 165-6, 174
Geiger, Eric (*Simple Church*) 186-7
General Pants 202
General Social Survey (Aus.) 18, 27, 247, 251
General Social Survey (US) 249, 251
Generation X 95
Generation Z 200
Geneva Push 186
Geoscience Australia 66
Geraldton, WA (World Winner for Community Participation) 205
Gillet, Ellie (Hunter Intrepid Landcare) 117
GiveDirectly 148
GiveEasy 146
GiveWell 147-50, 262
'giving circle' 142
Giving Pledge 142
Giving What We Can 147, 149
GIVIT 145, 216-19, 225, 267
Glenn, Alice (No Lights No Lycra) 130-2
Global Corruption Barometer Surveys 249
'Global Poverty Walk' (Matt Napier) 213-14
Global Priorities Institute 153
GoFundraise 146

'Going on a Bear Hunt' initiative 229
Gold Coast University Hospital 185
Golf Australia 32, 250
Good Cause Co. 263
Good2Give (Charities Aid Foundation) 146-7, 251, 262
Good360 (Alison Covington) 146
GoodCompany 78-9, 254
GoodGym UK (Coach Runs, Group Runs, Mission Runs) 119-21, 123, 135
Google 106, 187, 258, 259
  Books database 47, 252
  Digital Wellbeing 102
  Impact Challenge Australia 109
  Ngrams database 252
GoVolunteer 62
Graham, David 248
Graham and Louise Tuckwell Foundation 152
Granovetter, Mark (sociologist) 5, 37
Gray, Matthew 253, 268
'Great Leap Backwards' 30
Green Bans 193
Green Gym 118-19, 121, 125
Greenbushes community garden 126
Greening Australia 10
Greenpeace 16
Greenwood, Pete (Inner West Church) 185
Griffith University 26
Grill'd 202
'Grim Reaper' campaign 141
Grinham, Lisa (Good2Give CEO) 146
Guardian, The 254
Guides 8, 16-17

HabitLab app 104
Haggerty, Rosanne 195
Haidt, Jonathon (*The Coddling of the American Mind*) 96
Halpern, Sue 108
Hangout for the Homeless (Kids in Philanthropy) 141-2
Harassment Diary (Hospo Voice) 203
Harmony Alliance (Harmony Votes) 199-200, 265-6
Harris, Geoff (Flight Centre) 223
Harris, Tristan (design ethicist) 99

INDEX

Harrison, James (blood donor) 44
Hassenfeld, Elie (GiveWell) 147–8
Hausen, Eternity (Say Hello Kingston Facebook group) 108
Hawser, Fred 3
Heart Foundation 131
Hearth Italian restaurant Manhattan 104
Hearts and Minds Investments 145
Helen Keller International 148
heritage organisations 15
Hersh, Eitan (*Politics Is for Power*) 190, 265
Hervey, William 3
Hillman, Jeremy (NSW Office of Emergency Management) 55
Hillsong 179
Hillsong United 180
Hindu social group 20
Hireup 109
HIV/AIDS 261
hobby groups 15
Holmes, Kirsten 60, 70, 86, 126, 254
Honey Birdette 201
Hooked: How to Build Habit-Forming Products (Nir Eyal) 102
Hope Centre (Brisbane) 180
Horn of Africa Relief and Development Agency 83
Hospo Voice 200, 202–4, 266
Household Income and Labour Dynamics in Australia survey 97, 248, 256
Houston, Brian (*You Need More Money*) 179
Howard Hughes Medical Institute 152
Hudson, Wayne 248
Hunter Intrepid Landcare 115–17
Hustle 108
'hybrid vigour' 81, 185, 234

Ian Potter Foundation 152
Ibrahim, Mo 142
iGen 95
Impact100 ('giving circle') 142
Indigenous communities 1, 48–50, 109, 115, 152, 190, 209, 213, 219, 221, 237, 252
influencers 69
Influencers (Adelaide) 180
Infoxchange (Ask Izzy) 159

Inner West Church 185
Instagram 93, 95–6, 102, 258, 259
International Network of Churches 186
Intrepid Landcare 115–18, 135, 193
Intuit (Brad Smith) 100
Invercauld 3–4
Involve (public participation charity) 210
iPads 105–6
iPhone 96
   Night Shift 102
   Screen Time 102, 228
Ipsos Mackay Research 35
Isleib, Brandon 109
Italy 7

Jacobs, Nicky 248
JBWere 152
Jewish Australians 22
Jobs, Steve (Apple) 105, 258
John, Elton 107
Johnson, Alicia 221
Johnson, Emily 221
Johnson, Samuel 43, 252
Johnston, Governor General David ('My Giving Moment') 141
Jones, Kerry (Our Place) 155–6
Jorgensen, Astrid (Pub Choir) 133–4, 167
Junger, Sebastian (*Tribe: On Homecoming and Belonging*) 117–18
JustGiving 107

Karnofsky, Holden (GiveWell) 147–8
Kassem, Manal 10–11
Kasynathan, Sankar (My New Neighbour) 196–8
Keller, Helen 5
Kelly, Kevin (*Wired*) 139
Kenyon, Peter 235
Kids First 151
Kids Giving Back 83, 228
Kids in Philanthropy 141–2
Kindle 104
Kindness Pandemic 230–1, 233
Kingdomcity (Perth) 180
Kippax Connections 184–5
Kippax Uniting Church 184–5
Klinenberg, Eric (sociologist) 40, 251

INDEX

Knuth, Donald 105
Kobo 104
Kolt, Steven (FairShare) 145–6
KOTO ('Know One Teach One') café 223

Labour Force Survey 46, 50
Lady Gaga 107
Lakemba Mosque 182
Landcare 84–5, 114, 116, 118, 135
    Landcare Facilitator ACT (Rebecca Palmer-Brodie) 114
    Landcare for Singles 114–15
    Landcare Local Coordinators 85
    Landcare NSW 85
    Landcare Young Farmers event 114
language
    Australian 13
    individualistic 47–8, 50
    online terms 13, 50
Lauria, Patricia (Friendline) 161–2
Learning Through Lunch (Ardoch) 78
Lee, Mark 93
Lee, Victor (Communiteer) 63
Leigh, Andrew 8–9, 14, 35, 246, 259, 263, 267
Letter website 109
Lifeline 132, 161
Lilspace app 104
Lindsay, Norman 106
Lindt Café Martin Place 11, 19–20
LinkedIn 64
Linux 67
Lions 8, 16–17
Literacy Buddies (Ardoch) 78
Little Athletics 16
Lively (Anna Donaldson) 86–7, 107, 163
loneliness 38–9, 50, 86–7, 161–2, 251
Low, Liz (*Eaglehawk Girl*) 29, 250
Lower South West Football League 82, 254
Lowy Foundation 152
Lukianoff, Greg (*The Coddling of the American Mind*) 96, 256

ma'aser kesafim (Jewish giving) 143
MacAskill, William (Giving What We Can) 147, 262
Made With Love (Kids in Philanthropy) 142

Maesepp, Ella 114–15
Maisey, Nick (Befriend) 163–5
Making Democracy Work (Robert Putnam) 7
'Making of Men' camp 237
Manning, Ned 220
Manning Bancroft, Ella 222
Manning Bancroft, Jack (*The Mentor*) 213, 220, 225–6
Marchesi, Nic (Orange Sky Australia) 156–60
Markus, Andrew 248
Mayman, Reverend Margaret 184
McKinnon Secondary School 103
McLaughlin, Leigh 85, 254
McLeod, John (JBWere's philanthropic division) 152
McNamee, Roger (Facebook) 106, 258
McPherson, Miller 246, 251
Meal Mates (Suzanna Pawley) 162–3, 232
Meals on Wheels 162, 232, 268
Mecca Cosmetica 202
Medium 105
Melbourne Cricket Club 27
Melbourne Women's Fund ('giving circle') 142
mental health 6, 41, 70, 96–8, 245
micro-volunteering 64, 67–8
Millar, Mac 215
millennials 200
Minderoo Foundation 152
'Mistakenly Seeking Solitude' 227
Molloy, Julie (EVCREW) 59–60, 72–3, 87
Moltrasio, Michele 101
Moment app 104
Monarto Safari Park 83
Moore, Henry 67
Moore, Tom (former soldier) 107
Morgan, Geoff 222
Moriarty, Denis (Our Community House) 172
Mothers' Union 16
Mount Druitt Ethnic Communities Agency 76–7, 88
Mower Shed (Kippax Connections) 184–5
MS Research Australia 145
Murdoch, Alexi (singer) 159

INDEX

Murray, Kathryn (Sunday Assembly) 182
Murthy, Vivek (US Surgeon General) 39
Musgrave, Captain Thomas (Grafton ship captain) 3–4, 245
Musk, Elon 142
Muslim conversation groups 228
'My Giving Moment' (Governor General David Johnston) 141
My New Neighbour (Sankar Kasynathan) 197–8, 265

Napier, Matt ('Global Poverty Walk') 213–16, 225–6
Napier, Wendy 213, 215
National Aboriginal and Torres Strait Islander Social Survey 49
National Disability Insurance Scheme 193
'National Giving Campaign' 141
National Health Service (UK) 107
National Library Australia (Trove) 66–7
Natural History Museum London 66
Nature Conservancy 109
Navarro-Bustos, Lisa 259
NeighbourDay.org 235
Neighbourhood Care Network (Bellingen) 57
Neighbourhood Houses 74
NeighbourhoodConnect.org.au 235
Neighbours drama series 38
Netflix 95, 258
New York Botanical Gardens 66
New York Diamond Dealers Club 4–5, 238
New Zealand government 80
newDemocracy Foundation 205, 209
Newspeak (George Orwell) 57
No Lights No Lycra 130–2, 135, 260
No Lights No Lycra (Dance Break app) 131
Nobel, Dr Alfred (Nobel prize) 137–8, 154, 261
Noble, Denis 54
Northside Community Service 112–13, 135, 259
NRMA 254
NSW National Parks 118
NSW NRMA 77, 80

NSW Office of Emergency Management (Jeremy Hillman) 55
NSW Premier's Recognition awards 66
NSW Rural Fire Service 73
NSW State Emergency Service 73
NSW Year Book 247–8
Ntegrity (digital strategy firm) 69

Obama, Barack 211–12, 266
Oberg, Tim (parkrun) 122–4
Offtime app 104
Old Beechworth Gaol 173
Omnipoll 35
Open Philanthropy Project 149
open source data 159
Open Table 129
open-source code 61, 66
Orange Sky song (Alexi Murdoch) 159
Orange Sky Australia 10, 156–60, 174–5, 228, 263, 264
Ord, Toby (*The Precipice*) 147, 149
Organisation for Economic Co-operation and Development 246
Origin Energy 78–9
Orthodox Jews 5
Orwell, George (double-plus-good) 57
O'Toole, Tom (Beechworth Bakery) 107
Our Big Kitchen 82, 138
Our Community 172
Our Community House 172
Our Place 156
Outback Links 77

Palmer, Susan (Gather My Crew) 165–6, 174
Palmer-Brodie, Rebecca (Landcare Facilitator ACT) 114
Parents, Family and Friends of Lesbians and Gays (PFLAG) 192
Parker, Sean (technology entrepreneur) 105
parkrun 10, 122–5, 135, 144, 187, 199, 228, 260
Parnell, Karlya (After School Sport) 111–13, 259
Patchett, Lucas (Orange Sky Australia) 156–60

'Pathways to Womanhood' retreat 237
Paul Ramsay Foundation 151–2
Pawley, Suzanna (Meal Mates) 162, 232
Pay Checker (Hospo Voice) 203
Pazar restaurant Sydney 103
Pentecostal church 178–82, 187
Pfahlert, Matt (ACRE CEO) 173
PFLAG (Parents, Family and Friends of Lesbians and Gays) 192
Pham, Jimmy (KOTO 'Know One Teach One' café) 223
'philanthrolocalism' (William Schambra) 150
philanthropy 8, 10, 14, 41–4, 50, 137–42, 145–7, 151, 154, 218
    cultural *see daswandh*; *ma'aser kesafim*; tithing; *tzedakah*; *zakat*
philanthropy (corporate giving) 145
Philanthropy Australia 141, 262
'Pick My Project' (Victorian government) 210
Pickersgill, Eric (photographer) 94
Pinker, Stephen 139, 261
Pinterest 96
Pitt Street Uniting Church 184
Planetshakers (Melbourne) 180, 182
Plato (360 BC) 104
Play for Lives campaign 9, 10, 232–3
Pledge 1% 143
Pokémon 68
political engagement 7, 22–8, 49, 108, 190
political knowledge 24–5, 27, 210–211
Politics Is for Power (Eitan Hersh) 190
Pope Francis 94
Port Alegre, Brazil 206–7, 210
Posner, Judge Richard 153
Post, Stephen (researcher) 6, 246
'power of free' 144
Pozzebon, Guido (FairShare) 145–6
Price-Mitchell, Marilyn (psychologist) 6
Productivity Commission 247
Proust, Marcel 5, 245
Pub Choir 133–4, 167
Puddle Jumpers 70–72
Putnam, Robert (political scientist) 7–8, 19–20, 32, 47, 246, 247, 252, 253
Pyle, Kevin C. 258

Quality Time app 104
Queensland floods 58, 217–18
Queensland University of Technology 122

Rainer, Thom (Simple Church) 186–7
Raisely 146
Ramadan 74
Ramsay, Paul 151–2, 154
Rate My Boss (Hospo Voice) 203
reciprocity bonds 14, 19, 50, 204
Reconnected Australia 10, 188, 233, 235–8, 239–42
Record My Hours (Hospo Voice) 203
Recruitability Tool 86, 88
Red Cross 44, 50, 58, 73, 108, 233
    'Trauma Teddies' 229
refugee sponsorship 197, 265, 268
Reich, Rob (scholar) 153, 263
Reichstein Foundation ('Change not Charity') 153
Reid, Stephen 248
Religion for Atheists (Alain de Botton) 20, 181
religious communities 14, 19–22, 177–9, 183–7, 228
religious services attendance 8, 14, 19–22, 29, 49, 228, 247–8
Returned Services League (RSL) 15–17
Richman, Barak D. 245
Rio de Janeiro favelas 229–30
RMIT 224
Roberts-Smith, Ben (former soldier) 159–60
Rockey, Jeanne (Foodbank) 145
Rogers, Chanelle 201
Room to Read (Cambodia) 143–4
Rorris, Arthur 203
Rosenstein, Justin (Facebook) 105–6
Rosling, Hans 139, 261
Rosshandler, Ash 79
Rotary 8, 15–17, 239
Rouhan, Laura (Friendline) 161
Rourke, Josh 196
Rowlatt, Megan (Intrepid Landcare) 116–17
Roy Morgan polling 30–4, 42, 250
Royal Automobile Club of Victoria 224

INDEX

Rumi's Cave (UK) 183
Rummukainen, Danny 83
Russell, Wendy 207

Sabbagh, Saara (Benevolence Australia) 183
Sacred Heart Mission 151
Salvation Army 58
Sander, Thomas 253
Say Hello Kingston Facebook group (Eternity Hausen) 108
Scanlon Foundation 153
Schambra, William ('philanthrolocalism') 150
Schlessinger, Carole (Kids Giving Back) 83
School of Life (Alain de Botton) 181–2
Schroeder, Juliana ('Mistakenly Seeking Solitude') 227
Schwartz, Carol and Alan (Our Community House) 172
Scott, Bec (STREAT) 160, 213, 222–6
Scouts 8, 16–17, 239, 247
Screen Time (Apple) 102, 228
Seah, Winston 259
SecondBite (Ian and Simone Carson) 145
September 11 attacks 56
service clubs 15, 17, 49
Shared Space and the New Nonprofit Workplace (China Brotsky) 172
Sharp, Timothy 251
Simple Church 186–7
Singer, Peter (philosopher) 142, 151, 262, 263
Sinton-Hewitt, Paul (parkrun) 122–3, 125
skin cancer education 261
SkinVision app 93
Skype 9
Slavin, Laya (Our Big Kitchen) 138
Slavin, Rabbi Dovid (Our Big Kitchen) 138–9
Slip! Slop! Slap! campaign 141, 261
smartphones 37, 91–4, 96, 98–9, 102–3, 106, 254, 255, 256
  and texting. 57, 95
Smith, Brad (Intuit) 100
Smith-Lovin, Lynn. 246, 251

Smithsonian 66
Snapchat 93, 95–6
Snapchat Streak 99
Snowden, James 148
social and online media 2, 9, 54, 57, 64, 70, 72, 91, 93–6, 100–1, 103–6, 258
  addiction 99, 100–4, 106
  emails 57, 91, 100–1, 257
social distancing (coronavirus shutdown) 9, 232
Social-Emotional Wellbeing (SEWB) survey 256
Social Enterprise Academy (Scotland) 174
social entrepreneurs 2, 10, 56, 63, 86, 109, 130, 133, 155–60, 174, 213, 225–6, 228, 238–9
social isolation 5, 9, 38–9, 53, 161–2, 228
social justice 28, 117, 154, 179, 216
social purpose organisations 10, 155–6, 159–60, 164–74
social validation feedback loop 105
Sodexo 79
'Sojouners Church' 186
solo living 14, 39–40
Sorry Day Bridge Walk (2000) 193
South African diamond mines 4
South Coast Labor Council 203
Southport Church of Christ 185
Sowerbutts, Felicity (Young Workers Centre) 202
Spira, Henry 154
sport participation 30–4, 49–50, 235, 239
Spurr, Nicola 229
Srikanthan, Jonathan 262
St John First Responder app 93
St Michael's Uniting Church 184
St Paul's College University of Sydney 220–2
St Vincent de Paul Society (Vinnies) 69–70, 89
Stanford University 105
Stephens, Rhiannon (DigiVol coordinator) 65
STREAT 160, 223–6
Subway 202
suicide 40–1, 50, 96–7, 251
Sukumaran, Myuran (Bali Nine) 179
Sullivan, Andrew 99, 104
Sunday Assembly 10, 182

INDEX

surf life-saving 250
Sutton's Law of Social Capital 113, 125, 127, 135, 164, 183–4, 187, 199, 204, 234, 259
Sydney Children's Hospital 145

Ta'leef Collective (US) 183
Tate, Melanie (Puddle Jumpers) 70–2
Taylor, Rob (Veg Out) 128
TEAR (Christian aid) 170
technology 13, 65, 68, 91–2, 95–6, 105, 109, 146, 166, 202–4, 234
The Age of Surveillance Capitalism (Shoshana Zuboff) 106
The Coddling of the American Mind (Greg Lukianoff and Jonathon Haidt) 96, 256
The Mentor (Jack Manning Bancroft) 220
The Precipice (Toby Ord) 149
The Purpose Driven Church (Rick Warren) 186, 265
The Upswing (Shaylyn Garrett and Robert Putnam) 7, 47
The Vanishing Neighbour (Marc Dunkelman) 94
This Is Your Life 198
Thomson, Naomi 232
Tibben, Mark (Sojouners Church) 186
TikTok 96
tithing (Christian giving) 143
Tofler-Riesel, Ruth (Kids Giving Back) 83
Towards a Better World (Matt and Wendy Napier) 215, 267
trade unions 14, 27–9, 49, 200–2
Trammell, Phil ('patient philanthropy') 153
Transparency International 26
'Trauma Teddies' (Red Cross) 229
Tribe: On Homecoming and Belonging (Sebastian Junger) 117–18
Triglone, Brian (Alchemy Chorus) 167–8
Trithemius, Johannes (1494) 104
Trove (National Library Australia) 66–7, 253
'trust accelerators' 155
Tsirekas, Angelo 205–6
Tua-Davidson, Maia 73–5
Tufa, Zulfiye 183
Tumblr 96
Turkle, Sherry (social psychologist) 95

Twenge, Jean (researcher) 95
Twitter 54, 64, 94, 96
 #DeleteFacebook 102
 #NotYourHoney 201
 #ShowUsYourFridge 208
tzedakah (Hebrew) 143

Uber 108, 230
UN International Liveable Communities Award 205
Underabi, Husnia 248
UNHCR (refugee agency) 170
UNICEF (Spread the Net) 140
United States General Social Survey Data Explorer 249
United Workers Union 202–3
Uniting Church 22
UnitingCare (Newpin, HIPPY) 184
University of Chicago 227
University of Minnesota 129
University of Missouri 99
University of South Australia 68
University of Sydney 153, 220–2
Urban Harvest food swap 129

Valentine's Day Speed Planting 114
Van Der Heul, Teresa 65–6
Veg Out (St Kilda) 128, 129
Vermeulen, Richenda (Ntegrity director) 69–70
VicHealth 131
 Citizen's Jury on Obesity 208
Victorian government ('Pick My Project') 210
Victorian Trades Hall 201
video game technology 97–98
Vietnam moratorium 193
Vinokur-Kaplan, Diane (*Shared Space and the New Nonprofit Workplace*) 172
Vollie (Matthew Boyd) 63, 79
volunteer fire brigades 2, 18–19, 247
Volunteer Fire Brigades Victoria 178
Volunteer Makers (UK) 62
volunteering 5, 8, 10, 18, 48, 53, 63, 67, 74, 76
 benefits of 6, 68, 70–1, 74–5, 117, 125, 132–4

INDEX

volunteering (cont.)
   in community gardens 126–30, 260
   coordination and management of 84–5
   conservation 114–18
   corporate 77, 78, 80–1 *see also* 'hybrid vigour'
   and COVID-19 56–7, 64, 134
   decline of 49, 60, 82
   digital strategy platforms 68–70, 89
   disaster recovery 10, 54, 56, 58–60, 80
   driving mentors 80
   egalitarianism 7, 117
   emergency services 73
   emotional satisfaction 6, 68, 70
   experienced-based 82, 87
   and families 83, 87
   fitness communities 119–25
   recruiting and induction 88–9
   school-based 82
   sporting communities 73–6, 81, 111–13, 119–24, 240
   virtual 10, 63–9, 72
   volunteer database systems 59–60
   in the workplace 77–80
   young volunteers 69, 77, 82–3, 114–18, 138, 163
   see also Convertibility Calculator; episodic volunteering; micro-volunteering; Recruitability Tool
Volunteering Australia 62, 82
Volunteering Queensland 58–9, 72–3, 88
VolunteerMatch (US) 62
volunteer-matching websites 62–4, 71, 88

Ward, Mary 43
Warren, John 67
Warren, Rick (*The Purpose Driven Church*) 186, 265
Warton, Lisa (Ferrington Collective) 194
'Weavers' open-source model 254
Welcome to the Game 74–6
Welcoming Sport 73
West Australian Aussie Rules 81–2

West Australian Football Commission 75
WhatsApp 64, 95–6
Wikipedia 67
Wilkins, Craig 169–71
Wilkinson, Peter 248
Williams, Evan (technology entrepreneur) 105
Wilson, Edward O. (biologist) 129
Wired 106, 139
Wood, Terence 251
Worksafe 201
World War II 28, 47
World Wide Web (Tim Berners-Lee) 105
Wright, Juliette (GIVIT) 145, 213, 217–19, 225–6
Wright, Tony 250
Wyatt, Ken 251
Wyndham City Council 205

Xceptional 109

Yawuru people of Broome 48–9, 253
'Yes' marriage equality campaign 192
You Need More Money (Brian Houston) 179
Young, Bernadette (Giving What We Can) 147
Young, James (Cherry Bar) 91
Young Landcarers 114
Young Workers Centre 201–3
Youth Projects Melbourne 142
YouTube 93–4, 105, 182, 258

zakat (Islamic giving) 143
Zimmerman, Eilene and Peter 92, 255
Zoom 9
Zooniverse 67–8
Zoos SA 83–4
Zuboff, Shoshana (*The Age of Surveillance Capitalism*) 106
Zuckerberg, Mark (Facebook) 107–8, 142, 259
Zylo 143

Andrew Leigh is the federal member for Fenner. Before being elected in 2010, he was a professor of economics at the Australian National University. His books include *Battlers and Billionaires*, *The Luck of Politics* and *Randomistas*.

Nick Terrell is an adviser to Andrew Leigh MP. He has worked closely with Australia's charity and non-profit sector to protect the voice of community organisations and promote the value of their contribution to Australian communities.

www.ingramcontent.com/pod-product-compliance
Lightning Source LLC
Chambersburg PA
CBHW062153080426
42734CB00010B/1672